Japa Transformations

Other Books on Japa Meditation by Satsvarūpa dāsa Goswami

Japa Reform Notebook
Begging for the Nectar of the Holy Name
Japa Walks, Japa Talks

Latest Books from GN Press

Vaisnava Compassion
Write & Die
When the Saints Go Marching In
Visitors
Human at Best
My Dear Lord Krishna A Book of Prayers
Soul Eyes

Online Journals

www.sdgonline.org
Tachycardia: A Journal
Vrindavana Journal 2009
The Yellow Submarine: My Bhajana Kutir 2009-2010
Viraha Bhavan: A Journal 2010

Foreword by Dr. Kenneth R. Valpey, Oxford Centre for Hindu Studies
Cover design by Caitanya Candrodaya

JAPA TRANSFORMATIONS

SATSVARŪPA DĀSA GOSWAMI

Foreword by
Dr. Kenneth R. Valpey

Persons interested in the subject matter are invited to correspond with our Secretary, c/o GN Press, Inc.,
134 Glade Circle West, Rehoboth Beach, DE 19971

JAPATRANS.GNPRESS.ORG

JAPA TRANSFORMATIONS

ISBN-10: 0-982260-03-2
ISBN-13: 978-0-982260-03-6

Library of Congress Control Number: 2010923260

Library of Congress Cataloguing-in-Publication Data
Goswami, Satsvarūpa dāsa, 1939-
Japa Transformations/ Satsvarūpa dāsa Goswami
xvi, 274 pp. 2 cm.

1. Spiritual life—International Society for Krishna Consciousness. I. Title.
294.5/925—dc21

To His Divine Grace
A. C. Bhaktivedanta Swami Prabhupāda

Contents

FOREWORD

ACCORDING TO THE MONIER-WILLIAMS Sanskrit-English Dictionary (still considered standard after more than a hundred years), *japa* means "muttering prayers, repeating in a murmuring tone passages from scripture or charms or names of a deity..." In this book *japa* refers to the soft, devotional repetition or "chanting" of the particular mantra (sacred utterance) that is so central to the practice of "Krishna consciousness." It is one of the pioneers of the Krishna consciousness movement in the West and one of the first disciples of His Divine Grace A. C. Bhaktivedānta Swami Prabhupāda (1896-1977), Satsvarūpa Dāsa Goswami, who here invites readers to become privy to his own experiences during recent retreats in practicing the *japa* of this *mahā-mantra* (primary mantra)—*hare kṛṣṇa hare kṛṣṇa kṛṣṇa kṛṣṇa hare hare, hare rāma hare rāma rāma rāma hare hare.*

It has been over twenty-five years since Satsvarūpa Goswami published his first book on this subject, *Japa Reform Notebook.* Those who are familiar with that work may know that in those days, for some members of Swami Prabhupāda's ISKCON (International Society for Krishna Consciousness), the book was seen as quite radical or even inappropriate. How could a senior devotee, revered as a renunciant (*sannyāsī*) and as an adept spiritual teacher (*guru*), so openly communicate his own personal challenges in the practice of chanting *hare kṛṣṇa*? Yet others were enlivened to see that a frank discussion of the challenges to pure chanting was being aired, offering practical advice to avoid the ten "offenses" listed by earlier teachers of the tradition. Since then, several other books on the subject of *japa* by other practitioner-authors have appeared, and in more recent years there has been a burgeoning of well-attended "japa retreats" offering guided improvement of the practice of softly meditating on Kṛṣṇa's names.

As the title of the present book suggests, *Japa Transformations* goes more deeply into the subject than the author's first book. Transformations are deep changes for the better, personal revolutions in attitude and understanding that come about as the result of deep reflection and intense determination. As in the previous book, Goswami locates himself as both a student and a teacher—as one who continues to learn from his own guru and who aims to help others benefit from what he learns. In this book he asks readers to spend time with him as he questions the extent and depth of his own successes and the meaning of occasional apparent setbacks in practice as he takes one through a sustained personal meditation on the eight verses of the *Śikṣāṣṭaka*, Śrī Caitanya's verses that encapsulate his teachings.

Japa Transformations is no doubt primarily meant for "insiders," persons more or less committed to the way of life and the "belief system" embodied in the extensive canonical literature of Caitanya Vaiṣṇavism, especially as taught by Swami Prabhupāda. Only tangentially and occasionally does Goswami address those who are not thus committed. And for such insiders familiar with Goswami's profuse literary output, this will be a welcome further chapter in his ongoing documentation of his personal journey toward Kṛṣṇa through self-observation, confession, "free writing," poetry, reportage of insights from daily life, and preparation for life's final test.

Yet this can also be a fascinating document for "outsiders" who, though not committed to the practices of Krishna consciousness, are nevertheless either themselves seekers on way of spirituality or are appreciative of the wealth of literature that bears witness to the impact of spirituality in ordinary and extraordinary people's lives. Though there is a wealth of such literature associated with Abrahamic spiritual traditions, very little exists in the way of autobiographical literature from within "eastern" spiritual traditions. What Satsvarūpa Goswami offers here is a special opportunity to see the ways that a western-born practitioner of an eastern spiritual tradition endeavors to go beyond the superficialities of outward forms to get at the truth and reality of life in communion with God that the tradition repeatedly insists is accessible for one able to receive divine blessings. And for the scholar of religion who studies and theorizes about "religious experience," this book can provide a fresh look at how "experience" can be related to "practice" in the sense of competence through repetition and improvement.

In the early 1970s J. Stillson Judah published one of the first academic studies of the Hare Krishna movement, entitled *Hare Krishna and the Counterculture* (New York: *John Wiley & Sons,* 1974). In that study, he located the Vaiṣṇava movement brought to the West by Swami Prabhupāda within the frame of American social unrest in the 1960s and 1970s, seeing in Prabhupāda's message a powerful answer to youth's questioning of established values. He also wondered about the future of the movement. At the very end of his book, Judah asks, "The phoenix [the Hare Krishna movement] is born, but where will it fly?" To shift the analogy, an important part of the answer to this question is in the continuing appearance of literary fruits of Kṛṣṇa-devotion such as *Japa Transformations.* The tree has indeed set roots in western (and southern, and eastern) soil, so that fruits such as this are becoming available. And to shift the analogy back again, *Japa Transformations* is one such work, specifically about "taking flight" through the transformative power of conscientious chanting of the *mahā-mantra.*

Some persons have found cause for criticism of the Krishna consciousness movement: that within its institutional missionary setting current practice of devotion to Kṛṣṇa has become (to shift Judah's meaning) a "culture of counting" (preoccupied with counting the numbers of mantras chanted in daily practice). This book offers a response to this concern, clearly showing the intention and indeed the ability to go beyond mere counting (and related external concerns) to the substance of the *mahā-mantra*, which is the attainment of love of God, known by followers of Śrī Caitanya as *Kṛṣṇa-prema*. But for the *mahā-mantra* to take flight, the author insists, requires extreme patience and determination, and this book is a record of his own pursuit of these prerequisites. It is spiced with surprises (such as a poem to Rādhā, in the voice of Kṛṣṇa; or a line quoted from a George and Ira Gershwin song), and colorful analogies (being "only in the foothills of *harināma*" or "pushing [to be attentive in chanting] like a farmer with his ox and plow"). More importantly, it is the open display of a heart that yearns to transcend the limits of mundane existence and to relish, without interruption, the promised fruit of *Kṛṣṇa-prema*.

— Krishna Kshetra Das (Kenneth R. Valpey)
Oxford Centre for Hindu Studies, U.K.

AUTHOR'S PREFACE

THE WRITING IN THIS BOOK RECORDS the transformations I underwent in my chanting in my *bhajana kuṭīr* in Lewes, Delaware. There are ups and downs but I hope my attempt to describe my experience will provide dynamic and helpful reading for fellow chanters. All glories to Śrīla Prabhupāda, who gave us the holy names.

—SDG
14 December 2009

JAPA TRANSFORMATIONS

INTRODUCTION

Satsvarūpa Dāsa Goswami's new *japa* book presents the best of his recent *mahā-mantra* meditations from his sacred cyberspace, *The Yellow Submarine.* Following Śrīla Prabhupāda and other Gauḍīya masters, the writer-captain takes his reader-mates progressively deeper into the ocean of Hare Kṛṣṇa meditation.

Taking up his beads in the wee hours, Goswami first tackles the tongue 'n' jaws of chanting, creatively weaving sacred texts with personal appeals and stories from "happy days" with "Swamiji" at 26 Second Avenue. Now a whole life later, he writes and chants as one of us, who survives and thrives only by the mercy of the holy names, determined to go deeper into Their glories, and share Them in daily gratitude.

From his "First Transformations" early on to his *Reality* ruminations later, it is Goswami's determination to surrender to the sweet sacrifice of chanting Hare Kṛṣṇa, and living its deep meaning, that invokes the Names' blessings on both writer and reader, even when we seem to digress.

The writer's textual digressions into divine philosophy and play clearly enhance the chanting because they are all about *nāmi*, the person named by *nāma*, the Hare Kṛṣṇa mantra. But what about when our captain writes "in the mix," when he takes us to the ballpark or the jazz club? Is the Divinity there, too?

Divinity is everywhere, as we hear from the *Bhagavad-gītā* . But only a heart surrendered to sacred sound will see God in the flight of a ball, or hear Him in the wail of a sax, and then let himself be led back to the Names, where the

Divinity plays, and to Prabhupāda's sublime prescription for all wandering minds: "just hear."

In our self-obsessed times, *Japa Transformations* is a welcome reminder that the best way to find ourselves is to lose ourselves in loving service to the Lord's holy names. Whether Goswami is writing to chant or chanting to write, his whole life is rapt in sacred sound, as ours could be, and more than ever, his words are helpful and endearing.

"The end of my book will have to be discovered at the end of my life," Goswami concludes. Like a spiritual retreat that comes home with us, *Japa Transformations* is a valuable companion to help us surrender our life's breath to calling God's hallowed names, and to enter His eternal loving service at last.

— Suresvara Das (ACBSP), *writer & teacher*

INVOCATION

MY DEAR LORD. I PRAY FOR BETTER *JAPA.* The daily *japa-yajña* is a relatively easy thing. It only takes about two hours, and we can surely find that much time out of twenty-four hours. If we can chant more than the minimum of sixteen, that is good. But let's start with sixteen good ones, offenseless chanting. That means chanting while avoiding the ten offenses, which start with disobeying the spiritual master and include inattention while chanting. My chanting is not yet at the offenseless stage, and so I pray for Your help in transforming it. It requires Your mercy. Chanting without offences is also called *śuddha-nāma,* the perfect stage of chanting where one begins to experience ecstatic bodily symptoms and receives revelations of the name, form, quality, and pastimes of Rādhā and You. It is an advanced stage of spiritual life.

There are three stages of chanting: (1) offensive chanting; (2) the clearing stage, or *nāma-ābhāsa,* and (3) offenseless chanting. Sometimes, for part of my *japa,* I may be free of the major offenses and chant the shadow of the holy names. That is on my brilliant days. But that is not enough. I need to experience *nāma-ruci,* the taste of the nectar of *harināma.* And we need to not slide back down to offensive chanting.

Śrīla Bhaktivinoda Ṭhākura has written a book on chanting the holy names, *Harināma Cintāmaṇi,* and he analyzes the causes of the offenses and offers suggestions on how to avoid them. His analysis of inattentive chanting is particularly interesting. He calls it *pramāda,* or madness, and says, "One may carefully avoid all the other *nāma-aparādhas* yet still not experience the ecstasy of the pure name. This is an indication of another type of *nāma-*

aparādha known as *pramāda,* which restricts the natural growth of pure devotion." He says that inattentiveness is similar to negligence and is of three kinds. One is apathetic devotional service, or a lack of fixed resolve in *sādhana.* The second is laziness, or even inertia. The third is distraction, or misplacing one's attention in engagments not directly connected with *sādhana-bhakti.*[1] He recommends chanting with a pure devotee and increasing the number of rounds. But he also says it is important to concentrate on the quality of the holy names and not try to artificially increase the number of rounds. He also recommends spending "a little time alone in a quiet place and concentrating deeply on the holy name."[2] I have read this book several times and have tried to take its suggestions to heart. But Śrīla Bhaktivinoda Ṭhākura states that it is impossible to achieve pure chanting by our own endeavor. Your mercy is required.

Press gently but persistently on this vantage point of distinguishing distractions from the desire to be attentive. I'm trying to relieve myself of this *aparādha* called *pramāda,* the madness of inattention, which is due to laziness, lack of taste, and attachment to material pleasures.

That means I have to beg for Your mercy as I chant: "Dear Rādhā, dear Kṛṣṇa, please engage me in Your service." *Japa* is a crying out for Your mercy. If we cannot cry, then we should cry that we cannot cry. I know that improving my *japa* is very important and that it is only apparently an easy task; it requires great concentration. Please help me. Let my mind not wander or become apathetic. Let me come to the stage where I can serve Nāma Prabhu with a humble heart, realizing that the holy names are my only shelter and my only true happiness.

---

1 Śrīla Bhaktivinoda Ṭhākura, *Śrī Harināma-cintāmaṇi*. Trans. Sarvabhāvana Dāsa (Vrindavana: Rasbihari Lal & Sons, 2001), 81.

2 *Ibid.*, 84.

My dear Lord, if we want to chant with more devotion, we have to rise early and exercise with concentration in *japa-yajña*. Then we will receive the mercy. If we don't make the effort, it's like we're hiding from the sun's rays. What can the sun do for us if we don't go out and expose ourselves? If we hide from its rays, we will grow pale and unhealthy. We need a little sunlight. Similarly, we need to bask in Your mercy.

Your mercy is available in *sādhu-saṅga, guru-saṅga,* and *śāstra-saṅga.* They will rejuvenate us. We need to receive these not just by lip service but by actual participation and association. Sometimes we need to inquire directly, submissively from *sādhu* and guru, and we need to regularly read the *śāstra* with faith. Your mercy is available there.

My dear Lord, again I pray with a wish to know You better. As I know You more, I will love You more and serve You more. The ways to know You are standard, as given in *sādhana-bhakti* by You and the *ācāryas* in Your disciplic succession. I just have to follow them sincerely and seriously.

The first thing is chanting Your names (and Rādhā's names) in the Hare Kṛṣṇa mantra. How do I get to know You by chanting? You are nondifferent from Your names; You are present in the sound vibration. So the more I chant with the desire to be with You, the closer I will come into Your association, and You will reveal Yourself to me. It is a little bewildering how just by uttering these brief syllables we can accomplish what even great, austere yogis and meditators cannot attain, but that is the prime benediction for this age as given by Śrī Caitanya Mahāprabhu. He came to deliver the chanting of Hare Kṛṣṇa imbued with the sentiment of pure love for You, as carried in Her heart by Your chief consort, Śrīmatī Rādhārāṇī. Someone once asked Prabhupāda, "What do you gain by chanting?" He replied, "Chanting brings chanting." That's like saying chanting brings Rādhā-Kṛṣṇa. They will dance on your tongue. *Harināma* will cleanse the mirror of the mind, and you will see yourself as you are, as spirit soul. The chanting will increase the ocean of transcendental bliss and help us to taste the nectar for which we are always anxious.

The taste, *ruci*, comes, but not to a materially diseased person. First comes appreciation, then *sādhu-saṅga*, associating with devotees. Next comes *bhajana-kriyā*. He feels, "Why not become a disciple? Śrīla Prabhupāda, please initiate me." Next comes *anartha-nivṛtti*, observing regulative activities and stopping sinful habits. The next stage is *niṣṭhā*, firm faith. And then *ruci*, taste. A jaundiced person takes sugar candy and gets taste. You have to go through the stages to reach taste. If you continue to hear with faith and appreciation, you come to taste. Taste means you like it. Then you can go on nicely chanting. Śrīla Rūpa Gosvāmī Prabhupāda wrote, "If I had millions of heads, I could satisfy my desire for chanting." But for us, sixteen rounds is a big job because we have no taste. Taste is created by serving a pure devotee. If you satisfy a pure devotee, you get all good qualities. *Kṛṣṇa-bhakti* is in everyone's heart, but it is covered by dirty things. The more you chant and hear, you will become cleansed of dirty things and it will be revealed.

BLESSED ROUTINE

nikhila-śruti-mauli ratna-mālā-
dyuti nīrājita-pādapankajānta
ayi mukta-kulair upāsyamānaṁ
paritas tvāṁ harināma saṁśrayāmi

"O Holy Name! The tips of the toes of Your lotus feet are eternally worshiped by the glowing effulgence radiating from the strings of gems known as the *Upaniṣads,* the crest jewels of the Vedas. You are eternally adored and chanted by great liberated souls. O Hari Nāma! Clearing myself of all offenses, I take complete shelter of You."

— Śrīla Rūpa Gosvāmī, *Śrī Nāmāṣṭakam,* 1

JAPA WISDOM: OF ALL THE PROCESSES of devotional service, chanting the holy names is the best. It is taken up by the wisest persons. They may not be learned in Sanskrit or in the philosophical speculation of the *Upanisads.* They may not possess great yogic powers or be capable of yogic gymnastics, and they may certainly not be materially opulent or militarily powerful. But these things, which are all hard to accomplish, are of little importance in obtaining the utmost goal of human life. That goal is known as *premā pumartho mahān*—love of God.[3] It is also referred to in Sanskrit as *prayojana*, the highest goal. Love of Kṛṣṇa is the highest goal.

A person chants the name of God that he is attracted to, but Kṛṣṇa is most powerful name. A thousand "Viṣṇus" equal one "Rāma," and three "Rāmas" equal one "Kṛṣṇa." The Hare Kṛṣṇa *mahā-mantra* is the greatest mantra. It's made up of the names of Rādhā and Kṛṣṇa. It is quoted in the *Upanisads*, and Śrīla Bhaktivinoda Ṭhākura and Śrīla Bhaktisiddhanta Sarasvati Ṭhākura chanted it and advised their followers to chant it. Śrīla Prabhupāda brought it out of India and spread it all over the world. He recommended it as the great mantra for deliverance. He gave his disciples *dīkṣā* initiation with the order that they chant at least sixteen rounds on 108 beads daily. He started public *saṅkīrtana* on Sunday afternoons at Tompkins Square Park. Crowds gathered to watch. Some took part in the singing. He led the singing of *kīrtana* in the storefront temple three nights a week and every morning.

Those first months with Swamiji were wonderful. Taking lunch with him in his apartment room – "Take more." Rice, *dahl*, *sabji*, and plenty of *capatis*. Conversations with him. Jokes and *kṛṣṇa-tattva* and *līlā* while eating. He led us and took part with us. Concern with getting his visa extended. Raising money for expenses. Brahmānanda (a substitute high school teacher) and Satsvarūpa (a case worker with the Department of Welfare) donated their weekly checks. An occasional donation from a friend.

---

3 *ārādhyo bhagavān vrajeśa-tanayas-tad-dhāma vṛndāvanaṁ/ramyā kācid-upāsanā vraja-vadhū vargeṇa yā kalpitā/ śrīmad-bhāgavataṁ pramāṇam amalaṁ premā pumartho mahān/ śrīcaitanya mahāprabhor matam idaṁ tatrādaro naḥ paraḥ.* This verse by Śrīla Visvanatha Cakravartī can be translated: "Vrajendra-nandana Śrī Kṛṣṇa is the Supreme worshipful Deity. Śrī Vṛndāvana Dhāma is worshipful like Kṛṣṇa, being the place of His pastimes. Amongst all forms of worship, the *gopīs'* worship of Kṛṣṇa is supreme. *Śrīmad-Bhāgavatam* is accepted as the supreme, flawless evidence of this truth. This is the instruction of Śrī Caitanya Mahāprabhu."

Enough to get by. Talking with him in his room on Tuesday, Thursday, and Saturday, when he didn't hold a class. He'd talk about Kṛṣṇa, answer questions. Gradually teaching us Kṛṣṇa consciousness. The best friend and spiritual father. Living on the Lower East Side became a paradise after two years of living there in artistic, loveless frustration. New friends gathered around the Swami. Typing for him. Getting close to him.

As late as 1977, Śrīla Prabhupāda recalled that I used to bring him a fresh mango every day. He reminisced about 1966 and said, "Those were happy days."[4] For me, they were the happiest days of my life. One of the best times to chant was in the morning with Śrīla Prabhupāda. After *kīrtana*, he used to say, 'Chant one round.' We did it together. He usually finished before we did, and then we all trailed off, even if we hadn't finished the round.[5]

stotrair japaiś ca devāgre
yaḥ stauti madhusūdanam
sarva-pāpa-vinirmukto
viṣṇulokam avāpnuyāt

"A person who chants japa and offers prayers to Madhusūdana, Lord Śrī Kṛṣṇa, becomes free of all sins and returns to the spiritual world."

—*Nṛsiṁha Purāṇa,* as quoted in *Hari-bhakti-vilāsa* 8.348

---

4 One time, when Tamāla Kṛṣṇa left the room and I was alone with Prabhupāda, he continued speaking about his own preaching. "When I went to New York," he said, I simply sat down with a small drum. Many were dancing. Were you there? I was working hard then. Those were happy days. Three hours chanting in the park, then back to the temple for two hours. There was a bench in the kitchen, and I used to sit on it and watch Second Avenue at night. I couldn't sleep." see Satsvarūpa dāsa Goswami. "Chapter Five" in *Life With A Perfect Master* (Philadelphia: Gita Nagari Press, 1987).

5 For elaborations by Śrīla Prabhupāda, see Śrīla A.C. Bhaktivedanta Swami Prabhupāda, *Śrī Nāmāmṛta: The Nectar of the Holy Name* (Los Angeles, CA:The Bhaktivedanta Book Trust, 1982).

I am a *japa* chanter. I do not chant at the perfect stage (*śuddha-nāma*), but I am very fortunate. I chant sixteen rounds a day and try to avoid offenses. I am bathed in Kṛṣṇa's mercy, *harināma*. It is the best way to approach Rādhā and Kṛṣṇa and ask for *sevā*.

I like to chant my *japa* alone, or at most with one or two buddies. Some places practice *japa* in a packed room with many devotees. At 26 2nd Ave., Prahbupada used to chant a round with all the devotees. But I believe Raghunātha dāsa Gosvāmī and Haridāsa Ṭhākura practiced solitary *bhajana*. It is nice chanting alone with the Lord in intimacy. You hear your own sound vibration clearly, without mingling with others. It lends itself to good practice by the nature of its concentration. There are no hard and fast rules to chanting the holy names. Either with others or alone is allowable. I am just stating a particular preference.

Japa is a blessing. You bless yourself, as when taking *caranāmṛta*. It's like when you take the flame which is offered by the *pūjārī*, or when he sprinkles you with water or offers you the flower to smell. It is like honoring *prasādam*. Only it is better. It is directly Rādhā and Kṛṣṇa. You are nourished by your tongue and your ears. *Japa* is even more merciful than the *sākṣād darśana* of the Lord's form.

In different *yugas*, different methods of achieving it are prescribed. In Satya Yuga, when people lived for thousands of years, the prescribed method is meditation on the Lord. People lived long enough to achieve it. In Tretā Yuga, the method was performance of sacrifices by learned *brāhmaṇas*. In Dvāpara Yuga, the method was Deity worship. For various reasons, peoples' powers have been diminished. Their life duration has decreased, they have little money, and there are no qualified *brāhmaṇas* for performing *yajñas*.

In the present millennium, which lasts 430,000 years, only one method of achieving God consciousness is possible. That is the chanting of the holy names of God, specifically, the *mahā-mantra*: Hare Kṛṣṇa Hare Kṛṣṇa Kṛṣṇa Kṛṣṇa Hare Hare, Hare Rāma Hare Rāma Rāma Rāma Hare Hare. It is very easy to perform. It can be done by singing (even without musical instruments) or by chanting silently on beads, at least sixteen rounds a day while avoiding offenses, such as inattention to chanting and blaspheming devotees. By chanting Hare Kṛṣṇa, the reactions to all of your previous sinful activities can be removed, and you can become liberated from birth and death. Who is such a fool that he will not take up this process of chanting Hare Kṛṣṇa? The devotees of the Lord take up the mission of inducing people to chant. This makes them very dear to Kṛṣṇa. But before inducing others to chant, one must chant himself under the instructions of the spiritual master. Śrīla Prabhupāda has said that of all the instructions of the spiritual master, the instruction to chant sixteen rounds a day is essential. How about you, dear reader? Do you chant sixteen rounds? As a servant of my spiritual master and as your humble well-wisher, I beg you to do so.

I pray to keep attentive and to make my chanting more holy. It is sometimes difficult to meet Nāma Prabhu at a deeper level. I'm counting the rounds. But I tried my best and did not falter in the basic execution. I'll be able to chant twelve rounds before 5:00 A.M. That's a decent pace. I am thinking of Prabhupāda's translation of *Śrī Śikṣāṣṭakam*: "It increases the ocean of transcendental bliss, and it enables us to fully taste the nectar for which we are always anxious."[6] I'm not in the ocean of transcendental bliss, but I am anxious for the taste of the nectar. I am praying to Kṛṣṇa for effort and steadiness. I am calling to Him in my desperation. Please, Lord, let me keep steady and improve. Don't let me slip.

A routine day, struggling to stay with
Nāma Prabhu, begging my mind to stay
alert and fixed. I stay at a decent level
and do not submerge beneath the water
of consciousness. But I wish I was
better, fresher in the realm of the
Hare Kṛṣṇa mantra.

aham eva kalau vipra nityaṁ pracchanna-vigrahaḥ
bhagavad-bhakta-rūpeṇa lokān rakṣati sarvadā

"The Lord said: 'Concealing My real identity, O *vipra* [Mārkaṇḍeya Ṛṣi], I appear in Kali-yuga in the garb of a devotee and always protect My devotees.'"

—*Nāradīya Purāṇa*, 5.47

In Dvāpara Yuga, Kṛṣṇa was blackish, and the prescribed form of *yajña* was sacrifice. In Kali Yuga, the Lord is worshiped by *nāma-yajña*. He appears in a golden form. The Lord chanted, and the people followed. Just as in some of our pictures, the Lord is dancing, and the

6 Śrī Caitanya Mahāprabhu, *Śikṣāṣṭakam*, 1. Trans. Śrīla A.C. Bhaktivedanta Swami Prabhupāda, in Introduction to *Śrīmad Bhāgavatam*, Vol. 1, (New York: Bhaktivedanta Book Trust, 1987), 40.

devotees are dancing also. It is said that Lord Caitanya is present when the devotees are chanting. Pure devotees have no interest in material enjoyment. *Kṛṣṇa-varṇaṁ tviṣākṛṣṇaṁ.* (*Bhag.* 11.5.32) This verse from *Śrīmad-Bhāgavatam* tells how He is worshiped in Kali Yuga. The Lord is worshiped differently in different *yugas.* In Satya Yuga, he was worshiped by meditation. In Dvāpara Yuga, He was worshiped by sacrifice, and in Tretā Yuga, He was worshiped by Deity worship. In Kali Yuga, He is worshiped by chanting. In the *Śrīmad-Bhāgavatam,* when Mahārāja Pariksit heard the predictions of how the people would suffer in Kali Yuga, he became sad. To encourage him, Sukadeva Gosvāmī told him that in this bad age, there is one boon. Although the age is full of miseries, the first-class boon is that in the midst of catastrophes, one can be free of all contamination. These verses are from *Śrīmad-Bhāgavatam.*[7] There is also a verse in the *Padma Purāṇa.*[8] There are different *Purāṇas* for people in different mentalities. The Bible was written for a different age, when people were not so advanced. But they should be given a chance. Rajasic *Purāṇas* are for demigod worship to have material desires fulfilled. But the *Bhāgavatam* says thatif you have material desires, you should still go to Kṛṣṇa.[9] In all Vedic literature, the last goal is Kṛṣṇa. In Kali Yuga, we are so condemned, but even the demigods praise this age because simply by *saṅkīrtana,* all interests are served, both

---

7 *Bhag.* 12.3.51-52 *Ibid.*,

8 In the present Kali-yuga especially, as described in the following verse of *Padma Purāṇa,* Uttara, 72.25: *dhyāyan kṛte yajan yajñais/ tretāyāṁ dvāpare 'rcayan/yad āpnoti tad āpnoti/ kalau saṅkīrtya keśavam.* "Whatever is achieved by meditation in Satya-yuga, by performance of *yajña* is Tretā-yuga, or by the worship of Kṛṣṇa's lotus feet in Dvāpara-yuga, is obtained in the age of Kali simply by chanting and glorifying Lord Keśava." *(Caitanya-caritamrta, Madhya,* 20.346) Kṛṣṇadāsa Kavirāja, *Śrī Caitanya-caritāmṛta of Kṛṣṇadāsa Kavirāja Gosvami.* Trans. Śrīla A.C. Bhaktivedanta Swami Prabhupāda. Madhya Lila, Vol. 8 (Los Angeles: Bhaktivedanta Book Trust, 1996), 195.

9 *Bhag.* 2.3.10

material and spiritual. Therefore the Hare Kṛṣṇa mantra is called the *mahā-mantra.*

I spoke at a gathering of disciples. The talk went all right, but I didn't do well in the questions afterwards. Līlā-avatāra asked me why devotees aren't going on *harināma* in the streets and why they aren't distributing books like they used to. I had no good answer. I said they were doing it in some places. Someone volunteered that a new kind of *saṅkīrtana* is evolving where devotees go into yoga centers and perform *kīrtana* there. Śāstra said that Kṛṣṇa consciousness is flourishing in India and that if one feels discouraged, he should go to the holy *dhāmas,* and he will see that things are enlivening there. But I had nothing much to add to the remarks that others made. Bhāgavatānanda mentioned that the tactics for book distribution had grown excessive and that there was cheating. My inability to answer the question left me feeling depressed and out of the mainstream. In asking why we don't go out and do *harināma* anymore, Līlā-avatāra yesterday quoted the Sanskrit to the first verse of *Śrī Śikṣāṣṭakam*: *ceto-darpaṇa-mārjanaṁ bhava-mahā-dāvāgni-nirvāpaṇaṁ.* She said we could have gone out today and done *harināma* in Rehoboth, but probably there were good reasons for not doing so. She said she herself does not have good health. I said I also am not able to go out.

I received a letter from a Godbrother lamenting that he does not have access to taking part in *kīrtanas.* He cited a statement by Śrīla Bhaktisiddhanta Sarasvati Ṭhākura:

"Proper *japa* chanting is possible only in the mind. Then the chanter will achieve the desired perfection. Chanting audibly with lip movements is *kīrtana;* it is more effective than *japa* and brings about the greatest benefit to the hearer. *Saṅkīrtana* means 'complete *kīrtana,*' for it is unnecessary to perform any other devotional activities if one performs *saṅkīrtana.*"[10] My Godbrother wrote, "I know philosophically that the holy name is no less potent in *japa* than in *saṅkīrtana,* but the issue is not Śrī Nāma's potency; rather, it is my ability to be absorbed. It seems that *saṅkīrtana* is the particularly applicable and potent way to capture the consciousness in this age."

Today my mind has not been wandering but has been staying fixed on the utterance of the names, so I've come to expect this. It's a gain from my previous years' chanting. My chanting of eight rounds was below seven minutes a round. Aside from hearing the sounds of the syllables, my mind did not sink into the Rādhā-Kṛṣṇa meditation. But I *am* calling out just by basic faith in the *japa* operation. As when I speak to Kṛṣṇa in my afternoon free write, I have confidence in Kṛṣṇa's being open to me when I chant *japa.* My fixation on accumulating mantras is not the highest stage, but it is important work. For now, it is the heart of my practice. I pay attention and quickly add one mantra to the next. I *try* to do something besides counting. This morning I thought of the vintage Lough Derg diary I'm reading, and I was eager to read some more. I also anticipated my journal writing and prayed to be able to do some today. Aside from this, I could not think of Kṛṣṇa aside from the counting. After all, Śrīla Prabhupāda did advise, "Just hear." The names are absolute. You benefit just by touching them with your tongue. When you put

10 From Śrīla Bhaktisiddhanta's purport to the first *śloka* of *Śrī Śikṣāṣṭakam.* "*Sarvato-bhāvenakīrtana* means complete *kīrtana.*" see Śrī Caitanya Mahāprabhu, *Śrī Śikṣāṣṭakam,* ed. B.V. Narayana (Mathura: Gaudiya Vedanta Publications, 1995), 17.

your hand in fire, you'll be burnt. When you say the Hare Kṛṣṇa mantras, you become Kṛṣṇa-ized.

This morning my chanting was at a low audible whisper. When I chant in the mind, I think it's due to fear of overstraining (and getting a headache), or maybe it's laziness. But I remain attentive. Prabhupāda said we should cry like a child calling for the mother. That is a wonderful quality. He said Mother Harā (Śrīmatī Rādhārāṇī) would hear our cry and respond with Her mercy. Am I crying, at least a little? I think so.

I remember in 1966 I once walked out of a *kīrtana* engagement we devotees held at a public hall. I wasn't yet committed to being a devotee, to restrict my association to only devotees. I walked out of the building and wandered into the streets of the Lower East Side, observing the lights and the people. But then I felt a strong sense of estrangement from everything in the streets and a pull to go back and join my new devotee friends. I walked back to the hall and met them just as they were leaving. They joked with me about my walking out but welcomed me back to their group. That was maybe the last time I did anything like that. From then on, I always stayed exclusively within the ISKCON group.

You want to be on the side of good and free of maya. Some taints remain until you are perfectly pure. By hearing and chanting, which are pious acts, Kṛṣṇa in the heart works to cleanse out the remaining dirt. Śrīla Prabhupāda once said, "When you are seventy-five percent pure, you can go back to Godhead." He said that immediately after saying you had to be a hundred percent pure. Kṛṣṇa decides.

Writing to Kṛṣṇa. Running to You with my eyes closed. Praying to You with the *mahā-mantra*. Not knowing what to do for You. The best thing is to give people Kṛṣṇa consciousness. That is better than food or medicine or weapons or "education." Give them direct Kṛṣṇa consciousness. There are tactics for that. They used to do it largely by dressing as civilians and approaching people to sell them Prabhupāda's books. Dressing as devotees and going in the streets to sing the Hare Kṛṣṇa mantra. Lectures in the colleges. Giving out *prasādam* to materially needy people. Festivals on Sunday at the temple or Ratha Yatras in the streets and parks. Setting the example by running a "self-sufficient" farm, growing crops and protecting cows. Bringing people to the holy *dhāmas* of India. Teaching *aṣṭāṅga yoga*. Holding lectures, *kīrtanas* and feasts in your home and inviting neighbors and friends. Publishing books and *Back to Godhead* magazine; selling CDs, videos on the Internet; running a webpage on the Internet; building temples. And many more tactics performed by enthusiastic preachers.

From the beginning, *śraddhā*, to the end, *prema*, faith is the essential ingredient. A doubting person cannot make progress. Acting on our original faith, we can progress to associate with devotees, take vows of initiation, become steady, attached, and develop taste. Then the first bud of love of God begins to open. Faith is cultivated by good association and by chanting and hearing. Please, Lord, keep my faith protected and always growing, so that I may not stagnate at the neophyte stage of doubting. I shall practice faith and attain devotion to Rādhā-Kṛṣṇa without disruption or delay. That is my earnest request.

I LIKE CHANTING THE *MAHĀ-MANTRA*. I'm familiar enough with the words "Hare," "Kṛṣṇa," and "Rāma." They please me as they pass through my mind and lips. I've been doing it so long it's become a love and a deep attachment. I could never switch to another kind of prayer of another religion, or even another mantra in the Vedic religion. This is it for me. I began in 1966, and I'll continue it until the end. Śrīla Prabhupāda was so expert as to cement it to my being, and the mantra itself has the potency that once you chant it, you never want to stop. I'm like Gopa-kumāra, who, no matter where he went, chanted his Gopāl mantra, because it brought him more satisfaction than anything else, even when he was in the heavenly planets or Vaikuṇṭha. He was always restless unless he was chanting his *dīkṣā* mantra.[11] The Hare Kṛṣṇa mantra stays with you so that you chant it even in the dentist's office or in the car after you've chanted your minimum prescribed rounds.

Yesterday I chanted eight extra rounds after my minimum sixteen and wanted to do more, but I got distracted. If there was enough time in the day and I didn't think I had other things to do, I would chant even more. It doesn't get boring once you're actually sailing along in the mantras themselves. I'm chanting with my right hand now, even though it hurts a little with my shoulder. It's more "comfortable" this way, and more natural. I'm convinced that Lord Caitanya has given us the best thing possible for this age. It's amazing how simple it is. People think it's too simple to be profound, and so they don't take it up. But we need a simple thing because we're not competent to do meditation or we're not capable of performing Vedic *yajña*s or elaborate deity worship in place of the mantra. It's a beautiful conception that He packed all His potencies in

---

11 Śrīla Sanātana Gosvāmī, Chapter 5 "The Glories of Goloka," in Sanātana Gosvāmī, *Śrī Bṛhad-Bhāgavatāmṛta of Śrīla Sanātana Gosvāmī*. Trans. Gopīparāṇadhana dāsa. Vol. 3 (Los Angeles: Bhaktivedanta Book Trust, 2002).

these thirty-two syllables and places Himself there too in the most merciful form. The conception is beautiful, what to speak of the actual execution. We should always be very grateful to Kṛṣṇa for giving us the Hare Kṛṣṇa mantra, and we should show our gratitude by chanting it as much as possible. That way, we will bond with Him, which is our heart's greatest desire. Hare Kṛṣṇa Hare Kṛṣṇa Kṛṣṇa Kṛṣṇa Hare Hare/ Hare Rāma Hare Rāma Rāma Rāma Hare Hare.

Chanting *japa* is my solemn duty. Even if you get up late, you have to chant your *japa*, gradually catching up with the quota. Don't be sloppy because it's late. Slow down and be patient and execute the *yajña* with a sane mind. Repeat the syllables patiently. Try to think of Rādhā and Kṛṣṇa. Don't worry, they will get done, they will get done. It's a simple thing. Anyone can do it. We should not push it to a corner of the mind and dwell on other things because of its simplicity. Give the mind's full attention to this simplicity. It's a prayer to which you can give your whole heart. Call out to Kṛṣṇa, the Supreme Lord, by saying His name. Call out to Rādhā, our eternal benefactor, by calling Her name. They can help you. Be sure of that. Use your time for this, and other things can get done at another time. Let it be a day of catching up. But I can chant with leisure and steadfastness. It is not a day to rush. Neither is it a day to be remorseful, but just take it in stride that you have to give your time to the chanting and not to other things. The mantras are a gift and should be handled gratefully. It is no different from another day, except you have more time to dedicate, more time to build the quota, more time to do it nicely. Less time for other things, but that's all right, because you're doing the primary thing, and so your day is not wasted, not in the least.

I chanted my rounds with enunciation
calmly turning them over and over.

A feeling of warmth grew within my heart,
and I felt neither guilty nor rushed.

It was a day to dedicate to the *mahā-mantra*,
a special treat,
not a day of punishment
or regret. I took my time
as the hours went by,
absorbed in the holy names just like a dedicated chanter
from the times of Lord Caitanya. They had nothing to do but chant
and felt they were totally engaged.

They gave their minds and hearts to the mantras
and spent the day in trance.
Why can't you do that?

A few days ago Nārāyaṇa-kavaca said we should like to take a day off each week and rest. What he meant was we should use it like Ekādasi and do extra *sādhana*, chanting and hearing. A devotee wrote me and said that at the Alachua temple, many devotees take the weekend off and don't attend the morning program. He said he didn't approve and that this wasn't Prabhupāda's standard.

Last night I dreamt of Śrīla Prabhupāda. He was gathering all his disciples together and asking them if they took his instructions seriously. Different devotees spoke up and gave proofs of how they had pleased him and done outstanding service. I showed a proof from a newspaper that I had done some good service. Prabhupāda was very serious at the meeting and not easily convinced by the devotees' proofs.

I don't like it when I think of him as being so stern but prefer his being pleased with us. Some of us think that Prabhupāda will appear at the time of our death and speak up to Kṛṣṇa on our behalf. I guess the idea comes from our knowing Śrīla Prabhupāda was very compassionate and grateful for the services devotees rendered him. The *Bhagavad-gītā* states that even a little service will never be lost and will save us from the greatest fear. The greatest fear is that the Yamadūtas will come for us and punish us after death. We think of Śrīla Prabhupāda as a Viṣṇudūta who will come and stand between us and the Yamadūtas.

Chanting *japa* with a clear head is a great gift. I was able to do it, unaware of pain. The time went by slowly, although I was pushing. *Japa* must be an intense endeavor. It is not a laid-back thing. As you chant, you simultaneously brush out of the thoughts, like using a hand brush and a dustpan. You keep your mind clean. As for thinking of the pastimes of Rādhā and Kṛṣṇa, I have not reached that stage. I am a mantra chanter. I am trying to avoid the ten offenses in chanting. On one level, I'm doing it pretty well, but not going further. I don't blaspheme devotees, I don't consider the names of the demigods as equal or independent of the name Kṛṣṇa. I don't doubt the scriptures, I don't take the chanting as exaggeration or make an interpretation of it. I chant with attention. I don't commit sinful activities on the strength of chanting. I don't consider the chanting a material act of piety. I don't teach the chanting of the holy names to faithless persons. I don't chant for material benefits. I try to avoid these basic offenses. But I don't cry out to Kṛṣṇa and Rādhā, "Please let me serve You." I don't dwell on Their sweet pastimes. Śrīla Bhaktivinoda Ṭhākura has made a reversal of the ten offenses and taken them all in a positive way. As an example, instead of the first offense being, "Don't blaspheme devotees," he says you should always be happy when you see the devotees. I haven't achieved all his positive reversals. I don't chant fully from the heart. I don't manifest any bodily symptoms of ecstasy. So I still chant out of duty, not spontaneity. Don't be disappointed, but don't think you have reached the stage of *bhāva*. Keep chanting like a workhorse. Giddy-up.

Oh pitiful chanter,
when will you reach the grace
of ecstatic mantras
in the footsteps of the *ācāryas*,
who have won this race?
When will you chant
with happy face?

You chant your *japa* quickly and then slowly. Sometimes you get sleepy. You have heard that even negligent *japa* brings great benefit, so powerful is *harināma*. The names are more merciful than Kṛṣṇa the person. They are Kṛṣṇa in the form of sacred syllables. You try to vibrate them out loud, loudly, but you're not always successful. But you always push them out. When you are not writing, you are chanting. You ask your body to cooperate, but it is slowing down and ailing. Even Haridāsa Ṭhākura began to chant fewer rounds in his old age, but Lord Caitanya told him not to worry, he was already liberated. At his prime, Haridāsa chanted three hundred thousand names a day. They gave it all they had, and the Lord empowered them. Their chanting was *śuddha-sattva,* completely transcendental with no offenses. They saw Kṛṣṇa in His names. They loved to chant and never diverted their attention. Saint Thérèse of Lisieux compared herself to a little sparrow who looked up to the great eagles, the saints like Teresa of Avila. I want to be like that, a little worshiping sparrow looking up admiringly at the great ones.

You're not really chanting
as well as you claim you
are. There are mountains
and mountains ahead of
higher achievement. You are only
in the foothills of *harināma.*

But you're grateful to be
living in Hare Kṛṣṇa space,
breathing the rare air
of transcendental sound vibration.
Your spiritual master has given
you a great gift, you
owe it to him to lift yourself
higher to chant without offense.
Go into your heart and cry
out for the mercy,
don't be content with the quota.

Oh, the world's a fine place. Grab a little chaos on a couch. Eat what you can and enjoy your woman. It's a good place if you're a rich human being; in that species, you can go farthest to hell. And after that, you're reduced to misery as a sheep in the rain who awaits his slaughter. Or if you're lucky, in human life you can turn it all around and become Kṛṣṇa conscious. But that takes work. You have to be willing to perform *tapo-divyam*. There is no other way; *nasty eva nasty eva* in Kali. Just chant, *harer nāma harer nāmaiva kevalam.*

It's such a good thing when you chant your *japa* decently. It brightens your day. You feel hope for the ultimate goal. After all, chanting is the prime necessity, the easiest way to achieve love of God. In fact, it's the only way in Kali Yuga. I was happy this morning to do a decent job. Now

I'll go on to chant another eight rounds at the parking lot. I hope I don't fall asleep. Keep your determination, your prayers. Keep clicking away at a rapid pace, and stay alert. Chanting may not seem like a big celebration, like eating pizza or having a festival, but in its quiet way, it is actually the happiest time. The greatest self-satisfaction: you feel at peace.

Japa japa japa,
The repeating mantras roll.
When you're awake, you're happy,
your heart feels warm with joy.

Japa japa japa,
repetition without boredom
the repetition of the heartbeat
without which you will die.

Japa japa japa,
may I chant until my last breath.

Japa japa japa,
you put me to rest
but never resting, always more,
moving on to another life with
japa japa japa.

FIRST TRANSFORMATIONS

vācyo vācakam ity udeti bhāvato nāma svarūpa-dvayaṁ
pūrvasmāt param eva hanta karuṇā tatrāpi jānīmahe
yas tasmin vihitāparādha-nivahaḥ prāṇī samantād bhaved
āsyenedam upāsya so'pi hi sadānandāmbudhau majjati

"O Lord! You manifest in two different forms, as He who is Named and as the Name. Of the two, I consider the second to be more merciful than the first. Even if one has committed countless offenses to the Named, one can still be immersed in an ocean of ambrosia by worshiping the Name."

—Śrīla Rūpa Gosvāmī, *Śrī Nāmāṣṭakam,* 7

KṚṢṆA'S NAME IS CAITYA-GURU, "guru, spiritual master from within." So Kṛṣṇa is trying to help us from within, and He manifests again externally also as a spiritual master.

I offer my obeisances to Śrīla Prabhupāda and to Bhaktisiddhanta Sarasvati and Gaura-kisora dāsa Bābājī. These are the real persons in my life. I accept them as guides, not the persons I accepted earlier in my life. I am entitled to change.

I offer respects and loving prayers to the *paramparā*—Bhaktivinoda Ṭhākura, Narottama dasa Ṭhākura, Viśvanātha Cakravartī Ṭhākura, Kṛṣṇadāsa Kavirāja, the Six Gosvāmīs of Vṛndāvana. I pray to Lord Caitanya and all His associates, especially for the mercy of Lord Nityānanda.

I pray to Lord Kṛṣṇa and Śrīmatī Rādhārāṇī and all the Vrajavāsīs. I wish my *japa* was conducted in Vraja.

I pray to the holy name. Please forgive me. Please accept me. Thank You!

You can't speculate. You can do it for many years, but you'll never understand. Guru means weighty. People think, "I know everything." In the Vedic system, a child goes to *gurukula* and works as a menial servant of the guru. The guru can ask him to do any kind of duty, and he does it. Even Kṛṣṇa went to *gurukula.* Caitanya Mahāprabhu accepted a guru. Prakaśānanda Sarasvati was criticizing Lord Caitanya as a sentimentalist for chanting. Prakaśānanda asked him, "Why don't You study *Vedānta*?" Caitanya Mahāprabhu replied, "My guru found Me to be fool number one. He said, 'You can't read *Vedānta sutras.*'" Caitanya Mahāprabhu took the part of an ordinary person. Therefore, Caitanya Mahāprabhu said, "He advised Me to chant Hare Kṛṣṇa, and I'm getting the result." In the present age, people aren't interested in *Vedānta.* They are very slow. They are not interested to know that there is a life after death and that they may have to take an inconvenient position. Therefore, one should consider that Arjuna accepted Lord Kṛṣṇa as his spiritual master. "You teach me, and I will take Your lesson." It is meant for everyone.

The emperor Prācīnabarhi sent his ten sons, the Pracetās, to practice austerities in preparation for marriage. They met Lord Śiva, who, out of great mercy, instructed them about the Absolute Truth. Lord Śiva emerged from a great ocean of water and spoke to them: "Any person who is surrendered to the Supreme Personality of Godhead, Kṛṣṇa, the controller of everything—material nature as well as the living entity—is actually very dear to me" (*Bhag.* 4.24.28). He then began to chant a song. Lord

Śiva had come to bless the Pracetās by personally chanting the mantra. Śrīla Prabhupāda writes, "When a mantra is chanted by a great devotee, the mantra becomes more powerful. Although the Hare Kṛṣṇa mantra is powerful in itself, a disciple upon initiation receives the mantra from his spiritual master, for when the mantra is chanted by the spiritual master, it becomes more powerful. Lord Śiva advised the sons of the king to hear him attentively, for inattentive hearing is offensive" (*Bhag.* 4.24.32, purport).

śravaṇot-kīrtanādīni vaidha-bhakty uditāni tu
yāny aṅgāni ca tany atra vijñeyāni manīṣibhiḥ

As to the processes starting with hearing and chanting of the names, which are the ingredients of *vaidhī-bhakti*, the wise should know them to be essential at the stage of spontaneous devotion as well.[12] Śrīla Viśvanātha Cakravartī Ṭhākura points out in his comments to this verse, that the processes starting from hearing and chanting of the holy names, the *aṅgas* of *vaidhī-bhakti,* which are to be observed in the spontaneous stage, also include the submission to the spiritual master or *guru,*[13] without such guidance by the spiritual master there is no chance of the following in the footsteps of the residents of Vṛndāvana.

12 Śrīla Rūpa Gosvāmī. *Bhakti-rasāmṛta-sindhu*, Eastern Side. 2.296. see Rūpa Gosvāmī, *The Bhakti-rasāmṛta-sindhu of Śrīla Rūpa Gosvāmī with with Durgama-saṅgamanī-ṭīkā, a commentary called "Resolving the Difficult" by Jīva Gosvāmī, and the Bhakti-sāra-pradarśinī-ṭīkā, a commentary called "Revealing the Essence of Bhakti" by Śrīla Viśvanātha Cakravartī Ṭhākura. Trans.* Bhanu Svami (Chennai: Sri Vaikuntha Enterprises, 2005), 329.

13 Śrīla Viśvanātha Cakravartī Ṭhākura, *Bhakti-sāra-pradarśinī-ṭīkā,* 1. 2.296. see Ibid., 329.

4:29 A.M My beginning mood was "ready to go," glad to be up early and start the auspicious practice. My first round went quickly, and after that they continued fast, with a couple of slow ones. My mind went to hearing the syllables and thinking of chanting. I was pretty much occupied with the operation itself. But I also thought of books I wanted to read in Vṛndāvana. I took shelter in feelings of *harināma.* By the time I reached four rounds, I was alert and focused on counting. I was also taking shelter in the potency of *nāma bhajana.* That is, I left behind other things and simply absorbed myself in *japa.* As I continued, it didn't get *better,* but I stayed exactly on course, not wavering in my attention on the holy names. The speed was under seven minutes. The audibility was barely at a whisper. The most disappointing factor was that there was no deeper dimension of calling on Kṛṣṇa. In that sense, it is somewhat mechanical. I certainly hear the syllables and stay awake with trust in the process. It is working, even though I don't go deeper. The best thing was that I wasn't discouraged and went forward undistracted, round after round. My overall impression was satisfaction at completion. But I long for the day when I will feel emotions, as described in *Śikṣāṣṭakam.*

We are sleeping in the lap of mother material nature. We have the power to awaken by good association of *sādhu,* guru, and *śāstra.*

A little faith will help us. We are in a great, dangerous position. We don't know it because we are sleeping. Sometimes the person is killed while he is sleeping. It requires a third person to come and wake you and warn you. Hearing the Vedic mantra is required. The most important mantra is the *mahā-mantra.*

The greatest welfare is to chant loudly so that others can wake up. If we hear the Hare Kṛṣṇa mantra, it will cleanse the mirror of the heart. In the heart there is such a stock of impressions from different lives. Experience of material things is a dirty covering. There is the potency to hear and have the covering removed.

We should take help of the spiritual master. Lord Caitanya has given us this easy process. There is no loss if we chant. There are no hard and fast rules in the chanting. The gain is very great. If the mirror is covered with dust, you cannot see your face. Similarly, the heart is covered. If we try to clean, Kṛṣṇa will help. Kṛṣṇa is so nice as Paramātmā, *caitya-guru.* He is always ready to help. He sends his representative from without. A little faith is required. There must be inclination.

I woke at 3:00 A.M. There was loud thunder and heavy slashing of rain against the roof. Nārāyaṇa-kavaca was in the room, and I began my chanting. I was wide awake, but at first I had some negative thoughts. I thought, "What is this chanting? Why all this repetition of sounds?" But then positive thinking came to my rescue, and I settled into the comfortable execution of the mantras. I chanted my rounds at about seven minutes and forty-five seconds per round. I chanted mostly in my mind, but it was good, paying attention to the mantra's syllables and getting close to the Lord. It is a wonderful practice. Chanting snug under Kṛṣṇa's shelter, even on a rainy day. I'd like to say more about the chanting, but it is what it is: the prime benediction for humanity at large, it spreads the rays of the benediction moon, and it gives us a taste of the nectar for which we are always anxious. Everything already has been said about the glories of the holy name. We just have to enter them daily with a humble heart and determination. I've chanted eight rounds, but I still have more time to chant before taking my shower.

Chanting is shelter, like
living in a house. You're
with the Lord in private
meditation. It is cozy
and intimate and warms
the heart. It is better than
a fireplace on a winter day.

I long to spend many
hours with the *harināma* mantra,
improving the performance,
getting closer to the Lord.

This simple, personal
practice is better than pompous
displays and can carry you
back to Godhead.

When you are actually chanting, it's not laborious. Sometimes thinking about chanting and how many rounds you have to chant gets laborious or worrisome. Procrastination or panic become negative factors. But actual chanting is smooth riding, and it's actually fun and enjoyable. You just have to keep moving along and take the responsibility for the larger number of rounds still to do. As you chant, they always gradually diminish, and quickly, too. The absolute necessary of chanting should not be a burden but just a given factor. I actually like to chant and shouldn't forget that. I just get bothered when I run into conflict with other things on my schedule and the quality of the chanting is disturbed. On days when you are behind your schedule, you may have to sacrifice other activities, and you should do that willingly. Quality chanting always comes first.

Chanting behind,
I control my mind
and assure myself
there is nothing to fret.

You'll reach the goal
before the day is out,
so what's to worry?
You have to do it
so you might as well enjoy
the easiest practice
of the day.

Oh well, let's admit
it's not always so easy
and you are not always so willing
but it's do or die
so rest with that.

I woke at 3:45 A.M. and called Nārāyaṇa. He came up quickly and asked how I was. I told him I was late. Then he told me a story from *The Hobbit.*[14] The hobbit was waiting for the wizard to come. He finally saw him coming on his cart. The hobbit was overjoyed and ran up to the wizard and

14 J.R.R. Tolkein, *The Hobbit*. (London: HarperCollins, 1992).

jumped on his cart. He said, "I'm so glad to see you. You're late." The wizard replied, "A wizard arrives precisely when he intends to." Nārāyaṇa-kavaca applied this to me and said I should stop this anxiety over getting up late. He said it doesn't matter when I get up. That's clear. I've chanted three rounds. I'm trying not to be in anxiety about it.

A wizard arrives
precisely when he means to.
So I should not lacerate myself.
I should be assured I'll

get them done during the day,
even if it's later in the day.
The important thing is
to say them nicely,

not rushed but
say Hare, Kṛṣṇa, and Rāma
with fervor yet relaxed,
praying steadily to my Lords.

You're sorry when you start *japa* late because you fear you'll neglect the mantras. There's no need to neglect them, even if you start late. You still keep your pace, rapid but even, and clearly enunciating the words. So what if it takes you longer into the day to complete the rounds? You still have to do them all, and as nicely as possible. It's the duty of the individual. You made your individual vow to Śrīla Prabhupāda to do sixteen rounds. It's a solemn vow. Other things can be put aside in order to complete your *japa*. You hear yourself chanting and rumble along. You keep the same reverence. You restrain your impatience and irritation. It's just another day. Chanting gets done, rain or shine. You spend a late morning chanting. It means just as much to you on an early day as on a late day. There's not some great advantage on an early day. It just seems that way. A chanting career is built on steadiness day in, day out, and in attention to the mantras, no matter what the condition. You control yourself to keep the same quality and effort in hearing. There's no racing to get a "bargain basement" set done. Holy, holy, holy, merciful and mighty. Be careful you don't cheat yourself and do less.

The chanting of the holy name resonates in your mind and comes out of your mouth. You pay attention to the quality, that each mantra is uttered clearly, each syllable pronounced and heard. You try as usual for reciprocation with the Divine Couple. Have faith that They are hearing you and are pleased with your recitation. This is the most important part of your day. "Of all the orders of the spiritual master, the order to chant sixteen rounds is essential."[15] I am all right, don't worry about me.

Say it over and
over again, the
mahā-mantra.

Say it over and
over again, thousands
of times, from your
heart.

Let Kṛṣṇa's names vibrate
in your room as you

---

15 Purport to *Caitanya-caritamrta*, Madhya 22.113 by Śrīla A.C. Bhaktivedanta Swami Prabhupāda in Kṛṣṇadāsa Kavirāja, *Śrī Caitanya-caritāmṛta of Kṛṣṇadāsa Kavirāja Gosvami*. Trans. Śrīla A.C. Bhaktivedanta Swami Prabhupāda. Madhya Lila, Vol. 8 (Los Angeles: Bhaktivedanta Book Trust, 1996), 393.

finger your beads.
Let the early hours
go by, and repeat
the mantras without
cessation.

That's the way to Kṛṣṇa
in this age. It's
the best way to realize
that the name is Him.
By many repetitions
without offenses, you will realize
success in spiritual life.

Say it over and
over again, Hare
Kṛṣṇa Hare Kṛṣṇa
Kṛṣṇa Kṛṣṇa Hare Hare
Hare Rāma Hare Rāma
Rāma Rāma Hare Hare.
Say it until you're tired,
and then say more.

You'll get your second wind
and start to relish
the sound vibration
as coming from Goloka.
Keep chanting later in the day and
try to extend your
numerical strength until you're a lover
of the holy names.

sat-saṅga, kṛṣṇa-sevā, bhāgavata, nāma
vraje vāsa,—ei pañca sādhana pradhāna

"To be elevated to the platform of devotional service, the following five items should be observed: association with advanced devotees, engagement in the service of Lord Kṛṣṇa, the reading of *Śrīmad-Bhāgavatam*, the chanting of the holy names of the Lord and residence in Vṛndāvana."

—*Caitanya-caritāmṛita. Madhya,* 23.193.

They say it's important to associate with advanced devotees.[16] So today I'm associating with one, Girirāja Swami. We will eat lunch together in the yellow submarine. They say you should reveal your mind in confidence. So I'll tell Girirāja Swami something on my mind. Tell him about my six months of not traveling and what I hope to achieve. We're both on the physically weak side and getting older. We can share our aches and pains. We both know it's important to keep alive our relationship with Śrīla Prabhupāda. We'll talk about how to do it. I'll have to admit some shortcomings. I'll give him copies of *Human at*

16 "Associating with advanced (*uttama*) devotees, the neophyte quickly comes to the stage of an intermediate (*madhyama*) devotee and at the end he himself becomes counted among the advanced (*uttama*) devotees. As a neophyte (*kaniṣtha-avasthā*), the devotee spends some days diligently chanting the holy name. Because of his diligent chanting of the holy name he finds that his *anarthas* flee far away. When that happens he becomes qualified to chant the holy name purely and also to serve the Vaiṣṇavas." Footnotes by Śrīla Bhaktivinoda Ṭhākura, "Chapter Fifteen." In *Śrī Harināma-cintāmaṇi* (2003). Available in digital form from www.vedabase.com

Best[17] and *A Poor Man Reads the Bhāgavatam,* Volume 4,[18] but with some misgivings because he may not like them. But it's better to give the books than hold them back.

Japa requires our full attention. We can't let the mind wander into ethereal space. It has to be nailed down. First of all, keep up a lively pace and listen to the syllables of the mantra and remember whose names you are chanting. Chanting is a rigorous practice. When you're going smoothly, it doesn't seem to require so much labor. The rounds go quickly, and you elevate yourself to better chanting. But when you run into trouble, then you slow down, and the mind wanders. You have to get a grip on yourself and keep the pace. Otherwise, you get lost. When the mind goes vague, chanting veers off into non-intense *japa*. You need a wake-up call to return to the track. Otherwise, you fall behind and get disappointed.

Chanting in a lost way
is a sorry state of affairs.
You lose your strict consciousness
for what you're supposed to do.

The only remedy is to wake up
to your purpose and put your
foot on the accelerator, your
heart turned back to Kṛṣṇa.

It's an easy process, and
time lost can be regained
by a change in attitude
and making up for lost time.

---

17 Satsvarūpa dāsa Goswami, *Human at Best* (Philadelphia: GN Press, Inc., 2008).

18 *Ibid., A Poor Man Reads the Bhagavatam*. Vol. 4 (Philadelphia: GN Press, Inc., 2008).

Ask Kṛṣṇa for forgiveness
and show Him your better side.
Don't slide.

The discussion of materialistic *japa* is complicated. There is no benefit,[19] but there is benefit because of the kindness of the pure *mahātmas* who find good in the chanting. So it is the kindness and potency of the *mahātmas* that make it valuable and lead to higher states.[20] The materialistic chanters have confidential talks and come to the right conclusions as to how to improve. Then they have to actually apply these conclusions.

Japa walk: 6:55 A.M.
Yadunandana Mahārāja went on the walk with us to the beach. It was foggy, but the sun came up as an orange ball. People were out walking their dogs.

Chanting alone or chanting with a buddy is a sensitive thing. If you chant with a buddy, it has to be the right person who encourages you but doesn't disturb you or interrupt you.

Today I'm making a soft sound vibration and keeping a pace. I'm still trying to accept the absence of Nārāyaṇa-kavaca and accept Yadunandana Swami in his place. Yadunandana Swami has a perfect service attitude. He said he considers it a privilege to help me in any way. He is

---

19 *kṛṣṇa-nāme bhakta kabhu jaḍa-buddhi kore nā/ anartha nā gele nāme rūpa dekhā deya nā.* "The genuine devotee never maintains materialistic conceptions about the holy name of Kṛṣṇa. If the deviations that impede devotional service (*aparādhas*) have not been expelled, then the chanting of the holy name will never reveal the beautiful form of the Lord." Śrīla Bhaktisiddhānta Sarasvatī, *Prākṛta Rasa Śata Dūṣiṇī* (Mayapur: Sajjana Toṣanī, 1916), 29. Also available in digital form from www.vedabase.com

20 Śrīla Bhaktivinoda Ṭhākura, "Śrī Nagar-Kīrtan." In *Gitavali*, available in digital form from www.vedabase.com. Purport by Śrīla Bhaktivinoda Ṭhākura. *Ājñā-Ṭahal* 2.

not as materially competent as Nārāyaṇa. Our relationship is not as intimate yet, but it will grow and bond. I say he is not as materially competent as Nārāyaṇa, but he is good. It's just that Nārāyaṇa is expert. Yadunandana Swami is more even-tempered and constantly helpful. He is in good health, unlike Nārāyaṇa, and so he is not hampered in that way. We should be able to chant well together, because he will keep his chanting at a low volume out of deference to me. We both take the chanting as very important and consider our quotas as being of utmost priority. I'll be missing the beach and the association of Nārāyaṇa.

Yesterday I heard a lecture Śrīla Prabhupāda gave on November 13, 1968, in Los Angeles. It was a commentary on Śrīla Narottama dasa Ṭhākura's song *Hari-hari-biphale.* In this song, Narottama dasa Ṭhākura is lamenting: *hari-hari-biphale* – "I have uselessly spoiled my life."[21]

The human form of life is an opportunity to find out why we're wandering from one life to another. But instead of inquiring, we waste our lives in these material things. So Narottama dasa Ṭhākura is lamenting: "My life was meant for understanding Rādhā and Kṛṣṇa, but I spoiled my life." What is the lamentation? *Golokera prema-dhana, hari-nāma-saṅkīrtana*: "The chanting of Hare Kṛṣṇa is coming from Goloka."[22] The vibration is coming from Kṛṣṇa. Our heart is always burning, trying for sense gratification. Unless you come to the spiritual platform, you'll never be satisfied. "I did not search out the immediate relief of *harināma saṅkīrtana.*"

The chanting is coming from Śacīnandana. Kṛṣṇa likes being addressed by His devotees' names. Vrajanandana has appeared as the son of Śaci, and Balarāma has also appeared. Kṛṣṇa and Balarāma as Gaura-Nitāi are accepting

---

21 *Dainya-bodhika*, 4.1. see Śrīla Bhaktivinoda Ṭhākura, *Prārthanā* (Kolkata: Touchstone Media, 1999), 34.

22 *Dainya-bodhika*, 4.2 *Ibid.*, 34.

sinful persons. The evidence is Jagāi and Mādhāi. They are a sample of the population, and Lord Caitanya delivered them by chanting. Anyone who takes to chanting will become a pure person. When he comes to his senses that he's the eternal servant of Kṛṣṇa, he'll surrender. After many lives, when one becomes wise, he takes to Kṛṣṇa and realizes that Vāsudeva is everything. Lord Caitanya has made it very easy. "You are present before me with Rādhārāṇī. Kṛṣṇa is never alone. First Hare, then Kṛṣṇa. Don't neglect me. I surrender unto You"[23]—this is the purport of this song.

Japa requires alertness. If I feel myself going down, I have to become aware and pick myself up. Chanting in the mind without making a sound vibration is not as good.

> *Japa* is our daily bread
> of devotion. Don't starve
> the beads. Stay alert
> and devotional, move along
> at a lively pace.
>
> *Japa* is our daily prayer,
> don't go without it or
> your spiritual life will
> wither and die. Keep it
> up in spritely spirit.

Japa requires concentration. You obviously can't do two things at once, such as watch television and chant on your beads. If you attempt that, it is offensive chanting and of little value. So you have to make up your mind,

23 *Dainya-bodhika*, 4.4 *Ibid.*, 34.

"This is my time for chanting," and put other things aside. This includes not only other external activities but also the activities of the mind. The *Bhagavad-gītā* says that controlling the mind is as difficult as controlling the wind. (Bg. 6.34) But there is a surprisingly simple way to control the mind while chanting. Prabhupāda's famous expression is, "Just hear." To practice this, you should chant audibly. If for some reason you are not able to chant audibly, then you must chant the syllables of the mantra in your mind.[24]

By deliberately hearing the sound of each syllable, your mind will be occupied, and if you do this vigorously, there will be no chance for the mind to wander to other realms of thought. This method is so simple that chanters may overlook it, but if you apply it, it is very effective. There are further stages in chanting in which one thinks of the pastimes of Kṛṣṇa, meditates on His qualities, and even comes to see His form, but they all follow from the basic practice of attentive hearing. The reason this works so effectively is that the holy name is Kṛṣṇa, and the Hare Kṛṣṇa mantra is invested with all His potencies. Anyone who practices the "just hear" method will find great improvement in his or her chanting.

Chanting is a frolic,
chanting is hard work.
The inner workings of the mind
must cooperate with the movements
of the mouth and teeth.

There's a quiet satisfaction in completing your rounds
that equals nothing else.
You don't feel it as a big fanfare,
but without it, you're miserable.

---

24 Śrīla Prabhupāda advised me to do this while working in the welfare office in 1966 for chanting above my regular sixteen-round minimum. SDG.

With faith I follow the *ācāryas*
who insist that chanting is the all-in-all.
With faith I follow the scriptures
which praise the chanting
as sublime.
It's all a matter of
faith and experience, too.

As you increase your faith,
you increase your conviction,
and everything comes out fine.
I pray for the time when my chanting will be uplifted
to the higher realms described,
and in the meantime, I crawl steadily
like a caterpillar up the stem, step by step
without hesitation, without slipping.
You wait until one foot is well placed, and then
you place the next.
In this way you make progress.

Japa in flower-bearing spring. Sign on a bumper sticker: "Life Is Good." Put the Hare Kṛṣṇa mantra on your bumper sticker. Most people won't relate to it, but it's good for them to see. Allen Ginsberg wrote the Hare Kṛṣṇa mantra in one of his poems in a somewhat disparaging way. The poem was about all the mail he gets. Some Hare Kṛṣṇa devotees knew he was favorable to Hare Kṛṣṇa, so he sarcastically wrote that many of them send him letters that say, "Dear Allen, Hare Kṛṣṇa Hare Kṛṣṇa, Kṛṣṇa Kṛṣṇa Hare Hare, Hare Rāma Hare Rāma, Rāma Rāma Hare Hare." Despite his sarcastic intention, it was good that he wrote the mantra in his poems. Even if the mantra is spoken sarcastically, it is beneficial.

I do not chant the Hare Kṛṣṇa mantra perfectly, but it is always beneficial. Now if I can just say it with pure intention to serve and please Kṛṣṇa! Mechanical chanting is not good enough. It has to be done with love. And that is what I am praying for.

I've fallen into a pattern of getting headaches right in the middle of my morning *japa.* I may not go on the walk today. Yadunandana Swami is very considerate, and I should be thankful that he's here, especially in the absence of Nārāyaṇa and Bala. I'm hampered by my illness. Chanting requires alertness and good consciousness, and I lack that now. But I still have time before my 5:30 shower, and I will try to do my best. I'm chanting without using the stopwatch, so I don't know my time exactly. I'm chanting mostly in the mind, but moving my mouth and listening to the syllables. I'm yearning to chant better. I realize I'm in the most important period of the day. Haridāsa wants to come over and talk to me in the afternoon, but I don't know if I'll be able to do it. I may be behind in my journal. Haridāsa and Śāstra are coming for lunch. It's going to be a strain and an interruption of my regular schedule. This is not a *japa* essay *per se.* The *japa* essay should be written by an instructor, but today I am a struggler. Still, I can instruct from this position. A *japa* essay should talk about the nature of *japa* and be helpful to other *japa* chanters.

I can just tell you to be persistent no matter what your condition and never feel anxious that you won't get your rounds done. You'll always get them done, even if you have to adjust your schedule and tell people you can't see them in the day. Make the *japa* your priority. Pray to Kṛṣṇa in close intimacy. It's possible, even in this condition. You cry to Him pitifully and strive to reach Him. All things considered, I'm not really doing that terribly. I've chanted four rounds and it's 4:45 A.M., so I may expect to get four more done before 5:30 A.M., and that's not so bad. I wish I could bless all chanters to be encouraged in their chanting. I got a letter from a girl who is very discouraged. I wanted to reach out to her and assure her about taste in chanting and the need to keep it up. She was even thinking of giving up her chanting. I told her that would be doom. You want to help people like that. There should be no question of giving it up. There will be better times, and even in your weakened condition, you can push on and call out to Kṛṣṇa, and He will receive it kindly. At least that's my understanding. The chanting is absolute, and Kṛṣṇa knows the sincerity of the attempt.

Chant when you're tired
and have a headache,
and Rādhā and Kṛṣṇa
will be pleased with you.
They see you don't give up.

"When the going gets tough,
the tough get going." Be a Marine and fight
with valor.

Kṛṣṇa sees the good
in the undertaking, and His
name is *bhāva grahi janārdana*,
meaning "taking the good out of your effort."

Usually we go out for the walk at 6:30 A.M., but I decided to go out earlier to keep awake. You could hear winds roaring around the car, and heavy surf was breaking onto the beach. The sky was overcast. When we opened the car doors, we were met with gale-force winds that pushed at our backs as we walked the first one-half lap. It was very unusual.

I thought of the pastime of Kṛṣṇa and the Tṛṇāvarta demon. Tṛṇāvarta was a personified tornado. He was a demon sent by Kaṁsa to kill Kṛṣṇa. He swooped down from the sky and picked Kṛṣṇa up at a moment when He was unattended by Mother Yaśoda. Actually, Mother Yaśoda had to put Kṛṣṇa down because He was too heavy to hold. He was preparing Himself to combat with Tṛṇāvarta. The wind demon had created a dust storm all over Vṛndāvana, and he picked Kṛṣṇa up and carried Him high in the sky. His intention was to drop Kṛṣṇa from a great height so that He would be killed when He hit the ground.

But Kṛṣṇa grabbed Tṛṇāvarta by the neck and manifested the *yoga siddhi* of becoming heavier than the heaviest. Tṛṇāvarta tried to get out of Kṛṣṇa's grip, but Kṛṣṇa held onto his neck until the demon suffocated, then He dropped him from the sky. Kṛṣṇa fell down with the demon and pillowed His landing on the demon's body. Then baby Kṛṣṇa began to climb and play on the demon's chest. Kṛṣṇa's parents and relatives ran to the spot and were greatly relieved that Kṛṣṇa was miraculously unharmed and the giant demon was dead.

The wind at the beach was nothing compared to Tṛṇāvarta's whirlwind, but it tugged at our clothing and bodies and made it hard to walk. When we finished the half lap and turṇed around, the wind hit us in the face, and it became even more difficult to walk. We managed to get back to the car and take shelter inside. Nārāyaṇa said, "We got double our value on this walk, due to the wind resistance." I said, "Yes, I'll count it as two laps." Just yesterday, it was mild, without much wind. How quickly Kṛṣṇa can change the situation! We'll stay in the car a while and then head back to the house. We won't attempt to feed the seagulls because the wind would just blow the crumbs away. How mighty are Kṛṣṇa's material elements! As the pastime of Tṛṇāvarta shows, He can subdue them without the slightest effort. As for us tiny *jīvas*, we can be swept away at any moment.

I pray to my own mind, "Please be kind. Please act for our welfare (not our destruction) by patiently hearing the sound of the names and surrendering your propensity to wander all over the universe in search of mental food and plans for sensual enjoyment. Please be a servant of the Vaiṣṇavas."

When I said *gāyatrī,* my mind roamed elsewhere, to an advertisement for a book about baseball. Then it was too late. But I could perceive that you can bring the mind back from one preoccupation and fix it somewhere else. Lord Kṛṣṇa refers to the austerities of the mind. Śrīla Prabhupāda says we have to divert the mind to the Vedic literatures. With this predicament, I looked at the Avanti *brāhmana's* song in the Eleventh Canto.[25] I have only read a bit of it, not the song yet.

It's strange how the mind goes. It doesn't always go to things I love or which are of interest to me. Rather, it has a nondiscriminating curiosity. As a goat eats anything, the mind "eats" anything. It turns it over, sniffs at it. . . . Roaming through the worlds, without scruples, without considering my self-interest.

25 *Bhag.* Canto 11, Chapter 23.

I may bring myself to a nice situation, but the mind doesn't come along, or it comes only part of the way. For example, we will take a *japa* walk on the beach. The mind will appreciate this along with the senses. But that doesn't mean it will agree to hear the holy names. It will do its usual jumping from one train car to another. If I really bear down on the purpose of this *japa* retreat, I will see it as a stark battle between the higher self and the *cañcalā* mind. Am I ready to engage in hand-to-hand combat? I don't think so. I am hoping to win the mind over on friendly terms. Hope to gradually appeal to the mind and receive a drop of Kṛṣṇa's mercy. One drop will inundate the mind with pleasure, and it will gladly become a devotee. By force of attraction to the name and form and *guṇa* of Kṛṣṇa, the mind will give up its roaming and devouring, its sniffing in the garbage pails. I am trying for that. But until the drop of nectar falls, I will have to bring the mind back whenever I notice it roaming away, and do something Kṛṣṇa conscious. Writing is for that, and reading. Chanting Hare Kṛṣṇa is the most direct and easiest method of associating with Kṛṣṇa, but I can't convince the mind to do it. Sometimes it cooperates, but not for long.

Good mechanical chanting is not *śuddha-nāma,* but it's important. It means you're attentive, concentrated and conscientious. Today I've been chanting with good mechanics, and I'm gratified. Since I started a little late, I've only chanted eleven rounds, but I'm sure I'll make them up later—with good mechanics.

Chanting mechanically
sounds derogatory.
But if you chant well tuned,
you're on the good side. You handle
each mantra with care, like a part
of an assembly line. You've got

a long way to go to chanting with *bhāva,*
but you've made a good start.

Chanting as duty, the mind on the count,
struggling to keep alert. This chanting
is not what Prabhupāda said would equal
Dhruva's austerity. You completed
your assignment, but not
with the presence of mind that "here is
Kṛṣṇa, here is Rādhā, please engage me
in Your service."

mūrkho vadati viṣṇāya
dhīro vadati viṣṇave
ubhayos tu samaṁ puṇyaṁ
bhāva-grāhī janārdanaḥ

"At the time of offering obeisances to Lord Viṣṇu, an uneducated person chants *viṣṇāya namaḥ* and a learned person chants *viṣṇave namaḥ.*[26] But both achieve equal piety by their offering of obeisances, because Lord Śrī Janārdana sees the sentiment of the living being, in other words, He sees the degree of devotion, or in other words, He awards the result regardless."

— *Caitanya Bhāgavata,* Adi 11, 108.

I received a nice letter from Mālatī Prabhu. She agreed to meet with me at the Gita-nagari Ratha-yatra. She enclosed a nice *japa* prayer by Jagattāriṇī Prabhu: "Dear

26 *Viṣṇave namaḥ* is the correct Sankrit grammatical form.

Lord, these are my rounds, and they aren't so good at the moment, but they are the best I can offer." I thought that was a sweet sentiment, expressing one's inability, but humbly offering the best one can do to Kṛṣṇa.

I don't believe that a ghost can prevent someone from chanting his *japa.* If one is determined enough and chants loudly, surely the "evil" spirit, the mischievous jinn or whatever it is will be vanquished. As Jesus said to Satan, "Get thee behind me, Satan!,"[27] so the reformed *japa* chanter can chase away the haunting spectre or bad spirit. The devotee who has stopped his chanting because of the ghosts in his temple must be listening to "ghosts" within his own mind, because Kṛṣṇa in His holy name is more powerful than any material illusory energy. As Kṛṣṇa turned the two Arjuna trees into beautiful demigods by tearing them down, so the holy names can tear down the ignorance that frightens and dissuades one from chanting. We have read in the story of Ajāmila how when an old man inadvertently called out the name of Nārāyaṇa, even the Yamadūtas could not take his sinful soul to Yamarāja. The Viṣṇudūtas intervened and said that because this man has chanted the holy names even once, you cannot take him. Even Fear Personified (Yamarāja and the Yamadūtas) are afraid of the holy name of Kṛṣṇa, and one utterance of that name can chase a band of ugly, deformed monsters.

In *Harināma-cintāmaṇi,* Haridāsa Ṭhākura talks about the glories of *nāmā-ābhāsa,* or shadow chanting. Śrīla Bhaktivinoda Ṭhākura discusses many technical varieties of *nāmā-ābhāsa,* and he says it should not be underestimated. Some of the categories include negligent chanting and even chanting in jest. He says *nāmā-ābhāsa* can bring liberation. So I thought it was best to persist in chanting. I could not concentrate on prayer, but clung to the holy names like a life raft and proceeded at a rapid

---

27 *New Testament.* Lk 4.8.

pace. By now I have chanted twelve rounds. I think I will go on chanting some more until it's time for my shower, but I'm very sorry I have this pain, which is so distracting to smooth chanting. I cannot sink deeply into peaceful contemplation of Kṛṣṇa's qualities and form. I notice he has placed Rādhā and Kṛṣṇa a bit apart from each other. I wish they were closer. I like them when They are standing close together. Let me go on chanting for now, and I can rest later.

You long to reach pure chanting
and pray that day will come.
In the meantime, through
stuffed sinuses you
savor *harināma*.

I think my reports on my chanting give a worse picture than the actual performance. I pretty much accomplish the basic routine. I chant at a pace of less than seven minutes per round, I keep awake, I hear the syllables (although at a whisper), my mind doesn't daydream all over the universe, and I accomplish at least eight rounds before it's time to take my shower. It's not so bad, except that I have higher anticipations. No trace of meditating on the form of Kṛṣṇa (except when I gaze on my Rādhā-Govinda *mūrtis*), meditating on the qualities and pastimes of Kṛṣṇa, and climbing the ladder to *bhāva* and *prema*. These things are beyond my scope. I regularly keep up my basic routine. It disappoints me, and I sometimes give a negative impression of my *japa* sessions. I should be thankful that I'm keeping the basic routine and at the same time yearn and strive for inoffensive chanting. On some days, I fall below even the basic duties, and that's when it gets worse. But more or less, I keep to the standard I have achieved.

He does his daily *sādhana*
and laments he doesn't go higher.
What do you expect,
little sailor,—to achieve
the *sākṣād darśana* of the Lord?
To converse with Him like
Sanātana Gosvāmī with Madana-mohan?

To immerse yourself in His wonderful
qualities and His pastimes
with the *gopīs*?
Well, why not? That's the
goal of the chanting.

Ah, but He has to allow
you in those sacred
precincts, and He doesn't think
you're worthy just yet.
Chant with enthusiasm,
confidence, and patience
at the lower stage and
pray that the day will come.

My duties and what I expect my disciples to reciprocate with me: Haryasva is stressing that my disciples and I are together in *japa* and that I should speak on that. It is a strong point, and actually I believe in it. I believe in the importance of *japa* in my own life and in our bond. As Śrīla Prabhupāda said to us in 1967 when he was going to India and we feared separation from him, "I will be chanting in India, and you will be chanting here, and we will be packed up together." They can read my books, which offer guidance and personal relationship. They can keep the basic vows of their initiation. They can write letters to me and tell me of their lives. We can meet on occasions like this. *Vapuḥ* and *vāṇī.* I am here to rededicate myself to being your spiritual master, and I hope that you will rededicate yourself to being my disciples. I should talk like that.

3:30 A.M. Before beginning *japa,* I heard a tape of Draviḍa reading *Bhagavad-gītā As It Is.* He read the verse that one should approach a spiritual master and inquire from him submissively. The self-realized soul can impart knowledge unto you because he has seen the truth. Śrīla Prabhupāda says one has to pass the test of the spiritual master. One cannot just ask absurd inquiries but must accompany his questions with submissive service. The spiritual master has to come in disciplic succession and not manufacture teachings. This is a good verse to begin chanting *japa* because the third offense is to disobey the order of the spiritual master.

5:09 A.M. March mayhem, it's already spring. I feel alert for more chanting. I really don't know what the chant is. There are Sanskrit words for Kṛṣṇa and His consort. It's a mystery to me. I enunciate them in a "foreign" tongue. But it's not actually foreign, it's transcendental. I chant with trust in the *ācāryas* and the scriptures. They speak in highest terms of the purifying power of the holy names. It is an offense in chanting to consider the glories of the holy names to be exaggeration. You chant like a little baby, doing what your father and mother have told you to do. Eventually, you're supposed to grow up and have some realizations of the sweetness and potency. Until it comes, you cry for it. Or until you cry, you pray, "Please let me cry for it." Until you pray, you are chanting with offenses. But even that is beneficial.

My spiritual master has taught us the importance of preaching, and he has given us stern orders to carry it out according to our individual capacities.

He has taught us Lord Caitanya's method of chanting the holy names. It is easy to reach You by this method, but somehow we find it difficult. I pray to gain facility in *harināma* and to infuse it with some emotions of love for You and Śrīmatī Rādhārāṇī. Let me pray, Hare Kṛṣṇa Hare Kṛṣṇa, Kṛṣṇa Kṛṣṇa Hare Hare. Let me pray Hare Rāma Hare Rāma, Rāma Rāma Hare Hare. The prayer means, "O Lord, O energy of the Lord, please engage me in Your service." Let me enter the prayer-meaning and carry it out by Your strength infused in me.

When You play with the *gopīs* and tease them, it may appear like mundane dealings between a man and women, to those who lack the divine vision. To those who hear of Your *madhurya* pastimes according to the teachings of the *ācāryas,* Your sports with the *gopīs* are the purest and highest expressions of spirituality. I want to gradually know You in this way. Please accept me as a sober but enthusiastic student to learn of Your pastimes with Rādhārāṇī, so I can enter Her shelter and be protected from false conclusions.

I have at present no qualifications to approach You but ask that You help keep me attached to my *guru mahārāja's* teachings and actions. Only then may I hope to actually attain You.

KṚṢṆA IS NEVER TIRED WITH US. He never gives up on us, no matter how many times we fail Him. He's always ready to take us back. You'd think He'd be disgusted with us, but He's too magnanimous for that. Sometimes He destroys some worlds, sends people to hell, but nevertheless, it's never permanent. After some time, after remorse, He'll take them back and bring them to the highest point. That's Kṛṣṇa, the magnanimous one. Jesus Christ was like that, too. He forgave everyone. Sometimes you get exhausted physically. You've done as much as you can, and you lie down, exhausted. So tired. You wait for some refreshment in your body so that you can go on again. Life in this material world is hard. In the spiritual world, they don't get tired. They can dance the equivalent of twenty-four hours a day without getting tired. We're given just a little energy here, so that even if we're blissful, staunch devotees, we can't do much. We have only a little energy, and then we get tired. But as you build up your devotional service, you're able to chant longer, you're able to chant more beads. You don't get exhausted. You're able to read more books. It even happens as you grow older, so don't be tired. Don't give up.

Let's pledge never to get tired of serving Kṛṣṇa.

4:21 A.M. What I seek and feel is lacking is *bhakti.* I don't want to chant mechanically. I want to feel the meaning of the Hare Kṛṣṇa mantras as I repeat them. Please engage me in Your service. Please reveal the essence of *nāma* to me. This seeking and crying has to be there, beyond the accumulation of numbers of rounds. I chanted as quickly as I could while still uttering the syllables distinctly. I began averaging about seven minutes per round and kept that up for the eight rounds. I whispered audibly. My mind did not wander much to thoughts other than simply hearing. The room's quietness and the quietness of the house was conducive to good chanting. I did not think of much *japa* thoughts, or thoughts harmonious or advantageous to *japa* but just stayed on the recitation of the names themselves. The best thing about the session was that I kept up a speedy average and was not much distracted. The weakest thing was the lack of deeper devotion and exploring the meaning of the names. On winning the NBA championship, basketball star Kobe Bryant said, "I feel as if a huge monkey has been lifted off my back." When I finish my daily quota of *japa*, I feel as if a monkey has been lifted off my back. Of course, it is a guaranteed thing that I will finish my vow every day. But until it is completed, I am not relieved. Śrīla Prabhupāda has given us the sixteen-round quota, and it must be done.

It is a pleasure to be able to complete the quota and keep that bond with him every day. It makes you feel successful in your personal commitment to him. Sometimes some of the later rounds are not done as well as the beginning rounds. There is a touch of getting them out of the way. But sometimes that doesn't happen, and you go strong through the whole quota. That is best. The concept of completing a solemn vow every day is very good for one's *sādhana*. And chanting some extra makes you feel good. You feel clean and honest, and you wouldn't have it any other way. It must be done, even if you have a headache and some of the last rounds are of poor quality.

Initiated devotees who don't complete their sixteen rounds are missing out on spiritual life. Kṛṣṇa forgives them, but they have let themselves down in a basic way. Once a devotee who was not chanting anymore told me that he took the vow when he was only nineteen years old, and he did not feel responsible for a decision made at such a young age. But that is not the right attitude. There may have been a risk involved in taking a lifelong vow at a young age, but one should feel responsible for it and not take it as an immature decision. You came before Kṛṣṇa with an innocent and open heart and made the promise, and He accepted it. Life is short enough, and not that much changes in growing from nineteen to twenty-nine to thirty-nine and so on. At least not that much changes in a vow made to God, although much may change externally in one's worldly affairs.

Losing faith in the chanting is another thing. Such a basic commitment should not waver, even though one does not feel he is making progress spiritually by his daily chanting. We realize that we have a mountain of dirty things to chip away at, so it is no surprise that a lifetime can go by of steadily chanting and still unwanted things remain in the heart. That is not a reason to abandon the only chance one has for eradicating the dirt. It is important to keep the other parts of the vow made at initiation, the promise to follow the four rules—no intoxication, no meat-eating, no gambling, and no illicit sex. If these promises gradually drop away, then it will be hard to cling to the one promise of chanting in isolation in a life that has become totally materialistic. But even if all that remains is the chanting, one should cling to it like a lifesaver in the ocean and not drop it, thinking that one is too offensive or too sinful to chant.

I chant my rounds
as daily vow.
It's not so hard to
find two hours
when you have decided
it's a must.

Two hours out of twenty-four
as a promise made
long ago to the spiritual master.

"I can do it, I will do it," is the required resolution
to complete a task
of sustaining holy utterance.

Śrīla Prabhupāda recommends the chanting of Hare Kṛṣṇa as more possible than the *aṣṭāṅga yoga* practice. In a separate verse, he recommends hearing about Kṛṣṇa. He says the point is to fix the mind on Kṛṣṇa, as in the verse by Mahārāja Ambarīṣa, *sa vai manaḥ kṛṣṇa-padāravindayor vacāṁsi vaikuṇṭha-guṇānuvarṇane.*[28] It was good to hear the reassurance of these practices which I am already doing. It gave me hope to go ahead.

I began chanting at 2:57 A.M. I begin the first round with reluctance, a kind of grudge. But then I feel good about it. I feel good about accumulating the rounds. Numerical strength is very important for me. When I see the rounds quickly accumulating, I become confident. My speed was under seven minutes per round. I made audible sounds of the mantras, but barely audible, in order to keep the speed and not overexert. My mind didn't wander. It stayed fixed on whispering the syllables. I kept fixed on just hearing and did not have many good *japa* thoughts. I was content to just occupy myself in the *yajña* of the sound vibration. I didn't philosophize but kept myself compact in mind. The best thing about the session was that I chanted regularly, linking the mantras and not being distracted. The weakest thing was that I did not go deeper, thinking that this mantra is for Rādhā and Kṛṣṇa or that I am calling out to Them for service.

Chanting is a great endeavor. I want to give my full attention to each mantra and feel the pastimes of Kṛṣṇa in my mind. But I can't do it. I lower my standards and chant. I hear the syllables and keep a good pace. So many people chant without a higher taste, assured that they are doing the best thing. I am one of them. Chanting is like being

28 *Bhag.* 9.4.18-20.

with your best friend. I relax and utter Their names. Even if it is not topmost, I chant with reverence and attention as best as I am able. I ask Kṛṣṇa's forgiveness that I'm not doing better. I'm aware of all my physical and mental limitations that prevent me from soaring into the spiritual realm. At least I prevent my mind from ranging into other subjects. I keep it focused on the mantras themselves. Time goes by, and I'm very careful to use every moment for chanting and not something else. But the time slips by without top performance.

Chanting not so well.
You wish that it was better,
counting your favor.

Your bodily pains tie
you down, but you
send your messages through to
Rādhā and Kṛṣṇa
and hope They won't be displeased.

I wish I had a better report,
but need to tell the truth
and hope for better
rounds as the hours
pass by.

I'm sorry to say I didn't pay attention to the chanting on the deeper level. I'm sorry to report that. I remember in my public school days, the report card had a line where the teacher could fill in a comment. Often, the teacher wrote in, "Could do better," on my cards. There was "Excellent," "Good," "Fair," and "Poor." My parents used to preach to me about the meaning of this "Could do better" comment. It held some promise that I had hidden talents. That was reassuring to both my parents and I. At least I wasn't a dope; I was intelligent. But there was an implication of serious trouble unless I corrected myself. It was like getting cavities in your teeth—not a good sign. You'd have to pay for it by undergoing drilling at the dentist. "Could do better."

But what if he doesn't? What if he grows up and doesn't do better?

I'm feeling like that now with my *japa*. It seems I can't do better. Who's marking my report card? Whom do I show it to?

How fearful we were before receiving the card. You never knew whether you'd get a bad rating or a good one. It was up to the fates, the higher powers.

Now things are different. The guru is my friend. Lord Kṛṣṇa is my friend. I don't think of myself as a rebellious, confused kid. I want to serve and improve. Sure I can do better. In fact, I'm "Fair" only, or "Poor." I'm poor, but not out of rebelliousness so that the smart alecks in the class will approve that I'm not a brownie-point earner or a sissy. I don't care for their opinion. I'm a Hare Kṛṣṇa devotee now, so all smart-alecks and honor roll kids can have a laugh on me. I'm in a school for devotees now. I go on chanting. But what to do about the quality?

As the writing has its own discipline (keep the hand moving, etc.), so the *japa* has a different discipline. It requires bringing my attention to the quick utterances of the mantra and not indulging in other trains of thought. But at this point, I can't even try to think of Kṛṣṇa's pastimes or of Vraja worship.

I am usually sarcastic with myself. I could be lighter. As I am kind to good friends—do unto others as you would have them do unto you—seeing myself about to start a round (or at any time in the round), make a light, friendly suggestion, "Prabhu, since you're already making the effort to chant and since you're able to pay attention to the syllables, why not make a little more effort and think about Kṛṣṇa?" It can be expressed even more nicely than that.

A friendly reader recently said, "Why are you so hard on yourself? I can't accept the hard statements you make against yourself. Do I have to accept them?" he asked, "or can I turn away from them?" I answered him by saying I have to tell the truth about myself, but maybe I *am* too harsh. He, for one, doesn't like it. Of course, I can't write to please him. But I'm talking about *japa.* I haven't succeeded by my strongarm tactics in thinking about Kṛṣṇa. Perhaps a sweeter, encouraging approach might be helpful.

I do appreciate that I persist patiently and am able to control my mind, even when there is no nectarean taste in chanting. I'm just suggesting that if I could be alert and bring the mind back to hearing, then why not try to go further? All the authorities say that attentive chanting is very important and leads to thinking about Kṛṣṇa's form, activities, qualities and pastimes. They must be right.

utthāya gopyo 'para-rātra-bhoge
smṛtvā yaśodā-suta-bāla-kelim
gāyanti proccair dadhi-manthayantyo
govinda dāmodara mādhaveti

"Having risen early in the *brāhma-muhūrta,* and remembering the childhood pastimes of the darling of mother Yaśodā, the *gopīs* would loudly chant while churning the butter—'Govinda, Dāmodara, Mādhava!'"

—Bilvamaṅgala Ṭhākura, *Govinda-dāmodara-stotram,* 16

The *brāhma-muhūrta* hour is the most important time in the day, and you want to be awake for good chanting. If you're heavy-lidded, there's not much you can do but wash your face, grit your teeth, and do the best you can do. Don't give in to sleepiness. The regulated life of a full night's sleep is important. Conversing before your *japa* uses up energy and is a distraction and shouldn't be indulged in. Get right down to business as soon as you get up. Call to Kṛṣṇa for help, and He will help you stay awake. Keeping up a good speed is also helpful. Gradually, you gain your wakefulness and take advantage of it. *Harināma* deserves your best effort.

It was a sleepy morning,
but I succeeded and overcame
the drowse.
My words came quickly
and sheer determination
took over when spontaneity failed.

Kṛṣṇa likes to see you fighting
to say your rounds,
and He'll reward you with
wakefulness.
Just don't give up,
apply the pressure to your mind,
and the clouds will clear
away. I proved it.

Sometimes the *japa* is limping because of bodily pains or mental agitation or sleepiness. You regret that very much. You want the chanting to be a wholehearted effort of body, mind, and soul. That's why good health is such a gift, not for sense gratification but for service. With good health, you can perform your service unhampered and make a full offering to Kṛṣṇa. Ill health puts you at a disadvantage, and you have to apologize to the Lord for the inferior offering. You depend on His accepting you for your sincerity at such times, accepting the chanting as just as good as when you're healthy. People with physical handicaps should not feel inferior. They do the best they can and leave it at Kṛṣṇa's feet in humility. They should strive medically and sensibly to regain their full health so they can make the offering without limping. But Kṛṣṇa is kind and understanding. He fully accepts even the offerings of a blind *sādhaka.*

To be able to use the tongue and lips and utter the holy names is a great advantage. One has to sometimes do it even from a hospital bed. Kṛṣṇa counts sincerity, not Olympic athleticism in devotional service. But devotees should not neglect their health because it is always better to make an offering that is unhampered by physical handicaps.

Bilvamaṅgala Ṭhākura became a great devotee despite his blindness, and Sanātana Gosvāmī remained dear to the Lord even when his body was covered with oozing sores. Crippled and diseased *sādhus* in Vṛndāvana make their offerings to Kṛṣṇa with fullhearted enthusiasm and are received by Him with full reciprocation. King Kulaśekhara prayed that it would be better if he died while he was chanting in full health than to have to wait to the time of death, when he would certainly be incapacitated and not able to chant well due to his voice being choked up with mucus and to other impediments. So take advantage of your health and chant Hare Kṛṣṇa at full volume, but know that the Lord will accept you even in your weakened condition.

Chant Hare Kṛṣṇa as best you
can in strong or weak health,

and please the Lord.
He is interested in chanting from
the heart, even if the heart
is physically impaired.

Chanters in the hospice can
be as pleasing as robust
bhaktas out on *saṅkīrtana.*
He wants to see your bhakti *latā* growing
through the universe
despite a terminal illness.

He wants to see the
crying of the healthy
spirit soul, the
one who overlooks
his illness and
glorifies the Lord.

What is actually needed is the repeated effort, small though it may be, to bring the mind back to hearing the names. The mind will continually go off, and we have to continually bring it back. Unless we have a good-natured attitude, we'll become soured at the stupidity and stubborness of the mind. We'll call ourselves demons, and then the mind may be insulted. We are asking him to do something he can't do—give up all distraction. Rather than ask for the impossible, ask him to add something.

We tell newcomers they don't have to change their lives, but just add chanting. This is similar advice. . . . You are already chanting, so please remember to bring the mind back. The mind will be glad to do it, knowing he's not responsible for performing an impossible task.

Ask him and stay with him, "Shall we do it again, come back to the mantra? Time to come back again. Here we go again, let's go back. Hey, mate, let's go back and hear that mantra. Shall we hear it again? One more time. One more. Let's hear the chanting. What was that you were chanting? Hare Kṛṣṇa, Hare Kṛṣṇa."

> You calm your head
> and concentrate:
> the sweet participation begins.
> "I like this chanting," the
> mind admits, an accumulation
> proceeds. Up you climb
> and flashes of Rādhā and Kṛṣṇa
> enter your mind.
>
> The *japa* chanter is not
> trying to become God but
> to link with Him
> to be with Him
> And he accepts on his tongue
> the "holy Eucharist," God's
> body and spirit,
> and feels joyful and content.

10:37 A.M. It feels like my second headache of the day is on the way. I'll wait but I don't want it to develop to where it's too difficult to write. I'd like to keep writing a little "*japa* essay" in the morning, but they're hard to keep up. So far I've done three in a row. I borrowed them from earlier writings. To write them in the morning, just after completing eight rounds and my early-morning *japa* log is a pressure. People don't know how hard it is to write on spiritual topics from a personal point of view. It's easy to repeat the dogma or paraphrase the Bhaktivedanta purports, but to squeeze out your own human responses to practicing *bhakti* takes insight, patience, honesty, and courage. You can't be afraid to fail, or you won't be able to write at all. How many times have I opened the cupboard to find it bare? How many times have I had to serve a frugal meal? How many tricks have I used to try to make my serving look good?

On a morning walk in Māyāpur, Śrīla Prabhupāda said that if we had to choose between standing alone in the agricultural field or going to Calcutta, we would finally go to Calcutta, because we seek activity. The *bhakti-śāstras* state that even demons attain liberation, so how can it be more exalted than bhakti? Only bhakti brings us real liberation, which is to join with Kṛṣṇa and His entourage in the spiritual world and never come back to the material world of repeated birth and death. This is stated in the *Bhagavad-gītā*: "One who knows the nature of My appearance and activities does not at the time of death come back to this material world but joins Me in My eternal abode" (Bg. 4.9). The *bhakti-śāstras* soundly defeat the impersonal scriptures, and Gopa-kumāra gives up the desire for liberation and aspires to be a *bhakta*. He has met up with many different opinions in his traveling through the universe, but by steadily chanting his Gopāla mantra, given to him by his spiritual master, he remains steady in his resolve to worship Madana-gopāla in Vraja. By steadily chanting the Hare Kṛṣṇa mantra, we will also weather the storms of differing opinions, and even survive falldowns to maya. Chanting Hare Kṛṣṇa purifies us of all misconceptions and sinful activities.

5:34 A.M. I took headache medicine upon going to bed last night, and as a result, I didn't wake up at 10:30 P.M. with a headache. I slept all the way through peacefully.

Yadunandana Mahārāja didn't wake me up until 3:30 A.M. Therefore, I'm behind on my rounds. Otherwise, I'm feeling all right, without a headache or bone aches. I'll try to take a little walk. I've chanted five rounds.

Japa essay

When I increase the quantity, I may notice, as I've been noticing the past few days, that I can actually be aware of the things my mind is focused on, and I *can* curb them, or at least I can be aware. This morning I started chanting and also started thinking about my book production. I noticed it and said, "Okay, you're thinking about book distribution. It's a nice thing to think about, but this is *japa* time." That curbed the one line of thought. These little things come to me, and I am grateful. (1) I live within my limits; (2) I hope to improve.

Although I make fun of my duty-bound counting up of the quota, still, it's a virtue. Maybe I inherited it from my *karmi* parents. I learned (rather late) to be an achiever and study for exams, to be a punctual worker. I can apply that, and I count. It's small-time, and I don't mind if you joke about it. I'd rather be this way then slovenly and unable to take my quota seriously. I like to count. How many rounds done? How many left? How many minutes per round?

I don't mind that I'm such a slow chanter, sometimes averaging eight minutes per round, but if I can go faster, that would be better. And be an athlete or musician in bringing the mind back gently to hearing. Be a renounced person who humbly accepts whatever he can get, but who goes on chanting.

Not fixed on the target
in the heart,
the heavy-eyed chanter
completes his quota.

He chants quickly
but not hearing out loud.
We have to give him a C.

He's got time for more chanting
and hopes he will improve,
glances at Rādhā-Govinda
for encouragement.

Pray to the Lord,
"Please let me chant."
Stay with determination,
don't say you can't.

Keeping the mind concentrated on hearing the holy names and not straying to other thoughts requires a careful balancing act. It is like balancing yourself on a railroad track. You can't overconcentrate on your walk, but you have to go ahead, just keeping your mind on balancing and walking confidently ahead. It is like writing this *japa* essay. I can't think that I have run out of worthwhile things to say. I have to go ahead and keep moving. This means depending on Kṛṣṇa. It is beyond your own power. You keep a lighthearted attitude, always thinking that Kṛṣṇa will keep you balanced, Kṛṣṇa will supply you more words. Sometimes if you are riding on a bicycle, and see some object ahead of you, and you're afraid you will hit it, you may become overconcerned and get drawn like a magnet to hit the object you want to avoid. So in chanting, you have to keep hearing the holy names and not get overworried that you're going to start thinking of some other things, or else they'll start filtering into your mind, and you'll get stuck on them. Today I did not get stuck into deep, lengthy subjects other than the chanting of the holy names. Light thoughts came up that were distractions, and I had to put them aside again and again. You have to go ahead with daring, like a locomotive, planning that the tracks will be intact and that you will not go off them. This is why chanting requires a relaxed, easy-going mood, not an uptight attitude. Sail along through the minutes and through the rounds and accumulate your quota. But there is something else you can do besides keeping balance. While keeping balance, you can go deeper into your mind and think of Rādhā and Kṛṣṇa in Vṛndāvana. It should come naturally and not be an awkward juggling act, like doing too many things at once. Rumble carefree along the tracks, and use your extra concentration to pray.

He doesn't compose a poem while chanting, the poem composes him.

Is there any deep desire to improve the *yajña*? Yes, some. So please acknowledge you have come here for this. There may be some mental inconvenience, thinking, "I'm not in the temple right now," but there are many advantages for extra *japa* in this *bhajana-kuṭīr.* We read how Mādhavendra Purī, in a contrite mood, left the Remuna temple and went to chant his *japa* in the marketplace. Śrīla Prabhupāda writes, "This chanting can be executed anywhere, either inside or outside the temple." The Gosvāmīs chanted under the trees. And don't forget the importance of chanting and the fact that yours needs work—people are looking to you to do something about it. Let me put down the pen and pick up the beads—and put the mind on the names.

I find the very early hours so superior that I won't sacrifice them in sleep, even if it means I'm drowsy later in the day. My first sixteen rounds are better than the rest I do after breakfast. Chanting varies, with ups and downs, but it's usually best before breakfast.

Where is that little voice? What does he want me to say? He wants me to find the best way to chant and stay focused. I've touched on some vital themes, but now I have to live up to them, like caring and concentration and prayer.

Take the *mahā-mantra* seriously. I tend to think of writing as being more vital. Writing lasts, it's preserved, it's me. *Japa* doesn't get preserved; it's something I do, but even a small quantity leaves me broke (without capital). This attitude of minimizing my chanting isn't good.

Writing about my problems in chanting is valuable. Don't ask whether it will make interesting reading. I have to write to help myself and not worry about whether it's repetitious.

When I notice that one round has taken eleven or twelve minutes, I should immediately do something. Don't stay in the same chair, or even the same room. Where are other places I could go? The hallways are so cold! Outdoors means putting on a coat and walking around and around the house in the heavy wind, but it might be good. Let's try it in the late morning or afternoon when the "drowsies" hit. Chant faster outdoors.

Chant faster, even if you think it seems mechanical. It's better than sleepy-slow. Rapidly, rapidly. Other things fall away, and I'm left with concentration on the energetic, rapid chanting. I hope it works that way.

I just told myself to write to help my *japa,* and immediately I came up with a practical plan—going outdoors when drowsy. This idea never came until I wrote it. The writing has such power. Whatever I turn it toward, it starts my thinking creatively, productively. It's leading us somewhere, have faith. We are staying true to whatever comes. But when I can drift into vital concerns, that's welcome. In this new freedom of writing practice without making a book, I should never refuse a thinking session on the page, even if it's just practical plans. Not that I have to always be artistic. Be a practical *sādhaka.* Help yourself. Have fun, too. Use writing sessions as best you can.

Move through concerns one after another. If something I write is worth immediate action, write it separately in a *brief* note, and then back here.

Japa is very important. I need to keep that in mind. At every chance, think "this is important." Press down on the accelerator of good quality and good speed. Remember what the *śāstras* say about the holy name and the importance of it. Never think of it as something minor or as something that you have to get out of the way. It's the centerpiece of my *sādhana.* Early-morning chanting is the most important part up to breakfast. But after breakfast, when I have rounds left over, I also chant with concentration. And then in the late afternoon, I chant extra rounds, beyond sixteen. Don't forget to do those. I've been taking time out for reading Śivarāma Swami's book *Śuddha Bhakti-cintāmaṇi.*[29] I find it very absorbing, and it's good for me. He said that we can go back to Godhead in this lifetime. I was very encouraged to read that. So I have to spend some time in reading and not always chanting. Again, sacrifice and compromise. Use as much of your time as you can. It just shows me again that I can spend all my time in the yellow submarine and be fully engaged and preaching. Unless I improve myself and become convinced of things like going back to Godhead in this lifetime and reading deeply and chanting deeply, then I cannot be a preacher. I preach mostly in my journal, but there has to be good quality in it. I will also do other types of preaching, but this preaching comes first. The most important preaching comes when I can honestly say I'm a good chanter and that I'm putting my best time into it.

---

29 Śivarāma Swami, *Śuddha -bhakti cintāmaṇi: The Touchstone of Pure Devotional Service* (Hungary: Lal Kiado, 2007).

Very Early.

Very early–means at least about 1:00 A.M., no later than that. Or maybe 2:00 A.M. Prabhupāda used to get up and write his books. At that time, the world is peaceful and quiet, at least if you live in a civilized place, a quiet place. Otherwise, it's still noisy. What is night for the restless person is day for the liberated soul (or something like that). People live in different time zones. Night people and day people. The devotees like to get up early and chant their *japa* and go and see the Deity. Nondevotees never get up so early to go and see the Lord. Very early in the creation of the world, Lord Brahma rose on the lotus flower and tried to figure out how to do it. He was bewildered and didn't know what to do. He climbed down the stem of the lotus, very early. Kṛṣṇa told him two syllables, *ta-pa,* and Brahma grabbed ahold of it and performed austerities. Then it was still very early, but he was able to begin creation after his austerities, when the Lord shook his hand. Do you remember that early? No, of course you don't, because you didn't have the same body. We can't remember previous births. Very early meant when we were just babies in this body and have no remembrance of it. Very early in the history of our evolution to the species is beyond us. So all we can do now very late, when we've reached almost seventy years old is to try to love Kṛṣṇa and perform devotional service so that you can go back to Him. Otherwise, very early, you'll be born again, and that won't be very nice. Begin your devotional service very early in life. If you've got good parents, they can give you a jump start. They'll teach you to do *japa* at an early hour and have a morning program and do all your *sādhana* before it's too late in the day. Because very early, it's quiet and not so passionate.

The usual *japa* report. The association of a pure devotee is important. That is why some of the ISKCON devotees were inspired to go to Puri Mahārāja, who spoke often and intensely about "*nāma*." Each of us has to go alone and apply what we have learned. Now is my time for that. Think about it at least—how my rounds go by and I don't think of Rādhā and Kṛṣṇa or Their pastimes, or the fact that I am chanting divine names and that I should bring my mind to hear them.

Silent rounds are not so good,
but you keep an artesian well within your mind.
The mantras flow through
at rapid rate.

In your comfortable room
with an aching shoulder,
you live with *nāma*
as the minutes and rounds go by.

The work is accomplished
and you're glad for that
but you yearn for
something more.

A *japa* man
makes little pies in the oven
at the rate of under six minutes per round.
His cherry tarts are delicious to taste,
and he offers them to the Lord.

They're done in haste, but with diligent devotion.
He'll chant some more.
Because he's worked so fast,
he reached the quota.

He'll chant some more
as the sun rises at the beach.

Please pity the *japa* man, self-pity for his shoulder,
but he will keep making those pies
and be content with that.

6:13 A.M. I changed into my outdoor clothes but felt too much of a headache to go out, so I canceled the walk and lay back in my chair. I finished chanting my sixteen rounds.

It's worth it. This is the time in my life for doing this. Later, I may do it or not, but now it's ripe and right to be alone and practice the subtle art of *japa*. I have been doing it wrong. I say this so often it can become a kind of pose—humbly claiming I don't chant well. Secretly, I may think, "I don't chant so poorly. If I were to compare myself to others, I might not come out so badly. After all, I am sincere in seeing *japa* as important."

But then, don't I believe I need improvement? Yes! I need it. It's real. A bad habit has developed. I must try to do something about it. The first thing is to keep reminding myself of the obvious—my mind goes somewhere else when I chant. I'm not attracted while chanting to *śravaṇam kīrtanam*. Intellectually or theologically, I am attracted to *harināma*, but my personal practice is different.

My desire for reform is not just a literary dance so I can write books to help others. It's a real desire for improvement, although I can't seem to translate it into practical work. Each time I pick up the beads, it's the same thing more or less.

Increasing the number of rounds daily appears to have the potential to help me. That hasn't occurred yet, but it may. I will give this much effort and try for more, even if there is no tangible result.

Oh chanter, chant your best.
I forgive you for your lacking
but you must work harder
if you expect the Lord's blessings to rain on you.

I'm chanting fast, I'm chanting straight,
chanting for all I'm worth.
I watch the clock, I watch my watch
I strive to push them through.

This chanting is the greatest work
a man can do.
Please push on
and never give up.
I trust in you
and believe you will succeed.

Every day I try to write something about *japa*, just a little short essay. It's hard to think of something new. The experience is always new. There is always new opportunity. It's like life itself. Kṛṣṇa gives you a new day every day until your death. Yesterday Kaulini told us that when she was in the emergency room and they were taking blood from her, she was very staunchly chanting Hare Kṛṣṇa mantras. She said this is not her custom, as she is a shy person. Every once in a while she would say to the doctors and nurses, "I'm sorry, I hope I'm not disturbing anyone," but then she would get back to her life-and-death chanting. She knew that this was a crucial moment for her because she was near death, and she had to chant as the most important thing in her life, regardless of embarrassing people around her. We should always chant like that, knowing that this is our crucial hour. Think like King Kulaśekhara, as I mentioned, that at the time of death, it may be hard for me to chant, so let me die now chanting while I can in a healthy state of mind. By that he meant that while chanting in a healthy state of mind, he would not chant blandly but would chant with great excitement and fervor and concentration. This must be done by a serious person, and he should put all his energy into it. There are so many other things that we have to do in Kṛṣṇa consciousness, such as write books, broadcast Kṛṣṇa consciousness, do financial business, and tend to our material bodies. But when it is time for chanting the Hare Kṛṣṇa mantra, we somehow have to put these things aside and concentrate on the murmuring, Hare Kṛṣṇa Hare Kṛṣṇa Kṛṣṇa Kṛṣṇa Hare Hare, Hare Rāma Hare Rāma Rāma Rāma Hare Hare. We're like railroad trains that have to stay on the track. The tracks are very rigid. To go off the tracks would cause complete disaster and death. So we have to stay on the track. I stayed on the track today, but somehow I was not as enthused as I would have liked to have been, not so fully engaged. I may have been keeping other thoughts out of my mind, but the thoughts of chanting Kṛṣṇa's names were not foremost in my mind. I was just going on automatic pilot and concentrating on the accumulation of the rounds. Accumulation is very important, but it is not everything. I pray to improve.

Here he comes, another day
another chance given by the Lord.
Will he take the lead and win the race
or will he lag behind at an uninspired pace?
We should be rooting for our chanting
and if necessary applying the whip.
Chanting is a calm thing,
a peaceful, easy *yajña*,
but it must be done with fervor and grace
if you want to win the race.
By "win" I mean you pay attention

and your senses are enlivened.
Your heart beats Kṛṣṇa and Rādhā,
and you think of Them with precious mind.

A young man wrote me to ask a question about *japa*. His question was, "I have go to the office on a bike. It takes two hours, so can we chant on bicycle by counting on hands or beads?" I wrote him back that his question was a coincidence in my own life. I told him I had just fallen from a bicycle and broke my collarbone. My arm was in a sling, and I cannot write or eat with my right hand. My shoulder is painful. The healing period is indeterminate. So from my own subjective experience, I would never chant *japa* while riding a bicycle, either with beads or with hand. There are two reasons for this. One is that it requires concentration to ride a bicycle in traffic, and chanting while riding is dangerous. The second reason is that because it requires concentration to ride a bicycle, it is not possible to properly pay attention to the holy names at the same time. He obviously finds it convenient to use the two hours for chanting, but that convenience is counterproductive because of the danger and the lack of attention to the holy name. So I recommended that he find another time to chant his sixteen rounds.

Be brave and forthright.
Take your shower, stay wide awake
and go to the beach. Chant rapid rounds.
I'm ashamed before our Lord,
I'm ashamed before the names,
but He is kind. He will give me
another chance.

Japa is the life breath of the devotee—at least this devotee. It's the most important function, aside from writing. Writing and *japa* go side by side. I chant so that I can write about it. I write only because I have chanted. One cannot go without the other. It is a handsome thing to do. It is a beautiful thing to do. It makes you feel healthy and alive. Without chanting, life has no meaning. I would like to say that I would chant no matter what situation in life I was put in. I will try to chant under the most duress I have to face. Because by chanting, I can be with God, and when I'm with God, I'm safe. I believe that chanting brings me to Kṛṣṇa. Devotees call out the names of Kṛṣṇa when they are in an auto accident or when some emergency besets them. They chant routinely every day, they are accumulating numerical strength. It's something Prabhupāda taught us from the beginning, and it will stay with us until the end of our life. When we are physically unable to chant, we will chant in our minds, and if that is not possible, we will ask that devotees surround us and give us the benefit of their chanting. It is not a theoretical thing, but we can actually feel it. Even though we may not be advanced chanters, we feel the presence of Kṛṣṇa directly also on our lower status. And so we chant happily to sustain our lives. We are committed to this prayer on a daily basis. We refuse to go without it.

May Kṛṣṇa always bless us with taste and determination to chant our *japa* faithfully, day in and day out, and may He give us the attentiveness to make a decent performance. May we not cheat ourselves with inattentive chanting but do our part according to the free will given us to hear the holy names with attention.

The worst thing is being spaced out and unaware of your chanting. It goes by mindlessly. It's almost wasting your time. So I catch myself and listen to every sound vibration and treasure it. I tell myself to be aware that this is Rādhā and Kṛṣṇa and that They are the goal of my life. I'm not just fiddling around with an early-morning exercise, I'm diving into the most important portion of my day, praying to God and His Consort to bring me into the circle of love of God. It's such an easy practice, it can mislead you into thinking it's not important. But we need it easy because we're so slow and lazy. We need an easy practice, and Lord Caitanya has emphasized it, just because He knows we're so unqualified to do something more strenuous or complicated in this age of Kali. We're poor candidates for things like yoga or meditation. We should be grateful for the ease of reaching Kṛṣṇa by reciting His names over and over. It's not a boring practice or trivial, but once you get into the groove, it becomes fun, it becomes absorbing, it becomes deep and spiritual. You become excited by the accumulation and the speed. You keep it up like a jockey on a winning horse. You feel happy and triumphant. You feel like you're winning a prize. This is the result of decent morning chanting. Śrīla Rūpa Gosvāmī said, "I do not know how much nectar this name 'Kṛṣ-ṇa' contains."[30] He had reached the pinnacle of success, wherein the utterance of the name of Kṛṣṇa was putting him into an ecstatic state. Hare, Kṛṣṇa and Rāma combine to put an attentive chanter into a state of bliss and deep absorption. You can do it in the beginning stages if you just put your mind to it, remind yourself of the importance of the act and comfortably repeat the names. There is no better exercise than chanting Hare Kṛṣṇa.

---

30 Śrīla Rūpa Gosvāmī. *Vidagdha-mādhava*, 1. 15, see also Caṇḍīdāsa's verse cited in Chapter Thirty-four of *Jaiva Dharma*: *japite, japite nāma, avaśa karila go, kemone pāibo sai, tāre*. "I do not know how much sweet nectar springs from this name, Śyāma, for even just one moment my tongue can't be restrained from such relish." Śrīla Bhaktivinoda Ṭhākura, *Jaiva Dharma*. Trans. Sarvabhāvana Dāsa (Vrindavana: Brhad Mrdanga Press, 2004), 498.

Chanting Hare Kṛṣṇa, forgetful boy remembered
what he was doing
and returned to the thoughtful praise.
Nāma Prabhu picked him up,
and he sailed into outer space,
leaving behind the mundane dirt.

He cleansed his mind, like a new shirt.
He became happy just by sitting in his chair.
The air became purified
along with his mind and heart.
He thanked the Lord for the gift of the name
and pursued his numerical strength.

Yesterday I listened to an initiation lecture Śrīla Prabhupāda gave on September 4, 1969, in Hamburg, Germany. One may be in any condition, pure or impure—if he remembers the lotus-eyed Supreme Lord, that person becomes internally and externally purified, *suci. Suci* also means *brāhmaṇa.* One is not a *brāhmaṇa* by birth but by practicing. Kṛṣṇa consciousness is to purify people from their comtaminated condition. By nature a person is pure, but by contact with nature, he becomes impure. Initiation means he's being accepted by the spiritual master so that he can be in a purified condition to understand God. If you want to enter a place, you have to be adjusted. The moon is very cold, so if they want to go there, they have to wear warm clothing. If you adjust yourself, you can go to higher material planets. In India, the climate is different. When we go to Western countries, we wear more clothes. So those who have adjusted to come to Me can come to Me, says Kṛṣṇa in *Bhagavad-gītā.* After leaving this body, you can come to Me. That's a planet where one doesn't have to return. That is My abode. There is no need of sunshine or moon there. One who goes there never comes back. Cats and dogs cannot take initiation. Every human being, however, can take advantage.

Very early in His youth, Lord Caitanya gave us this *mahā-mantra*. Whoever chants the mantra becomes purified. Everyone should keep himself in touch with the chanting. It is the only way. One who leaves this body chanting will not come back to the material world. Read our literature also. In the ninth chapter of the *Bhagavad-gītā*, Kṛṣṇa says that this is the process, and by chanting, you can understand you are making progress. Students who are taking to this process know that they are making progress. Śrīla Prabhupāda said, "My request to the initiates is to please keep in contact and avoid the four sinful activities." Intoxication means even coffee and cigarettes. You make quick progress, and after leaving this body, you don't come back to another material body. Anyone in this world has to suffer. The spirit soul is by nature joyful, but it doesn't know how to become joyful. By intoxication, you may think something, but it's not actually joyful. Spiritual life is *sac-cid-ānanda vigraha.* It is up to you. Everyone has his free will to make a choice for God. He doesn't interfere with your choice, or what is the meaning of your independence? Don't misuse it. What is the proper use? Kṛṣṇa consciousness. You are meant to render service to Kṛṣṇa. Śrīla Prabhupāda said, "Here in Germany, you are meant to render service to the state. But now you have to make service to the whole cosmic universe." The conditioned state is due to rebellious acts against God. The Kṛṣṇa consciousness movement is to give people a chance to become free.

In a lecture, Śrīla Prabhupāda spoke on the verse that says, "By serving great sages, great service is done." He says this means rendering service to a pure devotee, a *mahat,* one who is serving the Lord twenty-four hours a day. The great soul is under the *daivi prakriti,* or transcendental nature. We are trying to be under the guidance of Rādhārāṇī. Those who are materialists take shelter of the material energy. The first stage in devotional service is to hear with faith. This is a development of appreciation. We must take the sword. Prabhupāda said, "I started in New York, and I had the sword. But not, 'Take the scripture or I cut off your head.' That is another *type* of preaching. I had chanting and hearing." No one was interested, but now thousands are following. *Kṛṣṇa-bhakti* is in everyone's heart, but it is covered by dirty things. "The more you chant and hear, you will become *cleansed* of dirty things."

Chanting *japa* is an all-around practice. It requires mental and physical alertness. It requires going into the heart and calling to Kṛṣṇa and Rādhā. When these things are missing, it becomes anemic. But you always take assurance that the names are potent and that any chanting is beneficial. Take refuge in the fact that you chant your quota, and you chant on time. Kṛṣṇa is kind and lenient, and He puts all His potencies in the holy name. "But I am so unfortunate that I do not have a taste for the chanting because I commit offenses."[31] Lord Caitanya's lament resonates with us if we do not have a good day. He was so kind to put those lines in the *Śikṣāṣṭakam* and show His compassion and understanding of us chanters. He calls out to be just accepted as an atom of dust at the lotus feet of Kṛṣṇa. In the *Śikṣāṣṭakam,* He goes on to higher states of chanting, feeling the world all void in the absence of Kṛṣṇa. These are the sentiments of Rādhārāṇī. They should enter the mind of the devotee who is properly chanting. The chanting is the *yugala-mantra,* a chant composed of the feelings of Rādhā and Kṛṣṇa. In successful chanting, one

---

31 Śrī Caitanya Mahāprabhu, *Śrī Śikṣāṣṭakam,* 2, see Śrī Caitanya Mahāprabhu, *Śrī Śikṣāṣṭakam* (Mathura: Gaudiya Vedanta Publications, 1995), 37-38.

enters that mood. Staying only with the outer syllables of the chanting is going through the motions. "When oh when will that day be mine when my offenses ceasing, taste for the name increasing, when will that day be mine?" Śrīla Bhaktivinoda Ṭhākura takes the position of a struggling chanter and encourages us who are actually in that position.[32] We aspire to improve and to chant with taste and offenselessly. One day we will do it by endeavor and the mercy of the *ācāryas.*

When things change you adjust to them and keep a new *japa* routine. But keep the same one as far as possible. Nothing should make you so anxious that you don't keep your regular *japa*. I don't have to have certain friends present to be with my friends Kṛṣṇa and Rādhā in the holy names. They are with me even in solitude or with substitute friends. You just insist that you have to do your *japa* and tell the people around you and make it set. "Do Not Disturb: Japa In Progress."

Your life is changing
for a while, but *japa*
stays the same. The
same three names
and thirty-two syllables
and early-morning sessions.

My life may change,
but I cling to my routine
and call on Lord Hari.
Lunch may be different,
and personal care and
even sleep, headaches,
but the anchor of
harināma stays the same.

---

32 Śrīla Bhaktivinoda Ṭhākura, "Kabe Ha'be Bolo." In *Saranagati*, Vijnapati, 1, available in digital form from www.vedabase.com

Japa requires attention. You can't go careening off into sleepiness and still count it as chanting. You must be aware of what you are doing. Drowsiness is due to not enough sleep. It's not a cardinal sin. It's something you have to get out of, the way Kṛṣṇa got out of the coils of the Kāliya serpent. (Krsna *book*, Chapter 16) But I'm not Kṛṣṇa. I'm a struggling *jīva* trying to get his rounds done nicely. I just need a few more rounds to make it a respectable showing. Whispering *japa*, but rapidly. That's how I have to do it nowadays. I remember Prahlādānanda Swami's three tips on chanting: (1) hear the syllables carefully; (2) have faith you are reciprocating with the divine couple; and (3) enjoy the chanting. I enjoy the accomplishment of numerical strength and try to chant with faith and attention. Śrīla Prabhupāda writes, "This transcendental inspiration is called *brahma-maya* because when one is inspired, the sound produced exactly corresponds to the sound vibration of the Vedas. This is not the ordinary sound vibration of this material world. Therefore the sound vibration of the Hare Kṛṣṇa mantra, although presented in the ordinary alphabet, should not be taken as mundane or material." (Bhag. 4.9.4, purport.)[33] But Śrīla Bhaktivinoda Ṭhākura states that if, when chanting, one is thoughtlessly going through the motions, it is the outer covering of the mantra and not actually the transcendental sound vibration. All I know is that if your chanting is offensive, the antidote is to go on chanting. Determined chanting will bring one to the stage of *nāma-ābhasa* (shadow of the holy name) and finally to the clearing stage. Śrīla Prabhupāda states that we should not artificially impose the form of the Lord on our chanting meditation but that the day will come when He will spontaneously manifest.

I've been doing better chanting with pain. My chanting is not of the highest quality, but I keep it up so that I keep

33 See also extensive research in Guy L. Beck, *Sonic Theology: Hinduism and Sacred Sound* (Columbia: University of South Carolina Press, 1993).

on schedule. I chant in softness, in the pain, and plead to Kṛṣṇa to let me keep chanting despite the inconvenience. He kindly lets me chant. Actually, we should learn to chant under any condition as far as possible. When we're in distress, the chanting is a remedy to distress. This is true of mental and physical stress. Who better to call out to than the Lord when you're in pain? The finer points of chanting, such as deeper meditation, are harder to attain, and the distraction of the difficulty makes it hard to pay attention to the syllables. If you practice, you can improve.

Today it's raining outside, and I have a headache, so I don't think we'll go to the beach. But I'll try to keep up my *japa* quota. I'm under the weather, and so the *japa* isn't intense. But I'm keeping close to Kṛṣṇa, my best friend, by chanting His holy names. I have found a way to do that and not be stopped by the pain. You softly chant the mantras and keep away from the tender disturbance. I chanted quickly, averaging six minutes per round. *Japa* is certainly a duty, and I don't resent it for that. It is good to be doing your duty early in the morning, unhampered by anything. The room was quiet except for the rain outside. I've already resolved not go to to the beach.

Hare Kṛṣṇa, although subdued,
gives comfort and a balm.
You're like a medical patient,
but still a spiritual aspirant,
and the chanting runs on
like a piece of equipment
measuring your heartbeats.
It's not so bad because you're
not alone but staying
close to Rādhā-Kṛṣṇa.

There are many obstacles in the path of devotional service, and sometimes we succumb to them. But if we stay rightly resolved as Your devotee, You forgive us and clear our path. By reengaging in devotional service, our offenses are automatically removed without separate atonement. The road of devotional service is the safest and easiest way to attain You. Prominent in the practices is the chanting of Your holy names. You have stated that Your holy names are even more merciful than Your form and that You are completely present in the chanting of the names.

I praise You for giving us the *mahā-mantra,* the great chant for deliverance. By practicing the chanting of Your names in *japa* and *kīrtana,* especially in the present age of Kali, a devotee can attain love of Godhead and free himself of all unwanted habits. The chanting alone can qualify a person to go back to Godhead to join You in Your eternal *līlās.*

The main devotional activity for this age (*yuga-dharma*) is the chanting of the Hare Kṛṣṇa mantra, and I must pledge myself to constant chanting. The *Bṛhan-nāradīya Purāṇa* declares, "*harer nāma harer nāma harer nāmaiva kevalam/ kalau nāsty eva nāsty eva nāsty eva gatir anyathā*": "In the age of Kali, the only means of God realization is the chanting of the holy names. There is no other alternative, there is no other alternative, there is no other alternative." (*Bṛhan-nāradīya Purāṇa,* 5. 47) It is stated three times for emphasis. I began this prayer by saying, "I pray that You will stay by me and protect me and save me." The best way for me to assure myself of Your company and protection is to chant Your names. I ask You to please remind me to regularly chant and to do so in a humble state of mind, keeping myself lower than a blade of grass, more tolerant than a tree, and ready to offer all respect to others without expecting any honor for myself. In such a state of mind, I can constantly chant Your names and achieve my cherished goals.

Time to get off this page and go to *japa*. (You are worried that this ink will smear with moisture before you can get it typed. If you really mean this, then use a ballpoint pen. But I like these better—they flow—and so far we haven't lost material because of smeared pages. So many fears and insecurities. It's a good plan to avoid them. But in the end, you can't protect yourself and your work from *erasure by time*. The soul, however, does not get moistened or dried out or shredded; it doesn't lapse, expire, or go out of print. It doesn't need money or food. It needs love—but it already has that—Kṛṣṇa loves us. You don't need to look for love or work or prepare. As Śrīla Prabhupāda said, "Everything is there." Just discover it.)

Now go and discover your own *japa-yajña*. Have a good time. See you later.

READY TO OFFER ALL RESPECT

tṛṇād api sunīcena
  taror api sahiṣṇunā
amāninā mānadena
  kīrtanīyaḥ sadā hariḥ

"One should chant the holy name of the Lord in a humble state of mind, thinking oneself lower than the straw in the street; one should be more tolerant than a tree, devoid of all sense of false prestige, and should be ready to offer all respect to others. In such a state of mind one can chant the holy name of the Lord constantly."

—*Śrī Śikṣāṣṭakam*, 3

My dear Lord Kṛṣṇa, where are You? There You are, in my heart. There You are, everywhere, in Your impersonal nature. There You are in Goloka Vṛndāvana with Your close associates. And where am I in relation to You? I am right now calling to You, seeking Your presence. My headache has mostly gone away. I have finally completed my minimum quota of *japa* after being behind since I woke so late (4:30 A.M.) this morning. I am at Your doorstep calling to You. Please enter my mind and never leave. I have recently read a statement by Śrīla Bhaktivinoda Ṭhākura about the qualifications for a competent chanter of Your holy names. He said, quoting Lord Caitanya, that we must be humbler than a blade of grass, more tolerant than a tree, not expect praise but give respect to others according to their position. If we chant Your names in this consciousness, we will feel impelled to chant always in transcendental bliss. It is comforting and convincing hearing Bhaktivinoda Ṭhākura speak on the glories of Your names. He cites many scriptures attesting that *harināma* is the most accessible method of reaching You. It is the practice and the goal itself. I just have to chant with his conviction as to the name's potency. That comes by my concentration, but ultimately, by Your mercy.

I must have faith that even mediocre chanting is well worth my effort and that I gain spiritual credit because You have invested all Your power in Your names. But unfortunately, I chant with offenses and do not feel the sublime pleasure of pleasing You when I chant. The remedy to this, You say, is to go on chanting, even at my offensive level. Keep on chanting, and the offenses will clear up. So I will chant more in the afternoon.

One should be humble and think of himself as "lower than the straw in the street." Kṛṣṇadāsa Kavirāja says he was lower than the worm in stool, and that if anyone remembered his name, that person would lose his pious credits. This argues on the side of admitting one's faults. Kṛṣṇadāsa Kavirāja felt this way about himself. And Haridāsa Ṭhākura counted himself a very fallen soul, born in a low family. But Kṛṣṇa considered these persons to be elevated, and Lord Caitanya designated Haridāsa Ṭhākura the *nāmācārya*. What is the balance? One should consider oneself lowly, but as Kṛṣṇa's representative, one can take a position of good standing in human society. He doesn't have to act like an inferior among his contemporaries. He can speak Vedic knowledge and criticize the foolish notions of the materialists. One should use his talents and resources in Kṛṣṇa's service in an intelligent way.

Last night I had a reading with Guṇagrahi Mahārāja. (As I write this, two sea swimmers continue stroking in the ocean—they must be really good swimmers. They've been at it for almost half an hour.) We read from the beginning of the Ajāmila section of the Sixth Canto. There is a discussion of becoming free from karma. Guṇagrahi Mahārāja asked me if we become free from karma at initiation. I remembered the letter Śrīla Prabhupāda wrote to me in 1971. He said that at the time of initiation, all past karma is removed. Any apparent reactions or sufferings a devotee experiences are like the movements of an electric fan after the plug has been pulled out. They are residual and will soon stop. He also referred to token karma, where a *jīva* commits an act for which he should get severe punishment, but Kṛṣṇa pardons him and gives him just a little pinprick. These statements in personal letters from Prabhupāda are articles of complete faith and conviction for me, and I always remember them when relevant topics get discussed. How fortunate to have a spiritual master whose words you utterly trust.

Initiation means one has taken the third step in Kṛṣṇa consciousness. The first step is *śraddhā*, having a little faith to give a donation or buy a book. The second stage is to come to the Kṛṣṇa conscious society and associate with the devotees. The third stage is the beginning of activities—how to perform and develop the perfect stage. The fourth stage is to give up misgivings. This means to follow the four rules—no meat eating, no intoxication, no gambling, and no illicit sex—and chanting sixteen rounds of Hare Kṛṣṇa. The fifth stage is becoming fixed up. The sixth stage is to develop a taste so that you go out to the people and chant. The seventh stage is attachment. In the eighth stage, you can't give it up. In the ninth stage comes *bhāva*, and then perfect love of Kṛṣṇa. Love of Kṛṣṇa is not a foreign thing. It is there in every person's heart. It simply has to be revived.

When a devotee suffers, he thinks it is due to his past misdeeds. He thinks, "Kṛṣṇa is making me suffer a little." How much Prahlāda suffered from his father, but he was silent. Haridāsa Ṭhākura was beaten by the Muslm ruler, and he tolerated. It is understood that when he was beaten, Lord Caitanya was on his back, and he did not suffer. A devotee is educated to tolerate. At the same time, he is compassionate and spreads Kṛṣṇa consciousness so others may be happy. Prahlāda said, "I know how to be happy, but I am suffering for these fools, and I don't want to go back to Godhead unless I can bring them with me." (*Bhag.* 7.9.44)

When the *śravaṇam-kīrtanam* is about Kṛṣṇa, then there is no suffering or unhappiness. Other hearing and talking will not reduce suffering. Devotional service is so nice that even in the material world, the devotee will not suffer material miseries. Because his mind is absorbed in thought of Kṛṣṇa, he does not suffer.

Japa Essay

I began chanting at 2:30 A.M. My *japa* began at an audible whisper, and I immediately tuned in to attentively hearing the syllables in my mind and in the sound vibration. My head was clear, and I felt grateful for that. I thanked Kṛṣṇa for allowing me to chant, and I thanked Śrīla Prabhupāda. I gained momentum of speed by the second round, which was five minutes and fifty seconds. Aside from paying attention to the syllables, I remembered again the King Kulaśekhara's prayer. He prays that now that he has good health, his mind could be entwined in thoughts of Kṛṣṇa, the way the swan entwines its neck in the stems of the lotus. Otherwise, at the time of death, his bodily condition will be very difficult for thinking about Kṛṣṇa. I thought of this in my new awareness that I should not take a headache-free condition for granted but should be grateful I'm clear to chant. Prabhupāda very much liked the King Kulaśekhara verse and would sing it and refer to it in his lectures. I also thought that Śrīla Rūpa Gosvāmī has written a beautiful prayer, *Śrī Nāmāṣṭakam,* praising the holy names. I have not memorized the verses, but I want to get become more familiar with it. I also want to become more familiar with Lord Caitanya's *Śikṣāṣṭakam,* which is so intimately connected with *harināma.*

Japa is the life and soul of this devotee, and so even when he just runs his motor well and traverses the track again and again without a crash, he feels he's accomplished something. And the *śāstras* back this up.

Chanting by the hour. We were making good time. Japa is mysterious. It's just a simple thing, but Lord Caitanya has said it is the most important thing, to chant congregationally or to chant alone, to say the holy names of God again and again. It reminds you of the essay by the anonymous Christian who chanted his *japa* of the Jesus prayer. [34]You go into it, and you don't come out of it. Even fair chanting is great chanting, because you're doing the most important thing. And you're doing it at the best time of day—early in the morning when there's nothing to disturb you. There was just a little snoring on the floor below from Muktavāṇyā, but I didn't let it bother me. A *japa* essay means you tell the essentials of *japa,* but I don't need to tell them to you because you already know. The *saṅkīrtana* is victorious. It increases the ocean of transcendental bliss. It makes us happy, it cleanses the mind of dirty things and gives us a taste for the nectar for

---

34 Anonymous. *The Way of a Pilgrim* (Pasadena, CA: Hope Publishing, 1993).

which we are always anxious. We chant in a humble state of mind. I think I was chanting humbly because I wasn't even thinking of it. I was just operating like a driver at the Indianapolis 500 race, paying attention to what I had to do, going on the inside rail, speeding ahead.

Oh *japa,* you're our favorite act,
you and writing.
Sometimes one can't even chant out loud,
sometimes one has to use a clicker,
sometimes one cannot even count due to
political oppression,
medical emergency,
crises of many sorts.

But as long as he can utter the holy names
in the core of his heart,
from the rays of his mind,
he's making success,
and he'll find a better day
not too long in the future.

For *japa* to really be done with feeling, you have to call out to Kṛṣṇa. Cry like a child calling for its mother. One gets so occupied with the accumulation of the rounds and the proper enunciation that he leaves out the most important part, the feeling. The feeling must be at the center of the exercise in order for the *japa* to be complete. One has to have faith in reciprocation with Rādhā and Kṛṣṇa, faith that the holy names are Kṛṣṇa Himself and Rādhā Herself. Otherwise, you are just chanting the outer syllables of the name and not chanting offenselessly. *Śuddha-nāma* is a rare, advanced stage. We have to be patient with our chanting and hearing clearly, making the sounds audibly and keeping the mind fixed on the utterance of the words themselves. From this stage, we can go to the upper stage, but we should not wait forever to inject the emotion into the chanting, to chant from the heart with the call. "When will the day come when my offenses ceasing, taste for the holy name increasing, when oh when will that day be mine?" The taste for Hare Kṛṣṇa comes when you cry out to Kṛṣṇa to please hear you and please let your stony heart be softened by emotions of *bhāva*. So many years of chanting, and we are waiting for that day to come. Therefore, we should pray while we chant and not be content to merely rattle the names off clearly. We should pray in the mood of Lord Caitanya, as expressed in the *Śikṣāṣṭakam*: "Oh my Lord, I am Your eternal servitor, but somehow I have fallen into this ocean of birth and death. Please pick me up from this ocean and fix me as one of the atoms at Your lotus feet." All of *Śikṣāṣṭakam* is rich with guidance for proper chanting.

Without feeling, the center is missing,
like the hole in the center of a doughnut.
We must fill it up
with tears in the eyes
and feelings of separation.

Dear Lord, I am tired of chanting like a machine
instead of a human being.
Please fix my sight
at the lotus feet of the holy names
and let my heart finally melt
with devotion.

I cannot do it by myself,
but with a drop of Your mercy,
my chanting will turn out successful.

The main thing is to be persistent and not give up. I'm accumulating rounds at a steady pace. They're not the highest standard, but they are not so bad either. My mind is wandering a little bit. I'm bringing it back to focus on the sound vibration of the syllables. Those syllables are absolute and bring Kṛṣṇa into my mind. According to our philosophy, great leniency is afforded in the chanting. Even offensive chanting removes sinful activities from the mind. I'm chanting with a great physical handicap, and so that has to be taken into account and not held against me. I forgive myself for the troubled performance and beg Kṛṣṇa to excuse me. As soon as I get better, with less pain, the chanting will improve, so this is evidence of my good intentions. Chant through the pain. See Kṛṣṇa waiting for you. For that, I'm making the effort. He sees the good and overlooks the bad.

Chanting Hare Kṛṣṇa,
counting up the rounds,
is not the highest standard,
but it's good you
haven't given up.

Chanting Hare Kṛṣṇa is the
merciful sacrifice.
You get credit for your effort,
you get comfort for your try.

We were reading *Rādhākṛpā-kaṭākṣa,* and I noticed that I wasn't paying attention to the meaning or mood of it. Then I thought how my *japa* is the same way. But it *is* possible to think of the meaning. This is the difficulty in *japa.* It also occurred to me that *no one can do this for me.* We're each entirely alone in the application of our minds to hearing the holy name. If we think we can allow someone else to do it for us, we are mistaken. Śrī Kṛṣṇa doesn't want to do our chanting for us. He wants us to chant. Our guru also wants us to chant; not that he chants for us or that we think an obedient disciple is mindless, a robot operating under his guru's will.

It is easy to be neglectful. No one will notice. I can satisfy the devotees by making an appearance, sitting with them, fingering my beads and enunciating the names. They see me and hear my chanting, but they don't know what I'm thinking while I chant.

I want to start noticing.[35] Thanks anyway, but I have to accept my *neophyte talk*—and guide others, too. When you accept priesthood, you don't give it up later. When you sincerely accept the responsibility of guiding others, you don't give that up. But I do want to stop the charade. Be as honest as possible—that truthfulness will be one of the important qualities I will impart to others.

So you chant with your
wing clipped. But it doesn't
stop you from clear enunciation.
Nothing stops a sincere devotee,
as long as he gets enough sleep.
I was alert today and happy
to report it.

Let's hold a little celebration.
I can't even take a shower
or dress myself, my
shoulder so pains me,

---

35 When I wrote about some of these struggles in a *BTG* article, one Godbrother wrote me and said that my words were those of a gross neophyte and thus my acting as spiritual master was a charade. He begged me to stop the pretense of guiding disciples. SDG.

but I can chant Hare Kṛṣṇa
Hare Kṛṣṇa, and there is no
impediment to that.
I am thankful, and even glad.
Now here comes a headache,
but there is a way to stop that too.

So thank the Lord
and come on board the Hare Kṛṣṇa mantra.
Even if you cannot stop the ache
be grateful for the whispers.
They are intimate words
and uttered without stoppage.

ENOUGH FOR NOW. GO AND CHANT and pray to Kṛṣṇa. This writing requires humility, and *japa* does also. All arts require humility and honesty. I am begging for attraction to the holy name.

There's nothing to say except, "Please help me." Other than that, I'm saying to myself, "Here are some ideas on how to help yourself." And I'm saying, "Here are some obstacles." And I'm saying, "This is what is happening" (when I write as a reporter on reality).

Japa is a grand feast of chanting the holy names. When it is going well, I feel happy. I know that Lord Hari and Śrīmatī Rādhārāṇī are hearing me. I have firm faith. Even if I can't chant loudly, I chant with inner attention and keep my mind fixed. I did all this today, and in a speedy way. So I am am not regretful, but thankful to Kṛṣṇa for the gift of *japa*. It is so easy to do, simply repeating those sacred names and coming closer to Kṛṣṇa in meditation. Even when I don't "meditate" in the deeper sense, I'm meditating by chanting the absolute sound vibration and keeping my mind away from the plethora of all objects in the universe. It's a chance to narrow my consciousness and pinpoint it on the most important thing. Lord Caitanya has given us a brilliant method just suitable for people in the age of Kali, and we should always be thankful to Him and take up His process.

Chanting the names,
don't exaggerate how well you did.
But you have to give credit
where credit is due.

The credit is due to Mahāprabhu
and His munificent gesture of
giving and emphasizing *harināma.*
I chanted this morning with most
working parts intact, and that
makes me very satisfied,
even though I know it
was not a brilliant session.

He's so kind He's made the names
absolute, so even feeble
chanting counts for a lot.
And He gives you hope you'll
get better.

"Better quality, better quantity" that's my private prayer-mantra. Today I feel patient with myself, assuring it will come. Adding times when I chant. But I rarely chant except with the beads in hand, counting it as my quota. I have a tape of Śrīla Prabhupāda holding kirtan at Dr. Mishra's ashram. When I play that, I sing along, and I continue singing when it stops.

Not eating too much, but I have a hearty appetite for what Bala gives me (as he lovingly cooks it). The walk at the beach is devoted to *japa*. Hear tapes. . . .

Although the interior speaks of frustrations—facing myself as a drowsy chanter—the overall purpose is one that seems right and brings fulfillment. I only gradually attempt to become acquainted with the workings of the mind and to gain control over it in *bhajana*. One devotee who has done *vratas* of 108 rounds daily in retreat settings told me he discovered that "the mind is an organ." He got to see that it works in the same way any other part of the body works. It can be pushed to perform, and it has certain limits and behaviors. Rather than think the mind is "you," or be helpless to the mind's dictation, we control it. *Vāco vegaṁ manasaḥ krodha-vegaṁ.*[36]

I want to be able to place the mind on hearing *harināma* and thinking favorably of Kṛṣṇa during *bhajana*—and take the mind away from distractions.

Also I want to feel devotion. Or pray to Kṛṣṇa to allow me to feel devotion, to feel remorse over my lack of devotion and my inability to purge out *anarthas* and *aparādhas*. This is the general work. I don't have a vigorous program for it. Years ago, I read St. Ignatius of Loyola's retreat program. I don't have some process like that—daily meditations upon one's sins, turning to God or Christ. . . . I have *japa* and writing. I'm moving more toward reflective statements about my life, where I am and where I'm going.

A groggy session is not so good,
your shoulder pain prevents a poem.
But early rising is a boon:
you know you'll reach your quota.

---

36 Śrīla Rūpa Gosvāmī, Verse 1 in Śrīla A.C. Bhaktivedanta Swami Prabhupāda, *Nectar of Instruction* (London: The Bhaktivedanta Book Trust, 1975).

I pray to Lord Kṛṣṇa for alert
mahā-mantras, but they do not come.
I am saddened but ever hopeful.

4:46 A.M. I see I am a mass of distracting thoughts and, separate from them, I see my desire to fix my mind on the holy names. Periodically, I catch myself and express at least the desire to hear the names as they vibrate on my tongue. No one knows, only me, how strong this bad habit is. I've indulged in it like any other addiction. To get free isn't easy. It's a mental habit of allowing the mind to go wherever it wants during *japa-yajña.*

There, I've said it concisely and accurately. Now stay on this one point. Whatever gain I can make, please do it. Continue to focus on that problem. Distinguish the distractions from the desire to hear. Start a new habit of deliberately taking the mind away from other thoughts and applying it to hearing Hare Kṛṣṇa Hare Kṛṣṇa Kṛṣṇa Kṛṣṇa Hare Hare/ Hare Rāma Hare Rāma Rāma Rāma Hare Hare. Don't expect this to be easy at first but be persistent. Just hope I can make some headway. I shall not indulge so wantonly, obliviously, callously in other thoughts while chanting the Hare Kṛṣṇa mantra on beads. I'll remind myself what to do.

Chanting so slowly,
I lament over the pace,
but hope springs eternal,
in the human breast.
I will gain back what I've lost
before the day is over.

Kṛṣṇa will give me a chance again
as He has many times in the past.

Now do your work,
the utmost duty
for a fallen *bhakta.*

I've already stated that the worst thing is to be sleepy during *japa*. It slows down your total count. It makes you inattentive. Sloppy and unholy. It's offensive. I must work at it. Everyone should do this. Sleepy chanting is a plague. Keep awake. You have to be mindful and always on the alert. You can't drift off. It's good to keep track of your numbers carefully to note that you haven't lost the count. So my *japa* essay for today is against sleepy *japa* in favor of awake *japa*. It's one of the most crucial matters. What good is it if you spend five minutes nodding over the chanting, doing "dive-bombing" chanting, drowsing off into spaced-out land? You have to keep on the track. Notice the mantras passing through your mind and your vocalization. Then you're approaching real chanting. Otherwise, you're wasting your time.

Having said the above and given myself a stern warning, I must say that I've improved this morning. I'm chanting more alertly. The worst thing about sleepy chanting is that it slows down your speed. I won't be able to chant eight rounds before 5:00 A.M. I'll be lucky if I chant five.

Japa is the life and soul of the devotee. The bead bag is his constant companion. He's always chanting whenever he has a spare moment. But it's best to chant a lot of rounds consecutively, not to chant one or two here and there at spare moments. It is good to save time for chanting lots rounds at a time. That way you build up momentum and concentration. We will do that this morning. It's fun chanting and hearing the rounds roll off your tongue, putting aside all other subject matters. It's a quiet, solitary activity, and one that is to my liking. I think of myself like

Thoreau out at Walden Pond, spending his time by himself, being content with it.

In my case, I'm content with being with the Lord as His holy names. Lord Caitanya has given it to us as a major method of overcoming maya in the age of Kali. It is so simple, it is so natural, it is so easy. Seeing that we cannot perform more difficult *yajñas* in this present age, Lord Caitanya has given us this easy method, and if we cannot do it, then we are lost. I can do it. I am doing it. You can do it too. It is the *japa-yajña*. It is best to save time somehow or other in your busy day and not do it while driving your car or riding your bicycle.

That's why early morning is a good time, but if you cannot spare it then, then do it in the afternoon when you save some time for it. But a good block of reserve time is essential. During that time, you should create an environment in which you're not being bothered by your children or your work worries. Even worse is externally dividing your time between chanting and other duties. Be determined to find a time in the day which is your *japa* time, and carry it out faithfully every day. Steady performance of this routine will bring you good results.

It does not exactly matter whether it is early in the morning or later in the afternoon, as long as it is a time of peace and uninterrupted chanting. Strive to find that time and carry it out for Kṛṣṇa's sake and for our sakes. It's too important to be neglected.

Everything can change, as it did for me. I was immersed in the sounds and atmosphere of the Lower East Side, not very happy, when suddenly I saw it standing right there—a little sign in the window saying, "*Bhakti-yoga classes three nights a week. Transcendental sound vibration.*"[37] And suddenly the sun was shining everywhere as I attended and gave

---

37 Satsvarūpa dāsa Goswami, *Śrīla Prabhupāda-līlāmṛta*, Vol. 2, *Planting the Seed*, Chapter 18: "Breaking Ground" (Bhaktivedanta Book Trust: Los Angeles, 1980).

up my bad habits and took up the good habit, which I've never stopped, or *kīrtana* with Swamiji. Sudden revelations can come like that after many years of stagnation and no breakthrough. Eureka, I've found it. It's called sudden illumination. It happened to me, and it can happen to you.

The love chant for this age is the Hare Kṛṣṇa mantra. Chant it sincerely to Rādhā and Kṛṣṇa, and They reciprocate in love to us. This is a short piece, but it gives the essence. Devote yourself to the love chant, and you'll get everything you want. Love, or bhakti, is the most important thing taught in all the Vedas. You have to target the love to Kṛṣṇa, and then it's actually love. Other "love" misses the target and doesn't bring the reward. So you need a spiritual master to show you how to pull that bow and arrow to hit the target. You need a teacher of the love chant. Love chant is between two people, the spirit soul and Rādhā-Kṛṣṇa. It's a complete circle, a complete satisfaction, a calling out and a response. Chant and response, chant and response. Hare Kṛṣṇa, Hare Kṛṣṇa, Kṛṣṇa Kṛṣṇa, Hare Hare / Hare Rāma, Hare Rāma, Rāma Rāma, Hare Hare.

3:32 A.M. For the time being, I whisper, but I don't have to be ashamed of it or feel guilty. I can get the same quality as out-loud chanting if I concentrate. The main thing is to hear the holy names and pronounce them clearly, and beyond that, to sink into alert meditation on Hare and Kṛṣṇa and Rāma, over and over. I don't get bored, I don't get tired. So what if I chant at a whisper? It's still heard by Kṛṣṇa, and He's pleased to see me trying despite my handicap. A loud chanter could just be "blowing in the wind" without paying attention. The main quality is attention. I point my consciousness at the Hare Kṛṣṇa mantra and exclude other thoughts. I put my feeling into it and call on Lord Hari. It's the quality that counts, not the decibels. While I admit that loud chanting is better, I move with my crutch, not wanting to be pitied or blamed, and make my progress through the rounds. I try not to let the headache distract me and instead become attracted to the sounds of the *mahā-mantra*. It's mind over matter. It's spirit over mind. Just as they have special Olympics for paraplegics and cripples, the whisperer can break world records and become a champion chanter. Kṛṣṇa wants to see the effort and the pleasure felt as the chanter immerses in the pleasure potency of Mother Hara and Kṛṣṇa. Oh energy of the Lord, Oh Lord, please engage me in Your service.

Japa is an open field in which you enter and do the best you can. With a physical handicap, I feel impinged upon and can't roam deeply into contemplation of the Hare Kṛṣṇa mantra. So I cut my losses and my lamentations and the bare mantras move along quickly. I sit back in the chair and watch the count rise. I draw satisfaction from the accumulation of rounds and don't get depressed by the lack of freedom to go deeper. I trust that Kṛṣṇa knows I'm trying. People who chant with a handicap have to remain brave and keep optimistic about the efficacy of the chanting. I should take stock in my sincerity and plead to Kṛṣṇa that I may do better. I take satisfaction in the accumulation and the fact that I am not stopped by the impairment. All will go well somehow or other, and Kṛṣṇa will take the difficulties into account. He wants to see me trying, and that is my success. A person who does not give up despite difficulty is a good chanter. Try to reach further. Improve the quality of the names and think of Kṛṣṇa and Rādhā. I let a certain sorrow set in, but I restrain it also. It is a kind of war, or at least a struggle, and in times of difficulty gains are made.

THE TASTE

yad brahma-sākṣāt-kṛti-niṣṭhayāpi
vināśamāyāti vinā na bhogaiḥ
apaiti nāma-sphuraṇena tatte
prārabhda-karmeti virauti vedaḥ

"O holy name! The seeds from which sin sprouts within the heart are not burned to ashes by realization of the impersonal Brahman or by constant meditation on eternal consciousness. But, O Holy Name, as soon as You appear on the tongue of a sincere chanter, all the karmic seeds are burned to ashes. Thus all sinful reactions are finished. This is proclaimed by the Vedas."

—Śrīla Rūpa Gosvāmī, *Śrī Nāmāṣṭakam,* 4

I WOKE UP WITH a stomachache at 10:30 P.M. I took an antacid and went back to sleep. I got up at 2:00 A.M. and began chanting.

Nārāyaṇa-kavaca came up and began talking about my chanting. He said he was reading my old book *Dear Sky,*[38] where I repeatedly said that I was chanting just out of determination and that I did not have a higher taste. He said that nobody could chant for forty years just out of sacrifice. I told him I do have a taste, but I also struggle. He said that maybe my taste and personal reciprocation with Kṛṣṇa is a private thing. I think it is private. I think it's private even to me, and I'm not aware always of my taste

38 Satsvarūpa dāsa Goswami, *Dear Sky: Letters From a Sannyasi* (Philadelphia: GN Press, 1993).

in chanting. I remember one of my disciples once wrote to me to express annoyance with me for always talking about struggling with chanting. That disciple wanted me to write in my books that I was chanting at the *rāgānuga* level. But I have to be real. That's more important than making higher claims. Prabhupāda himself says, "These boys and girls would not continue chanting Hare Kṛṣṇa unless they had a taste." So it's true. He used to say that we couldn't chant the word "John" over and over and over, but we can chant Hare Kṛṣṇa twenty-four hours a day. I chant Hare Kṛṣṇa every morning with taste. But I lament that it's not the topmost. I admit it. I don't experience bodily symptoms of ecstasy, I don't see the whole panorama of Kṛṣṇa's name, fame, activities, and qualities when I chant. Sometimes my chanting is mechanical. I think the whole question of taste is something that is private and that I can't discuss because I'm not so much aware of it myself. Well, do you either taste or not? Yes, you taste, but you want to taste more, more and more. And you admit your chanting is flawed. O Kṛṣṇa, I know that I am personally reciprocating with You in *japa*, but You are withholding from me until I improve.

By 4:45 A.M., I had finished sixteen rounds. It was really nice to get them all done in a row like that. I was chanting at under six minutes per round for the first twelve rounds, then I became tired and slowed down. I even began to develop some head pressure, but persisted and finished the sixteen. Yes, Nārāyaṇa, there is a taste.

My dear Lord, I pray to please You. This is the aim of bhakti, of the pure devotee. He has no other motive or goal in his life. He is above the *mukta,* or the one who seeks liberation from birth and death as the result of his austerities and spiritual purification. I do not claim to be a pure devotee with no other motive in my life but to please You, but I've heard from my spiritual master and from Lord Caitanya's words in *Śikṣāṣṭakam* that this is the highest standard, and so I desire to attain it. I'm serving You and practicing *vaidhī-bhakti*, and I wish to do so for Your pleasure. I want my acts to be pleasing to You.

Personally speaking, I am on Your path back to Godhead. But one has to practice to perfection, or else one must return to the material world in his next life to finish his advancement. Sometimes, even if one has completed his progress, Kṛṣṇa sends him back to the material world to assist in missionary activities.[39] In His *Śikṣāṣṭakam*, Lord Caitanaya prayed, "Oh My Lord, I do not desire wealth, fame or beautiful women. All I want in My life is Your causeless devotional service, birth after birth."[40] By this prayer, Caitanya Mahāprabhu bypassed even the desire for personal liberation in favor of eternal devotional service, even in the material world.

In a *Śrīmad-Bhāgavatam* purport, Śrīla Prabhupāda wrote that even if a devotee doesn't desire to go back to Godhead, the Lord takes him and brings him to live with Him and His eternal associates in the spiritual world. It is comforting to know that You want us to come join You in Goloka Vṛndāvana and that You personally initiate our going there. I must admit that I desire to be with You in Your abode with Your intimate devotees. I pray that, by Your mercy and my own endeavor, I may come to the standard of desiring eternal devotional service and that I be satisfied with wherever You place me.

---

39 Conceptually, this is roughly similar to the *bodhisattva* teaching of Buddhism, where perfected beings are sent back to the material world to assist in missionary work until all living beings attain *nirvana*. SDG.

40 Śrī Caitanya Mahāprabhu, *Śikṣāṣṭakam*, 4. Trans. Śrīla A.C. Bhaktivedanta Swami Prabhupāda, in Introduction to *Śrīmad Bhāgavatam*, Vol. 1 (New York: Bhaktivedanta Book Trust, 1987), 40.

When a *Village Voice* reporter visited Prabhupāda at the Bowery, he wrote in his article, "I just plain liked the guy." Similarly, I just plain like the Hare Kṛṣṇa mantras. I enjoy chanting them as a man would enjoy having a tasty meal. I am very grateful to have attained this taste. The pain obstructs the feeling of enjoyment. You might think that the enjoyment is coming from the pleasure potency, and so it should overcome the headache, but it doesn't work that way. Nevertheless, I still feel the pleasure of the mantras, although they are impaired

Japa essay

If my main purpose is *japa*, I might think how writing could support that more. Yet what can I do? When I chant, I chant. I know I should bring the mind back into prayerful hearing—mostly I can do it. How can writing—a separate discipline—help *japa*? I'm not writing a sequel to *Begging for the Nectar of the Holy Name*[41], where I'm thinking of the reader and how to help him chant.

Okay, tell yourself, "Man, why don't you pay attention when you chant?" Soon I'll be out facing the sea—as the sun rises, the sea will be blue and brilliant under a clear sky. At least for a while. Don't mind that my words are repetitious. The sea itself is not restless with boredom, although it has repeated the same movements since the beginning of creation. It's beyond boredom. My truth is to see and hear the sea. Tell us again, in slightly different ways, how the waves splash, about the light, the colors of the sea, the foam, the cool air blowing, your windproof hooded coat. What do you feel when you sit here and face outward?

Bring yourself toward prayer. Surely writing can help with that, with a literary version. O God, O Kṛṣṇa, O spiritual master, allow me to be sincere. I wish to chant

41 Satsvarūpa dāsa Goswami, *Begging for the Nectar of the Holy Name* (Philadelphia: GN Press, 1992).

with devotion. I don't know what to do. All I know is to count and pronounce the names and surmount drowsiness and to sometimes notice what I'm thinking, and then correct myself.

Chanting deserves the best.
But when your sleep was
interrupted, you can't stay alert.
It's a problem I don't know
how to solve. Keep trying,
keep moving the beads.
Kṛṣṇa will help you.

I will do better, and whatever
I do is something worthy,
because the names are so potent
even a mediocre session
is brilliant.

Japa is serious business and requires full concentration in order to do it right. Your main interest can't be caught up in rattling off the numbers. You have to dive deeper for spiritual emotions. Ask Kṛṣṇa to accept your offering as a serious service. It's not a physically active performance but requires mental energy and prayer, which are not easy to come by, especially when you're just starting after waking up in the morning. Quickly you must progress through proper enunciation and counting and go on to further things. This takes a serious chanter and one who is in good spiritual shape, like an athlete. Mental and physical preparation is required. Don't forget to be serious and attentive from the very beginning. You have no time to lose. It's like the scoring in the basketball game. The very first points are important. It requires agility, balance and speed. All the players are required, not just a superstar, to move, pass and coordinate around the court. Try to keep count of the scoring as soon as possible. Bring the time down from very high numbers to lower numbers. Don't be afraid you'll wear out. Eight rounds is not long, and so speed should be emphasized. You should be expert at keeping alert and pushing with the fingers. A good start indicates good, complete rounds.

Kṛṣṇa is sweet, sweet, sweet: madhuram, madhuram, madhuram. *That's the best kind of love of God,* madhurya, *or sweet. There's no room for awe and reverence, it's just sweet and lovely exchanges of the most intimate kind. How nice it would be to go there where there's no* kuṇṭha, *or anxiety. It's not sentimental, it's not sticky-gooey. It's actually sweet, like the lilacs, like the call of the cardinal. Sweet like things we know in this world that are actually lovely—the lotus. In the spiritual world, it's beyond comparison. We can only sing a song of sweet and lovely thinking of this world, but if you let me, I'll transform it to the spiritual world, where you can think of it in that way.*

Haridāsa and I spoke on the phone, and he shared a *japa* thought with me. He mentioned how Kṛṣṇa in Dvārakā sits early in the morning and meditates on Himself. As He does so, His meditation expands and expands (because He's unlimited). Haridāsa said that when we chant *japa*, Kṛṣṇa can expand in our hearts. For so long, we haven't been open to Him, and if we chant with attention to the heart, Kṛṣṇa can expand and expand to us, His knowledge of Himself and our devotion to Him. Just as Kṛṣṇa's meditation on Himself expands, so can ours.

Sixteen rounds done,
pin a medal on your chest.
It's the bare minimum,
but your mind can rest.

You've paid your dues,
and there's time for more.
This is the honest life.
A happy Hare feels at peace.

He's accomplished his duty.
Kṛṣṇa kindly gave him
time and attention,
and he broke through the finish line.

Now we must work more on the quality
beyond mere numerical counting.
Trace your heart with loving mantras
of the dearmost, Rādhā and Kṛṣṇa.

Your Speed

Speed isn't everything. You have to chant at a comfortable rate, where you're actually chanting and hearing. Prabhupāda did indicate a general average and said the chanting of sixteen rounds should take from two to two-and-a-half hours. To chant 16 rounds in 2 hours, one would need to chant at an average rate of seven and a half minutes per round. To chant 16 rounds in 2.5 hours, one would need to chant at an average rate of 9 minutes, 22.5 seconds per round. That's not slow. One has to learn the art of chanting the mantras quickly while paying attention to them and not going too slow. Developing the art takes time, so that you're paying attention and moving along at a decent pace. Outsiders to Kṛṣṇa consciousness who hear a group of devotees chanting their mantras tend to think they're going too fast, and they would even recommend a very slow uttering of the words to be sure that each word is said thoughtfully. Devotees learn to be thoughtful while simultaneously moving along at a pace. You really have to be hearing each syllable, or you're chanting too fast. Dwelling methodically on the mantras so that they come out twelve minutes per round is too slow. In time, we find the balance that's right for us.

The most important thing is quality, not quantity. We have to go deep inside ourselves and chant from the heart, calling out to Rādhā and Kṛṣṇa to please accept our service. It needn't take "all day" to utter this sincere cry, but we have to be sure we do not rush over it thoughtlessly. That's why a stopwatch is not a bad idea for those who are uncertain whether they're chanting too fast or too slow. "O Lord, O energy of the Lord, please engage me in Your service" has to be felt with each mantra. How long that takes is up to you to find out. There is an early tape of Prabhupāda chanting *japa*,[42] and that can give you a good idea of a suitable pace for *japa*. All this is relative and can be learned by each person with time and practice.

I chant my rounds
at a go—
the seconds fly by.

I'm paying attention to the
mahā-mantra, and I feel
it in my bones.

I'm not too fast or slow,
but average, as advised,
now it's up to me to
find out the heart

42 Not the recording where he's chanting in public at an initiation, where he says, "Sit properly." SDG.

and call to the Divine Couple
without too much frenzy
so that my words aren't just a slur.

Everyone can do it—it's
easy and sublime.
Practice makes perfect,
and you're feeling on time.

Chanting out loud is better than chanting in the mind, but sometimes you just fall into the habit. As long as you are attentive, it is not so bad. Chanting out loud captures more senses and benefits others who hear. But *japa* is mostly a private conversation. Each mantra is distinctive and separate. Sometimes you get a little tired of chanting and you have to prod yourself and remember the importance of what you're doing and overcome the lack of taste.

Japa operates mechanically and then opens to the heart. It rattles along the rails like a speedy train. No danger that it can be derailed. The only danger is not opening to the heart. Listen to the mournful train whistle.

Today I woke at 2:55 A.M. but on my third round I got a headache. The more intensely I chanted, the worse the headache got. But I didn't stop chanting intensely. I wanted to get them done. I wanted to persist in the *yajña*. I've chanted thirteen rounds, but I'm not in good shape. I chanted at a whisper, but I went down the track at a rapid pace—six and a half minutes per round. If only I could chant with a clear head. If only I could chant with an open heart. At least I was chanting, no doubt about that. My mind stayed on the track without going disastrously to other thoughts. It was a strain with the pain. My *japa* train hurtled through the barrier regardless. Nothing can stop it from its charge. Now I am left shattered. Better to have gotten them done than to have laid back sleeping, nursing your wound.

The engineer stokes his locomotive
and charges down the track.
He chooses *japa* over pain
because the holy names come first.
We can always repair the engine,
but we don't want to miss the
golden opportunity of early-morning
yajña speeding through *brāhma-muhūrta.*
You take your choice and favor *nāma.*

Chanting is the most important thing for keeping focused on your Kṛṣṇa consciousness, especially early in the morning. Repetition of the mantras is like a heartbeat to keep you in touch with Rādhā and Kṛṣṇa. I like to do it and don't find it boring. I like the climb in numerical strength. It requires awareness that you don't drift off into la-la land. It's so easy to lose concentration, but it's also easy to keep it if you just keep your wits about you and remember the important *yajña* you're performing. Being aware of the importance of the Hare Kṛṣṇa mantra keeps you on the track. You easily utter the mantras and hear each syllable clearly. It's not a difficult thing when executed properly. It has to be taken seriously, and preferably with love. Routine love. You have come again another morning to be with the holy names. In your remaining lifespan, no time should be wasted. It should not be done with dull mechanism but by taking a fresh opportunity on a bright new day. Take shelter at Kṛṣṇa's lotus feet. The wonderful opportunity of another day, another chance offered by Kṛṣṇa to come close to Him and build up your devotion.

Each day you can either do it successfully or blow it. Each day Kṛṣṇa wants you to chant successfully. He's giving us access to the easiest form of meditation, as endorsed by Lord Caitanya and to the stream of sacred *paramparā* of chanting *ācāryas.*

The whole twenty-four hour day has to be arranged so that *japa* is chanted under the best conditions. You have to go to sleep early so that you're not tired in the morning. Alert, awake chanting is very important. Drowsy chanting is no good. A round should not take nine minutes, as one of mine did today. Chanting should reach meditation or calling out, like a child calling for the mother. It should be a real emotional confrontation, not a mechanical act. We're calling to the persons Rādhā and Kṛṣṇa from our needful position. We need Them; we need the holy names. We're up early to call on Them. It's the most personal devotion of the day. Attentiveness is key; inattention is madness (*pramāda*). Your lifestyle, your daily duties, your health and mental state should all be contributing so that you are in top condition for this period of a few hours. That's how the priority should be arranged. Not that the chanting gets neglected because of other considerations. Chant as many rounds as possible in good time. Your life is molded so that it's the life of a Hare Kṛṣṇa chanter.

Chanting Hare Kṛṣṇa is
the most important thing.
It's the sword that cuts
the knots of karma,
it's the song that you sing.

Up early in the morning,
you strive to keep awake
and utter sacred mantras
from heart with nothing fake.

The timing should be rapid
but with attention to the words,
the mind is fixed on chanting
and not on morning cares.
This is the life of chanting
in dedication fixed
and not in morning mixed.

A memory from Boston, 1969: The devotees gathered in the back of the Dodge van, preparing to go out on *harināma saṅkīrtana* at the Boston Commons. Both men and women filled every inch of the spacious van. They were all dressed in devotee clothes and made a brave and merry pose for the camera before the doors were shut. Once at the Commons, they piled out and formed a long line facing the avenue. People began to gather, and a few hecklers cried out. Soon the loud singing of the mantra drowned out the opposition. Baradvaja led them, playing the *mṛdaṅga*, and several devotees clashed pairs of *karatālas*. It was a balmy summer day. As a crowd gathered, Girirāja and Yadurāṇī circulated among the people seeking donations for *Back to Godhead* magazines. The Hare Kṛṣṇa mantra chorus ebbed and flowed in a wave that would have pleased Śrīla Prabhupāda. This was a daily affair in the summer, and the devotees enjoyed their exhibition in the celebration before the crowd. They chanted for about forty minutes and then took a break. If the crowd was not too unruly, one of the devotees would give a short speech. Prabhupāda had instructed that if the people were too noisy, they should just go on chanting. Control the mind and chant. Hare Kṛṣṇa, Hare Kṛṣṇa, Kṛṣṇa Kṛṣṇa, Hare Hare/Hare Rāma,

Hare Rāma, Rāma Rāma, Hare Hare. You can chant that all the time, that's the main thing—you can chant the mantra wherever you go.

Japa is a big sea. You have to steer your ship through it with careful navigation and concentration. Otherwise, you won't reach your destination. Going around in circles is not chanting with direct, on-course meditation. Chanting is done by a competent captain and navigator with enunciation and alertness at every moment. It's not just a seaworthy act but a devotional, religious act, calling on God and His Consort to help you to stay in the waters on the direct path. Sometimes I chant as if I have the anchor down and go around in circles. Not much benefit in that. But the chanting is so wonderful that even the anchor trip is filled with absolute sound vibration. You make progress in Kṛṣṇa's realm. But real chanting is staying on course. A straight line is the shortest distance between two points. Reaching the goal is meditation on Kṛṣṇa's qualities, names, and forms.

When you miss your big block of *japa* in the morning, you have to remain calm and assure yourself that you'll get the rounds done during the day. There's no doubt about it. Just be sure you don't rush them. Stay calm and enunciate the mantras. Try in the future to ensure you get those big blocks in the morning, when you can stretch out and chant lots of mantras. We'll be going to the beach, and I can chant there in the car. Keep the mind fixed on the goal of the mantras, the yearning to reach Rādhā and Kṛṣṇa. Reciprocate with Them in your mind. Chant from your lowly position, and reach out. You have nothing to regret, no reason to panic. Everything will go all right. You may just have to chant a little more in the late morning. But that will be fine also. Relax in your chair and utter the Hare Kṛṣṇa mantra in peace. With such a high priority to the mantras, you cannot fail. The pain of missing the big block of chanting early in the morning creates a greater desire to do them. Chanting Hare Kṛṣṇa is your greatest friend. You will not desert Him, and He will not desert you. Better than writing this essay, I should go and chant.

Chanting in a hurry
creates a worry.
Better to slow down
and reach the crown.

There's no question you'll reach the quota
not even an iota.
So don't be anxious,
just feel your pulse
and pray to Hari
without hurry.

The time is the same,
the boy is the same,
it's just a little time difference,
so don't make a big inference
that you failed Nāma Prabhu.

I have a small wave of loneliness nagging me in my own life. I don't desire a wife or fame (*na dhanaṁ na janaṁ na sundarīṁ*),[43] but I sometimes feel low because of the aloneness of my life. Most of the time I feel right about it, so I wouldn't even call it a conflict. It is not something I am motivated to change. I don't want more people in my life. But occasionally, a little voice of unhappiness speaks to me. I think it is my general lack of Kṛṣṇa consciousness. As Lord Caitanya prays in *Śikṣāṣṭakam*, "I do not desire a wife, fortune or fame. All I desire in my life is Your causeless

---

43 Śrī Caitanya Mahāprabhu, *Śikṣāṣṭakam*, 4. *Ibid.*, 40.

devotional service, birth after birth." I need to desire more to serve the Lord. I like the occupations I have—chanting, writing, living with my friends. I don't need a change in my activities. But I hanker for more taste from them, just as this morning's *japa* was not so good, as well as my noon *gāyatrī.* I shall pray to Kṛṣṇa for more taste in my devotional activities.

The Christian monks used to say, "Stay in your cell, and your cell will teach you all you need to know—about prayer."[44] My *bhajana-kuṭīr* is a safe and exciting place. I can have fun here. I can be with Kṛṣṇa, our Beloved.

I have come to improve the quality of my chanting and hearing. I'll do it at the time of death, but I need to practice so that I can be attentive. Give to this practice. Make the mental effort. We learn from the words of Vṛtāsura that a devotee of Lord Viṣṇu should not desire *dharma, artha,* or *kāma.* "But a devotee has no other desire than to serve the Supreme Personality of Godhead, both in this life and in the next" (*Bhag.* 6.11.23 purport).

My book *Begging for the Nectar of the Holy Name* contains statements on inability in chanting. They are clarified to show faith in the *śāstra*'s statements of the absolute mercy and power of the holy name. Thus, it is an acceptable book for devotees.[45] What did I mean when I said that my

44 Abba Moses in John Chryssavgis, *In the Heart of the Desert: The Spirituality of the Desert Fathers and Mothers.* (World Wisdom, Inc, 2008), 41.

45 Another book in the series on *japa* is: Satsvarūpa dāsa Goswami, *Japa Walks, Japa Talks* (Philadelphia: GN Press, 1994).

present writing is not helpful? Because I can't guarantee beforehand the neat resolution of my doubts or the release from *aparādhas* like inattention. I have to go through them. They are not already solved, and I am not already redeemed because I am the author of *Begging,* who brings Vedic texts to our rescue. I can't wrap it up in the canon so quickly. Go the whole route. It may not be assuring enough for readers. But my primary act in writing is not to provide assuring reading but to help myself in my struggle.

This kind of writing is not selfish; we found it can produce the best kind of communication and assurance on a deeper level for more serious devotees.

Have faith in that process, despite critics.

The anonymous monk who wrote the book about the Jesus Prayer said that he had reached the stage where the chanting automatically continued in his heart without any effort on his part.[46] The Gosvāmīs of Vṛndāvana also chanted like that. They were so enamoured by the Hare Kṛṣṇa mantra that it filled them with love for Rādhā and Kṛṣṇa and kept them always connected to the Divine Couple. I usually don't remember to chant when I am in the dentist's office because I become so distracted, but I'm going to make more of an effort today. It really should be easy to take shelter when there is possible pain. Sometimes, however, others start talking to you, and if you are chanting, you can't pay attention to what they are saying. As the Cub Scout motto says, "Do your best." The Boy Scout motto is even better: "Be prepared." Set your mind in advance with resolve to chant, and you'll be prepared for whatever obstacles arrive.

All right, let's go back to our car chanting . . .. "Do your best" implies you are just a little boy, and so you may fail, but try anyway. "Be prepared" is something higher than

46 R. M. French. *The way of a pilgrim; and, The pilgrim continues his way* (Pasadena, CA: Hope Publishing, 1989), 182.

"Do your best." It implies that you should have intelligence to think in advance what may go wrong and avoid it. So "be prepared" to feel drowsy now, but avoid it with well-planned strategy. Oh well, do your best, and Kṛṣṇa will make up for what you lack.

Japa *should be chanted from the heart, the seat of affections. It is an act of love toward Rādhā and Kṛṣṇa. Short of love, it is a pleading. Anything less than that is just reciting the outer covering of the* mantras, *the syllables without the heart. I should not be satisfied with my little speed rituals in the morning. It is a desperate act, with time running out. When will you love Rādhā-Kṛṣṇa while reciting Their names? When will you dare to ask for service? There is a legion of lackadaisical chanters, and they are not appreciating* śuddha-nāma. I *have far to go, but seem stuck in* nāma-ābhāsa. *Chanting more is one remedy. Praying at other times for improvement in* nāma bhajana. *Even writing, ask for it.*

The *japa* is a chore at the beginning, but soon that feeling is overcome, and you're sailing into stringing the mantras together effortlessly. They're slow for the first couple of rounds by the stopwatch, but then fast. I averaged under six minutes per round. My mind stayed focused on the mechanical act of hearing the syllables, not daydreaming or roaming over other subjects. But I was rushing too much. Neither did I think of Rādhā and Kṛṣṇa in a natural way. Today I folded Śrīmatī Rādhārāṇī's shawl over Her hand so that She would not be guarding Her face from Kṛṣṇa's sight. Dattatreya remarked yesterday that She was being shy and was hiding Her face from Kṛṣṇa, so I've adjusted that. Her face is now visible to His.

A person should be always thinking of Kṛṣṇa. Kṛṣṇa is the Vedic word for God. Allah means "all" Kṛṣṇa means "all-attractive." People cannot understand how God can be so playful. But Nietzsche said, "I would believe in God who could dance."[47] Kṛṣṇa is the best dancer. He is also a romancer. He kills great demons from the earliest age. He is in love with all the residents of Vṛndāvana—the cows, the birds, even the grass and Govardhana Hill. And all the Vrajavāsīs love Him. When they thought Kṛṣṇa was going to be killed by the Kāliya snake, all the Vrajavāsīs (except Balarāma) fell unconscious and wanting to give up their lives. When they saw Kṛṣṇa walk into the mouth of the Aghāsura demon, the demigods cried from heaven, "Alas! Alas!," and they thought that they would die from grief. But Kṛṣṇa killed these demons (danced on the heads of Kāliya until they were smashed and bleeding, expanded in Aghāsura's neck and made him suffocate and die), and the demigods and Vrajavāsīs cheered with joy.

Japa is fun. But it's hard work, too. You have to keep your mind controlled, and controlling the mind is as hard as controlling the wind. But with the right determination, it can be done.

Chanting Hare Kṛṣṇa is a daily routine
but it's more than that.
It's not just like brushing your teeth.
Concentrate your mind.
Recall the urgency of your diminishing time
and your need to improve.

Fight the drowse, fight complacency.
Rise, spirit soul,
and meet the mantra in a higher place.

---

47 Frederick Neitzsche. *Thus Spoke Zarathustra*, "On Reading and Writing" (Kessinger Publishing, 2004), 153.

You just streamline. You ride horseback with no saddle, like an American Indian. You don't think of anything else but the sound of the syllables. It's really not so hard to do. You just cling to the mantras, ride fast, and let the wind blow through your hair (if you have any hair). "Hare Kṛṣṇa Hare Kṛṣṇa." . . .that's good enough. "Just hear." Prabhupāda's famous signature. Of course, there's more to it than that—there's seeing Kṛṣṇa's form, qualities, pastimes, etc. But if you can simply "just hear," you have made a good start. The rest will come gradually. If you can think of Kṛṣṇa, that's so much the better. But on the other hand, what is there to think? The name of Kṛṣṇa is as good as Himself. The name Kṛṣṇa is more merciful than the form of Kṛṣṇa. So it's really complete in the chanting and hearing process—just keep it streamlined, without catching cows on your locomotive's cowcatcher. Just keep the flocks of birds out of your jet intake, pure and simple, with no obstructions. Cry to Kṛṣṇa to do this and your meditation is complete: "Please let me chant Your names, O Rādhā, O Kṛṣṇa, please let me serve You!"

We should be determined to steal moments from the material activities. If you have a fifty-hour-a-week job, you should not settle for that. You should steal moments from material life, steal moments from family entanglements, steal moments from all the things that keep you from practicing Kṛṣṇa consciousness. All those hours in front of the TV set and frivolous talk in gatherings. Steal them! You'd be surprised how much time you can save for Kṛṣṇa if you're just determined about it. So that's what we should do. The stolen moments are used in the service of Kṛṣṇa. A beautiful flute comes on, reminding you of Kṛṣṇa's flute. He is the one who steals the moments when He plays His flutes. He steals the hearts of the *gopīs*, who run out of their houses to go and join Him in the forest. He steals their hearts, He steals their lives by the sound of His transcendental flute.

So there is something good in thievery when it's stealing from forgetfulness of Kṛṣṇa. A calm, tenor saxophone comes on. It's stealing more moments for sublime jazz. Jazz steals moments from the mundane doldrums, brings us into a wonderland of delight. It's not illusion if you can listen to it in the right way, as we are doing in these prose improvisations. We're stealing moments from our late mornings. We're not stealing them from our *japa*—oh, no. But from time to time we might be drowsing or sleeping or just spacing out. We're using these moments in Kṛṣṇa consciousness. So if you call that stealing, then stealing is good.

Kṛṣṇa Himself is the greatest thief. He used to steal butter from the *gopīs*' homes. When He was caught, He denied it. Kṛṣṇa was an honest child. But He did cheat sometimes. He was stealing moments in the sense of stealing hearts through attraction to Himself. He made the cows stop eating grass and just stand motionless with the grass in their mouths. He let the calves steal the milk from their mothers' udders because they were in ecstasy over Kṛṣṇa's flute. Or they stopped drinking the milk entirely, and the moments of their nourishing were stolen while they listened to His flute. Let everything be stolen and placed at the lotus feet of Kṛṣṇa. The cows in Goloka Vṛndāvana are far superior to the deer. When they hear the sound of Kṛṣṇa's flute, they stop chewing the grass in their mouths and stand stunned. The Pulinda aborigine women are superior to the cows. They take the red kunkuma from Kṛṣṇa's feet and rub it on their breasts and faces, relieving themselves from lust. (*Bhag.* 10.21.17) The *gopīs* observe these things and lament their misfortune at not getting Kṛṣṇa's association.

Kṛṣṇa had mad celebrations, deep in the forest of Vṛndāvana when His parents weren't around. He'd play with the *gopīs*, and sometimes they'd get intoxicated.

The *sakhīs* would play the rhythm of many *mṛdaṅgas* and whompers and *karatālas*, and Rādhā played Her exquisite stringed instrument, and they would dance like wild people, spinning around and around, more exotic than any mideastern city. The drums thunder together, many pairs of *gopīs*' hands on the left- and right-hand side of the *mṛdaṅga*, making a suitable rhythmic storm for all the other *gopīs* to dance for Kṛṣṇa. All nonmoving living entities start to move, and the moving living entities stand still. The calves stop chewing the grass and stop drinking the milk from their mothers' udders. Śiva and Brahma, who are expert in music, become puzzled by this music, and they can't understand it. Can you? Can you understand Kṛṣṇa's flute? If you can, you're the most fortunate person in the world. If you can understand Kṛṣṇa's flute, you're in more than heaven. You're in Goloka, the epitome of existence. Just by hearing.[48]

The *gopīs* were envious of the flute. They said he was taking all the nectar from Kṛṣṇa's lips and leaving none for them. They said they were the rightful inheritors of that nectar because they knew Kṛṣṇa from their birth, whereas the flute—a dry piece of bamboo—had become acquainted with Kṛṣṇa only since His taking the cows into the fields. Nevertheless, Kṛṣṇa gave the touch of His lips to His flute. He has several flutes—a *veṇu,* and a *muralī,* and others, too. He puts the beautiful touch of His lips to the holes of His flute and fingers it, and out comes music that enchants the

---

48 Jīva Gosvāmī in his commentary to *Bhakti-rasāmṛta-sindhu*, Eastern Side. 2.296, confirms that "Without hearing, there will be no manifestation of Their basic forms and pastimes. Hearing about Kṛṣṇa and the *gopīs*, even without seeing, is also effective." see Rūpa Gosvāmī, *The Bhakti-rasāmṛta-sindhu of Śrīla Rūpa Gosvāmī with with Durgama-saṅgamanī-ṭīkā, a commentary called "Resolving the Difficult" by Jīva Gosvāmī, and the Bhakti-sāra-pradarśinī-ṭīkā, a commentary called "Revealing the Essence of Bhakti" by Śrīla Viśvanātha Cakravartī Ṭhākura,* Vol.1. Trans. Bhanu Svami (Chennai: Sri Vaikuntha Enterprises, 2005), 329.

whole world.[49] The parents of the flute—the trees and the ponds—are proud of their offspring. But the *gopīs* suffer from the wounded pride. They say it's better to take birth as a flute than to take birth as a *gopī.*

Did you ever think that love had a sound? It's in the sound of sweet music. Best tunes are sounds of love. They can be played in the present, and they exist now. The sound of love is embracing and feeling love right now. The sound of love is music. The sound of love is you talking to me and me talking to you in affection, laughing together, having a good time. The sound of love is Hare Kṛṣṇa when it's chanted with emotion and devotion. The sound of love is Kṛṣṇa's words when He says, "Bow down to Me, offer homage to Me, and you will come to Me."(*Bg.* 18.65) Those promises of Kṛṣṇa are sounds of love. The sound of love is sweet and tender. It's not fighting, raucous voices. The sound of love is tender. It's confidential words, and sometimes just whispers. Words that don't really mean so much but are just spoken in the ear, the way the cowherd boys sometimes talk to Kṛṣṇa with not much meaning but lots of bliss. The sound of love is blissful, although not always coherent.

Having heard the music, let's go back to *japa*, another type of music. Music for the soul. A whispered music from my own lips. Today we're going to Mahāhari's and Yaśoda's for lunch. That will be a treat. But a little more time taken off my day. Thinking of *japa* as music is an interesting parallel. It's not really the same, but when you glide along through the mantras, it has a similar effect. Maybe not. Maybe I'm just making it up. But I did enjoy the music. And now I have to return to *japa*, so I'm just giving myself some

---

49 "Hearing the sound of Kṛṣṇa's flute, Lord Śiva's intelligence became completely disoriented and he began to roar so loudly that the dynasty of the demons became vanquished." *Bhakti-rasāmṛta-sindhu*, 2.2.11. see *Ibid.*, p. 658-659..

solace. Go, my friend, listen to the music of the holy names. Accumulate your rounds.

It is so much better to chant early in the morning, when the mind is calm and the atmosphere is quiet. It's the best time of the day to chant. You're usually alert and awake for an early-morning burst. The mind is willing to go along with attentive chanting for a stretch. It seems the later the morning gets, the less your potency. The *brāhma-muhūrta* hour is recommended as the best time for spiritual duties. Devotees who have fulltime jobs should try to make the sacrifice of going to bed early at night so they can get up early. But it may be that they cannot do it because they get tired later on the job. Still, the earlier, the better. Little children and the wife may still be asleep, and you have a clear stretch to be alone with Nāma Prabhu. Or husband and wife can both make a pact and be up early for the sacred *yajña*. A temple room in your house and deities are helpful, or at least an altar with pictures as an aid for concentration. Śrīla Prabhupāda used to chant rounds after his very early morning translation of *Śrīmad-Bhāgavatam*. He would chant before his morning walk. Before the sun rises, before the birds start chirping and the car engines start revving, in the still of predawn, chant the holy names.

In my *bhajana-kuṭīr*
before Rādhā-Govinda
I start my daily *japa*.
There's no one stirring in the house,
the only sound, my own vibration.

I reciprocate with Nāma.
My head is clear
or almost clear,
I pray for clarity
and push on with the beads.

The numbers rise,
a headstart feeling.
Your heart is calm,
your mind is clean.

2:30 A.M. Before going to sleep last night, I had a bedtime headache. I woke up at 2:30 A.M. But then I had another headache and had to take medication. Nevertheless, I felt a fighting spirit to go ahead with my *japa.* The *Bhagavad-gītā* excerpt that caught my attention was the discussion of what happens to the unsuccessful transcendentalist. Arjuna expresses this doubt to Kṛṣṇa because there is no one else who can alleviate the doubt but Kṛṣṇa Himself. Kṛṣṇa says that one who engages in transcendental life never meets with failure, whereas the materialist always fails. (*Bg.* 6.37-47.) This again was reassuring and convincing. It is nice to know that Kṛṣṇa is the only one who can resolve our doubts. I began my *japa* at 2:55 A.M.

Japa is an art. It's a gift from Kṛṣṇa. We have to take advantage of it. You have to put your heart into it and not just chant off rounds mechanically. Feel your chanting, believe in it, adhere to it, and be sorry you're not doing better. But rise to the occasion. There's always another chance, another bead, another round.

Yesterday I read aloud to Guṇagrahi Mahārāja. In the purports, there was a lot of material about how we have to go alone in our Kṛṣṇa consciousness. Śrīla Bhaktivinoda

Ṭhākura was quoted as saying that we're in the ocean by ourselves, and we have to swim with no one else's help. Prabhupāda said a similar thing, that there is no help for us except Kṛṣṇa. Guṇagrahi Mahārāja commented that of course, devotees and the spiritual master help us, so we're not alone. Yet in these purports, Prabhupāda was emphasizing that as long as we think we're this body, we're alone, and we have to die, life after life. No one can help us, neither mother nor father nor friend. Only Kṛṣṇa can help us. We have to surrender to Him. So while chanting, I turn to my own self and my own recitation of the mantras. This morning I chanted at a barely audible whisper, but chanted quickly. My rounds were under six minutes. I began to pay attention to just the syllables of the mantra. I could not think about Rādhā and Kṛṣṇa but just the sound vibration of the *mahā-mantra*. That was good enough for me. I was especially pleased at how speedy the mantras were going, and the enunciation was clear. It was a good "just hear" session.

When we chant *japa*, we're alone. We should not be thinking of other people or other things. It's a time to be alone with Kṛṣṇa in the form of His sound vibration. Prabhupāda repeatedly quoted the verse, *sarva-dharmān parityajya mām ekaṁ śaraṇaṁ vraja/ ahaṁ tvāṁ sarva-pāpebhyo mokṣayiṣyāmi mā śucaḥ*. "Give up all forms of religion and just surrender unto Me. Do not be afraid. I will protect you."(*Bg*. 18.66.) We should give up all forms of altruism, philanthropy, and other "isms." Just concentrate on surrendering to Kṛṣṇa. Getting out of the cycle of birth and death is very difficult. Prabhupāda gave the example of the silk worm who makes a cocoon out of his own saliva and is then trapped in that cocoon. He compared this to life in the material world. Once we get in here, a choice we make out of our own mistake, it is very difficult to get out. We cannot get out without Kṛṣṇa's help. In this age, that help comes primarily in the chanting of His holy names. Kṛṣṇa comes to rescue us, as the Viṣṇudūtas came to rescue Ajāmila from the grip of the Yamadūtas. (*Bhag.* 7.6.11-13) By chanting the holy names, we become unsinful and eligible for liberation. So chant, chant, chant. It is the only way out of the silkworm cocoon, the only way out of our self-made prison.

In his cave-*kuṭīr,* Haridāsa Ṭhākura
chanted all the time
and was free from all the chains
that bind one in material life.
He depended on the holy names
as his exclusive shelter
and became the *nāmācārya*
to lead all souls by his example.

Just by chanting
you can fee yourself
and gain self-realized knowledge
of the soul and the Lord.
You can gain *kṛṣṇa-prema*
by the chanting of the names
done alone in concentration
with all other worries pushed aside.

Just you and Kṛṣṇa
through the medium of the sound.
It's the prescribed method
for all souls who are bound.

Japa cannot be compared to anything. You pray from the heart. Yet *japa* can be compared to championship golf. Sometimes you use the heavy driver, sometimes you use the iron, sometimes you use the putter, sometimes you make a birdie or an eagle, or you make a lot of bogies, or you make par. Sometimes you wind up in the water. Sometimes you wind up in a sand trap. Sometimes you do real well and move up in the competition. You play it carefully and measure your shots. You don't have to wear special shoes or shirts. There are no hard and fast rules. You can even chant in your pajamas. The main thing is to keep trying sincerely and stay awake. This morning, I've been alert for eight rounds so far, and I'm hoping to keep it going. I'm chanting mostly sub-par in audibility. But I'm paying attention.

I love *japa*. It's my favorite sport. But I'm not a champion. I'm just an amateur. I've been working at it for a long time, and yet I remain an amateur. Sometimes I have to cry out, "Fore!" as my ball sails into the crowd. You wouldn't expect that from me after all these years. But I keep trying. I honestly keep trying. *Japa* is the easiest form of spiritual meditation. Many people enter the competition, and many people improve over the years. They attend seminars. They go on *japa* retreats. They study books. They get down on their knees and pray. They get frustrated and throw the club down. It's done on beads or clickers. You don't use a caddy. You do it on your own. *Japa*, please let me perform you to the end of my days. Don't let me break my legs or need surgery so that I have to lose a year of *japa*. I'm already chanting less because of my shoulder. I'll get better, though. You'll see me. I'll get better. *Japa* is my favorite sport. *Japa* is my most serious meditation. *Japa* has been given to use by Caitanya Mahāprabhu, and Prabhupāda says the order of the spiritual master to chant at least sixteen rounds daily is the most essential one. So I'm working at it. I pray to Kṛṣṇa to bless me.

A *japa* poem
without a pen or typewriter [50]
is very hard to do.
You do it from your tongue,
you do it from your mind.

You're happy when it's going well.
Birds chirp in the air. You're depressed
when you hit a drowse
or inattention comes.

Japa is a daily challenge,
and so is a poem in praise of it.
I make this poem today.
I hope it will be accepted
by the *japa* master in the sky
by the *japa* master on the earth
by the *japa* masters in *paramparā.*

They're like golf champions
making holes in one, making birdies.
Today I'm not doing so bad,
and so I hope this poem will serve
to cheer me on to better things.

---

50 Written after a falling accident, with a broken collar bone.

je vaiṣṇava haibe laibe harināma
sankhya kari nāma laile, krpa karena gaurādhāma

"Those who are Vaishavas must chant the holy names in a particular number everyday. Then Lord Gauraṅga, the supreme abode of love will be merciful to them."

—*Prema-vilāsa*, Chapter 11

Some of the Gauḍīya Vaiṣṇava *ācāryas* are known for chanting many rounds of Hare Kṛṣṇa mantra on beads. Foremost is Nāmācārya Haridāsa Ṭhākura, who chanted three hundred thousand names a day. Raghunātha dasa Gosvāmī used to chant a hundred thousand names a day, and other Vaiṣṇavas also spend great quantities of time on their beads. When Bhaktisiddhānta Sarasvatī Ṭhākura formed his Gauḍīya Math, he required his initiates to chant sixty-four rounds a day—a feat which takes quite a few hours. Nevertheless, he considered it so important that he made it a requirement. When His Divine Grace A. C. Bhaktivedanta Swami Prabhupāda came to America, he saw that the young men and women were not capable of such sustained chanting. There is a famous conversation recorded in *Śrīla Prabhupāda-līlāmṛta* between Prabhupāda and his young disciple Mukunda dāsa.[51] Prabhupāda told Mukunda dāsa that he should chant sixty-four rounds, and Mukunda dāsa said he could not do it. Prabhupāda asked if he could chant thirty-two rounds a day. Mukunda dāsa said no, he could not do that either. Prabhupāda then

51 Satsvarūpa dāsa Goswami, "Swamiji's Departure" in Satsvarūpa dāsa Goswami, *Śrīla Prabhupāda-līlāmṛta: a biography of His Divine Grace A. C. Bhaktivedanta Swami Prabhupāda*, Vol. 1, Second Edition (Los Angeles: Bhaktivedanta Book Trust, 2003), 704.

asked him, "Can you do sixteen?" Mukunda agreed, and out of this informal conversation came the institutional requisite for initiation into the Hare Kṛṣṇa movement, or ISKCON: every initiated devotee must chant sixteen rounds.

Some devotees chant more than sixteen rounds; they have vows of seventeen, eighteen, twenty, twenty-five or thirty-two rounds. Some devotees chant an extra hour without counting. Some devotees chant sixty-four rounds on Ekādaśī days and Janmāstami.

Is there any benefit in chanting larger numbers? Yes, there certainly is. Prabhupāda was right in ascertaining that his devotees could not chant sixty-four rounds every day because they lacked the concentration. Also, he assigned them so many other duties to do for active preaching. But on several occasions, he remarked to his disciples in conversations that it would be good if they could chant more than sixteen rounds. If you chant over sixteen rounds, you feel like you are doing more than your bare duty. You get extra strength. You go beyond the period of boredom by chanting "extra," and enter a stage which is actually advanced, just like the previous *ācāryas* who chanted many rounds. So it is good advice to try to chant a little more than the bare sixteen and make a higher quota for oneself, if at all possible. The benefit will be self-evident in the good feelings and the strengthening that comes with the practice.

Japa should be done in a composed way, without being frantic or losing track of your count. If you lose track of your count, then you have to arbitrarily set a new count and just go on with that. Make the best of the bad situation. Try to do your best, giving the benefit of the doubt to the count rather than to cheat. It's always best not to cheat Kṛṣṇa in your *japa*. When you don't know the count, you'll have to do it with a guess. The exact count is really not the most important thing. The important thing is chanting sincerely and with dedication. You can make up your count eventually later in the day, to make sure you've done your sixteen. My shoulder hurts, and that's a distraction. But the most important thing is to move on sincerely. I'm doing the best I can. I beg that Kṛṣṇa will forgive me for my discrepancies.

> Wheeling 'round the *japa mālā,* pointing
> finger doesn't touch the beads.
>
> A bulky knot between each red bead
> from many years ago. One hundred and eight and you
> reach the head bead and say another
> mantra on it and start back in the
> opposite way.
>
> Don't touch the head bead, but circle
> back again, wheeling on the wheel of
> fortune, the Vaiṣṇava rosary.
>
> Wheeling around, you chant out loud
> Hare Kṛṣṇa Hare Kṛṣṇa
> Kṛṣṇa Kṛṣṇa Hare Hare.

Harināma is the tonic for the anemic soul. It is the panacea for all spiritual ills. It goes far beyond Ayurveda, which is the medicine that purports to treat material ills. But Ayurveda is still a material medicine. It cannot alleviate the terrible condition of alienation of the soul from Kṛṣṇa. *Harināma* is the "silver bullet" which medical practitioners have sought in their attempts to find a cure-all.

Harināma is Kṛṣṇa Himself, and by touching the *mahā-mantra* to the tongue, you contact the all-purifying source of spiritual health. Spiritual health is more important than material health. One may live a perfectly healthy life but die in the state of sin and suffer with death, disease and old age in the next life. Even if one is physically ill and about to die, the taking of *harināma* will keep him from suffering in the next life. When Prabhupāda was at the end of his life, his doctor asked him which treatment he wanted. Prabhupāda told him that all he wanted was the medicine of chanting and hearing the names of Kṛṣṇa.

Prabhupāda was not an avid prescriber of any particular medicines for himself or any of his ailing disciples. He told them to take what was practical but mainly to depend on Kṛṣṇa. After all, we each have to suffer and die, but if we take to the chanting of Hare Kṛṣṇa regularly and with devotion, we can save ourselves from the most dangerous type of illness—entering the cycle of birth and death. Chanting Hare Kṛṣṇa will bring us to the lotus feet of Rādhā-Kṛṣṇa for a healthy life of eternity, bliss and knowledge.

Wheeling round the Lord's names,
wheeling around your head and dancing
on your tongue.

It's a miracle a sound vibration that
contains the Lord as person on a wheel
of beads with knots in between.

Wheeling around sixteen times is the
number, and it takes over two hours
when you say them swift and smooth.

It's the most essential instruction
of the spiritual master to say at least
sixteen and don't slur them. Don't

swing the wheel but keep it in a cloth
bead bag, and your pointing finger
pokes through and the strap that
goes around your neck.

The Hare Kṛṣṇa mantra is Him. It's nothing else. It's not *about* Him, *it's* Him. The song is made up of His names—His name and the name of Rādhā. The song is Him. The song is Her. Listen closely and you won't miss it. The song is Kṛṣṇa embodied, Kṛṣṇa personified. The song is not another thing but Kṛṣṇa Himself, and that's what's so wonderful about it. The song is Rādhā, the song is Kṛṣṇa.

The song is *prakaṭa* Kṛṣṇa and *aprakaṭa* Kṛṣṇa—Kṛṣṇa seen and with us, and Kṛṣṇa beyond us, unseen. In any case, it's Him, it's Her. There's nothing but the song and you.

Chanting is progressive. You become more expert, learned and happy with the practice. You just have to keep it up. Don't fall back into old ways. It takes some effort, but it's well worth it. You grow stronger, and your muscles stay stronger. You become more fit to chant Hare Kṛṣṇa. It's all a matter of consistency and stick-to-it-iveness. To the sincere chanter goes the prize. Rādhā and Kṛṣṇa begin to reciprocate, and you know They are there. Your faith builds.

Wheeling around the horn, around the
circle of the *tulasi* beads with a hole
drilled in them and they're either smooth
or rugged. You can pick your choice
and oil them, and the bead bag should
be saffron if you're a sannyasi.

It's a prayer wheel of 108 plus
the head bead, which has a different

> shape. You don't have to say the Panca-tattva mantra at the end of a round, although some folks have made it a custom.
>
> The wheel can be taken out of the bead bag sometimes and hung like a necklace around your neck and fingered in that way.
>
> It's a simple labor, and you'll see devotees throughout the day finger on their mantras if they haven't finished the quota early.

In fifteen minutes, I'll start my first hour of chanting. Śrīla Prabhupāda says *japa* gives the mind no chance to deviate because it's always engaged in hearing the holy name. But I haven't learned how to do this yet. The mind does other things and doesn't sit submissively at the *mahā-mantra's* feet. The mind says, "I can do the chanting and think of other things at the same time. Chanting isn't enough." It's a struggle. Writing seems more successful than chanting in reining in the undesirable mind and its bad behavior. Chanting is more demanding.

Anyway, I chant and I have to accept it as it is. I chant with faith in the absolute benefit of the holy name. I shouldn't think I can't improve. I may try to hear the syllables of the *mahā-mantra*, and to meditate on the mercy of the holy name, on my need for the holy name, on my unworthiness. As for the higher stages— Rādhā and Kṛṣṇa's pastimes in Vṛndāvana, that would be nice. If it comes, I'll be most fortunate. That seems to be only within Kṛṣṇa's power, not mine. But He should see that I do desire this stage of advancement and that I am making an endeavor to achieve it. I am not being indifferent to the holy names.

The *japa mālā* was used thousands of
years ago and is still in style.
It introduces people to Kṛṣṇa
consciousness when they buy their first
set of beads at a temple store or order
in the mail.

You can spend more money and get a set
of big beads in the bazaar, as big as a
big marble, or some are very small.

Get your wheel out each morning and
start your *japa-yajña.* Wheeling around
the circle with the holy names
is one of the best things you can do
in ISKCON.

Devotees have their photos taken with
their hand in the bead bag and their
lips moving.

That's all external. The important thing
is what goes on in the heart and mind
as he utters the sacred sounds, the
holy names of God.

The internal spirit is the thumping
of the *bhakta's* heart as he or she
says the names Kṛṣṇa Kṛṣṇa,
Hare Hare, Hare Rāma, Hare Rāma,
Rāma Rāma, Hare Hare.

"Hare Kṛṣṇa, Hare Kṛṣṇa"
is repeated without boredom,
you can't do it by saying "Coca Cola"
or "Mr. John," but "Hare Kṛṣṇa"
you can do for 24 hours.

Keep saying the names and the time
will come when you'll cry tears, your
voice will choke up, your hairs will
stand on end.

These are the symptoms of *bhāva,* the
advanced stage of Hare Kṛṣṇa
mantra. Keep at it and your time
will come.
You'll chant with bliss.

Dear Lord, I am conscious of many of my failings in my career in devotional service, but I don't claim I have attained the admirable quality of *dainya. Dainya* is when one is acutely aware of his unworthiness. I'm still proud of my accomplishments and puffed up in various ways. Just the fact that I do not chant offenselessly should make me cry tears of remorse, but I go on stoneheartedly in my mechanical chanting. My lack of intense preaching endeavors in recent years—these things and more do make me feel lowly, and I try to assess myself accordingly. I know there is a difference between material low self-esteem and Vaiṣṇava humility. Because I am following the rules and regulations of devotional service and am engaged in *bhajana* and service, I should not feel miserably unhappy. I should feel assured of Prabhupāda's and Kṛṣṇa's goodwill toward me, and I should not be psychologically or clinically depressed. I am not. On a certain psychological level, I feel contentment and well-being because I am a servant of my spiritual master and Lord Kṛṣṇa. I feel fortunate. But I need to feel humble as part of my constitutional nature. I have come to this material world out of misuse of my free will and committed many misbehaviors before coming to Kṛṣṇa consciousness. In the Ajāmila section of the *Bhāgavatam*, Prabhupāda writes that we should always remain aware of what we were before we became devotees. This will make us aware of our failings. (*Bhag.* Canto 9, Chapter 10).

I have heard that real humility means not mere meekness but positive action on behalf of the spiritual master. Hanumān, the great monkey warrior, is cited as an example of a very humble devotee. He always thinks of himself as the lowly and loyal servant of Lord Rāma and never acts out of pride or false ego. Yet his humility took the form of violent, brave attacks singlehandedly upon the kingdom of Rāvaṇa. Prabhupāda was humble, never taking credit for himself but saying that whatever he did was by the empowerment of his spiritual master. Yet he acted boldly and defiantly against the Godlessness of the age. He was, like his spiritual master, a "*Simha guru.*" So I pray that I may assume some of that boldness of the truly humble Vaiṣṇavas.

Therefore I have a long way to go before I become actually humble. I do not possess the *dainya*, or keen awareness of my unworthiness, and I am not a bold servant acting like a humble soldier on the front lines. Please let me become more aware of my actual lowly position, and let me act more assertively in Your mission. Without Your help, I will remain proud and self-satisfied. Please inspire me to be humble.

Now I'll have to make it up.
It's so sad when you don't do well.
All you can do is gather your wits
and push forward, like a losing team
trying to rally.

A Plea for Connection

kabe mora sei din ha'be
mana sthira kori', nirjane bosiyā,
kṛṣṇa-nāma gā'bo jabe
saṁsāra-phukāra, kāne nā poṣibe,
deho-roga dūre ro'be

"When will that day be mine? With a steady mind, sitting in a secluded place, I will sing the holy names of Kṛṣṇa. The lamentable bondage of worldly existence will no longer echo in my ears, and the diseases of the body will not disturb me."

—Śrīla Bhaktivinoda Thakura, *Bhajana-lālasā,* 12.1

DON'T GET AGITATED AND DEPRESSED over your lack of attention and devotion in *japa.* Be grateful for what attachment you do have and capitalize on that. Build up. You watch yourself merely counting the minutes and seconds per round, the number of rounds, the time of day. . . . the progress that any worker feels as he shovels his way or as she types her way or he reads his way through a designated amount of work. Think of pieceworkers who get credit for so many items sewn. Any worker with his eye on the clock, waiting for the coffee break, the lunch hour, the 5:00 P.M. whistle . . .

There's that level of my *japa* reality, but I assume there's more. I know there's more. I keep going with it yearly, my whole life is only one life-chapter in a career that may take many lives of improving chanting. (Kṛṣṇa *prema* could happen in a moment, or it could fail to happen for many births.)

I don't want to fake my actual attitude. I mean I shouldn't be overly dramatic about my disappointments. I'm not that upset about it. It's a longstanding fact that I'm not ecstatic when I chant, I don't experience that Kṛṣṇa and Kṛṣṇa's name are nondifferent. Yet I chant every day. I feel good about fulfilling that obligation.

I also dearly love the practice. If a nondevotee sees me chant, I feel worlds apart—how much I value these prayer-bead mantras and how he or she cannot understand. If I cannot chant my mantras aloud and privately because I'm with *karmis,* then I feel how I love *japa,* how it's like my life and breath.

But we accept more as a matter of fact that we chant with no taste. "When oh when will that day be mine when my offenses ceasing,/ taste for the name increasing—/ when in my heart will Your mercy shine?"[52] When I read those lines, I think he's describing me. But it's no big deal. It's like the way I accept my somewhat crippled left ankle or my headache syndrome. I live within those limits, and I don't necessarily lament. If I can walk for half an hour a day, that's fine. I don't expect to walk more than that. If I can go for half a day without a headache, that's wonderful—and I try to get as much done as I can within that no-headache zone. But when the pressure starts coming again, I live with it. I have no other choice. The loveless, inattentive chanting is another part of my life and conditioning.

Besides, I have the hope that I can improve. It's up to Kṛṣṇa. Within my power is the ability not to worsen. I can occasionally take a *japa* retreat.

---

52 Śrīla Bhaktivinoda Ṭhākura, *Śaraṇāgati: Surrendered to the Lord's Shelter,* Vijnapati, 1.1. available in digital form from www.vedabase.com

I GO THROUGH MY DEVOTIONAL SERVICE in a routine way, following the path of rules and regulations out of obedience toward my spiritual master. There is some spontaneity in it, but not enough to be called pure love.

So I am lacking, and I do not know if the sheer faithfulness and repetition of my acts of *vaidhī-bhakti* will bring *rāgānuga* upon me. I know I cannot "jump over" and exclusively hear Your pastimes of amorous affairs with the *gopīs* and by this means awaken my own advanced sentiments of love for You. I have to await the descent of Your mercy upon me. I can pray to You to invoke love in me. And I can work harder to please my spiritual master, which will please You to bestow that mercy upon me.

In a lecture Prabhupāda gave on September 30, 1968, in Seattle, he started off by singing the Govinda prayers: *govindam ādi-puruṣaṁ tam ahaṁ bhajāmi.* The devotees responded three times. He said our purpose is to worship Govinda. We are teaching people to love Kṛṣṇa. You have to place your love in the proper place. People are being frustrated by placing their love in the wrong place. They love the body, family, community, nation, and world. But if you love Kṛṣṇa, you'll be satisfied. You throw a pebble in the middle of the water, it will make waves that will continue out to the shore. If you directly touch Kṛṣṇa, you'll be satisfied. Lord Caitanya Mahāprabhu said we should become subordinate to Kṛṣṇa and to His place, Vṛndāvana.

How to love Kṛṣṇa? Lord Caitanya says the way is to follow in the footprints of the *gopīs*. In the beginning, we worship God for necessities—daily bread. But the perfection is the love of the *gopīs*. Kṛṣṇa would go to the pasturing grounds. The *gopīs* stayed at home, thinking of Kṛṣṇa's feet being pricked by thorns. They're not thinking,

"Kṛṣṇa, what have You got in Your pocket for me?" They dress nicely just to satisfy Kṛṣṇa. The *gopīs*' love was so unalloyed, Kṛṣṇa said, "I can't repay your love." The *gopīs* are on the highest platform, and Rādhārāṇī is the highest *gopī*. Lord Caitanya also said to read *Śrīmad-Bhāgavatam*, the *amalam purāṇam*. In the very first verse of *Śrīmad-Bhāgavatam*, it says that, "I offer my love to the Supreme Lord, from whom everything is coming."[53] The preliminary study is *Bhagavad-gītā*, which is the entrance to love of God. The next study is *Śrīmad-Bhāgavatam*. After that, the Ph.D. study is *Śrī Caitanya-caritāmṛta*. The human form of life is meant for loving God. We have the instinct to love others, but we are frustrated until we love Kṛṣṇa.[54]

Today, after the first round, I averaged about six minutes per round. That's moving as fast as I can without blurring or mispronouncing (not hearing). Quality is still more important than speed. I'm grateful that I'm not thinking of other aspects of my life while I should be chanting. Fortunately, other thoughts are not coming, and I streamline my consciousness to that of a *japa* chanter. If other thoughts do come, I gently put them aside and return to my business. Kṛṣṇa has been kind to me to let me perform like a single-minded athelete. Today I was able to do that. The biggest defect today is the abiding fact that my chanting is not deep. I say the names, but I don't feel them. I chant at the surface. So I was moving along like a railroad train without heart. The high point in the day was that I was chanting so quickly. The overall impression was that the chanting was short of the *śuddha-sattva* stage.

---

53 *janmādy asya yato 'nvayād itarataś ca. Bhag.* 1.1.1.

54 Śrīla A. C. Bhaktivedanta Swami Prabhupāda, Lecture in Seattle, September 30, 1968. available in digital form from www.vedabase.com

hari hari hena dina haibe amara
dunhu anga parasiba
hunhu anga nirakhiba
sebana kariba donhakara

"O Lord Hari, O Lord Hari, when will this day be mine? When will I see Your lotus feet? When will I drectly serve Your lotus feet? When will I touch Your lotus feet?"

—Śrīla Narottama dāsa, *Prārthanā, Svabhiṣṭa-lālasā*, 1

The Divine Couple intoxicate each other. Sometimes Kṛṣṇa gets the *gopīs* to drink an intoxicating Vāruṇī liquor, and their eyes roll. It goes to their heads. But even without that, they're intoxicated by their Kṛṣṇa. All He has to do is stand there in His threefold bending form and put His flute to His lips. All Kṛṣṇa has to do is just appear before them, and it goes to their heads. In fact, He doesn't even have to be there. He goes to their heads even more when He's gone. He goes to their heads in separation. Their heads are full of lamentation, and their hearts, too: "Where is Kṛṣṇa, our beloved Lord, that beautiful cowherd boy? Where has He gone to? Where is the Lord of Mathurā? Is He there with the ladies of Mathurā? Have they attracted Him, so that He doesn't think of us any more? Does He have time to think of His *gopīs*, or is He just enchanted by the sophisticated ladies of Mathurā?" Kṛṣṇa goes to the heads of the *gopīs* until their heads are reeling and they don't know where they are. They can't do their household duties. Sometimes they just stand frozen stiff like statues in trance. Sometimes they're restless, and they run here and there. They even imitate Kṛṣṇa's pastimes, and one of them says she's lifting Govardhana Hill by raising the sari of another *gopī.* Their dealings are not staid and calm but like the effect of champagne on the head of an uninitiated drinker. He gets them spinning.

guruḥ śāstraṁ śraddhā rucir anugatiḥ siddhir iti me
yad etat tat sarvaṁ caraṇa-kamalaṁ rājati yayoḥ
kṛpā-mādhvīkena snapita-nayanāmbhoja-yugalau
sadā rādhā-kṛṣṇāv śaraṇa-gatī tau mama gatiḥ

"Śrī Śrī Rādhā-Kṛṣṇa, at Whose lotus feet stay the spiritual master, the scripture, faith, love, following, and perfection, Whose lotus feet are my everything, Whose eyes are flooded with tears of mercy, and Who are the shelter of all, Who have no other shelter are my only shelter."

—Śrīla Jīva Gosvāmī, *Bhakti Sandarbha,* 1

YOU'RE MY EVERYTHING. This is a Rādhā-Kṛṣṇa song. A song of every pure devotee toward the Lord. King Yudhiṣṭhira had opulence beyond the king of heaven, but he didn't care for it. All he cared for was serving Kṛṣṇa. Kṛṣṇa was his everything. We should strive for this. You're my everything, Rādhā-Kṛṣṇa. I don't want anything else. I just want to love You and serve You. "You're my everything" is a tender sentiment and one to be kept true. It's the highest thing. You're mine, *mamata.* You belong to me, and I belong to You

Lord Caitanya came to teach the *ujjvala-rasa,* the most radiant mellow, conjugal love, and He personally took on the complexion and mood of Rādhārāṇī and expressed Her emotions of separation from Kṛṣṇa in the Gambhīra at Jagannātha Puri. The greatest followers of Lord Caitanya, the Six Gosvāmīs, as well as Viśvanātha Cakravartī and other notable *ācāryas,* were all *gopī mañjarīs* in their *siddha dehas,* or eternal spiritual forms. So there is no doubt that Śrīmatī Rādhārāṇī and the *gopīs* are the most intimate devotees of the Lord.

3:57 A.M. The early-morning *japa* session was performed out of duty and adherence to the vow. I came to it with enthusiasm. I chanted the first four rounds quickly. The second four rounds were slow, and I was sleepy. On the whole, the time went by in average measure. My mind was occupied only with the chanting. I did not have distractive thoughts. Attentiveness became bogged down during the second half by fatigue. I enjoyed it because it is life's morning *yajña.* It is the best thing I can do. I like saying the names one by one. The biggest defect was the fatigue which came upon me. The best moments were when I heard the names and took shelter. I thought a lot about faith that Rādhā-Kṛṣṇa were responding. I kept going to that idea.

Chanting Hare Kṛṣṇa is a daily chore. But as I said, it has to be done with enthusiasm, not like brushing your teeth. You may be a little lethargic at first, but then we have to remember, "This is Kṛṣṇa. This is Rādhā." I'm doing the greatest thing when I am chanting. The lethargy of taking it as an ordinary thing is just an illusory covering. My heart really loves the Lord, the Lord's name. So I have to get past the mundane feeling. It happens if you just persist; the covering just starts to fall away, like layers of dirt in the shower. You start to feel refreshed and clean.

Even if I was not filled with Their pastimes or qualities, I was fixed on the idea that They were hearing and that I was chanting to Them. These were the best moments. Do I have faith that They are responding? Chanting is not a dead stone. It is the same as Rādhā and Kṛṣṇa. So even though I "feebled out" somewhat in the second half, I kept clinging to the idea that I was crying like a child for the mother, Mother Harā. I cried like a child crying to its mother in my chanting. I believe in the chanting because it has been given to me in disciplic succession and because I have chanted for many years with solidity. Chanting is real exchange. Chanting is Kṛṣṇa Himself. I will never stop chanting, because of my vows and because of the taste I receive. I believe that I have to chant in order to practice for leaving this body and getting a next body favorable to Kṛṣṇa consciousness. I will never stop chanting because I believe it is the highest form of worship of Kṛṣṇa. It is easy, and it has been given to use in Kali Yuga as the only means for God realization. One should never think of stopping. This morning's chanting was good because I hung in there and did not give up, despite obstacles. The rest of my morning's chanting at the beach will be even better. I will be determined.

It is interesting how Śrīla Rūpa Gosvāmī links up enthusiasm with patience. We have to be patient, even if we don't seem to make great strides in our daily *bhajana.* The cowherd boys had to execute "heaps of pious activities"(Krsna *book*, Chapter 12). before they could play with Kṛṣṇa as an equal friend. Haridāsa Ṭhākura retained his fervor for completing his *japa* even when the beautiful prostitute came to seduce him. His patience conquered her to become a great Vaiṣṇava. When Mukunda Datta offended Lord Caitanya by listening to Māyāvāda philosophy, the Lord say he would not see him for millions of years. Mukunda became joyful on hearing that the day would come in the future when the Lord would accept him again. Lord Caitanya became so pleased with Mukunda Datta's patience that He asked to see him at once. (*Caitanya-caritamrta*, Adi 10.40) We should be confident that our chanting and hearing will accumulate like a bank balance and that the practice is never in vain. Prabhupāda used to say, "Don't be discouraged."

My dilemma over Rādhā-Kṛṣṇa *kathā* is a good sign. I see that "fools rush in where angels fear to tread," and I am not ready for the most *rasika* descriptions. But I am not satisfied to have nothing. I think I'll start reading the first part of *Bṛhad-bhāgavatāmṛta,* where the conclusion is that worship of the *gopīs* is highest form of worship.[55] Nārada goes to all great devotees of the Lord, and they humbly admit they are not very exalted. They recommend that Nārada go see a higher devotee. But each devotee he approaches says, "I am not much of a devotee. The Lord doesn't show me much mercy." Finally, he approaches Kṛṣṇa's best friend in Dvārakā, Uddhava. But Uddhava says he is nothing compared to the *gopīs.* Uddhava went to visit the *gopīs* in Kṛṣṇa's absence from Vṛndāvana, and he was astonished at their love in separation. He prayed to take birth in a future life as an herb or blade of grass in Vṛndāvana so that he might be touched by the footdust of the *gopīs.* You can find literature about *gopī-bhāva* and Rādhā-Kṛṣṇa that is not so amorously explicit and keep your growing desire to adore Them alive.

A Plea for Connection to Rādhā and Kṛṣṇa

Oh Rādhā and Kṛṣṇa,
can You be mine?
Can I worship You as
the Divine Couple?

Can I accept my lack
of qualification to enter
the *kuñjas* and see
the scratches on Rādhā's breasts?

---

55 Sanātana Gosvāmī, *Śrī Bṛhad-Bhāgavatāmṛta of Śrīla Sanātana Gosvāmī.* Trans. Gopīparāṇadhana dāsa. Vol. 1 (Los Angeles: Bhaktivedanta Book Trust, 2002), 10-11.

Shall I accept that I am
not qualified to hear
how Kṛṣṇa is the aggressive rake
who physically attacks a *gopī* messenger
and pulls her to His bed?

Shall I worship You as Lakṣmī-Nārāyaṇa?
But I want to be with You in Vraja.
Please solve this dilemma for me,
let me serve at the proper distance
but be connected with Your *madhurya rasa,*
not thinking myself a *gopī-mañjarī*
allowed to come upon the Divine Couple
in Their most intimate moments.

Please purify me in simple
worship of Rādhā-Govinda,
dressing Them, and praying
Hare Kṛṣṇa mantra before Their
forms, begging, "Please let
me serve You."

Let me not lose the vision
of You standing together in
the contemplation of Your
exclusive love, but protect
my fragile creeper from
sahajiyā and wrong *siddhānta.*

Please, Lord, give me mercy to cry out Your names in the *mahā-mantra.* Let me do it better. The daily *japa-yajña* is the most important thing, and yet I cannot cry out with tears of love. You have made Yourself most accessible in

Your holy names, but unfortunately I commit offenses and do not have full taste for chanting. Somehow I have fallen into this ocean of material suffering, and I cannot extricate myself. I beg You to pick me up and make me one of the atoms at Your lotus feet.

aghadamana-yaśodānandanau nandasūno
kamala-nayana-gopīcandra-vṛndāvanendrāḥ
praṇata-karuṇa-kṛṣṇāv ity aneka-svarūpe
tvayi mama ratir uccair vardhatāṁ nāmadheya

"O killer of the demon Agha, O son of Yaśodā, O son of Nanda, O lotus-eyed moon of the *gopīs*, O Lord of Vṛndāvana, O merciful to the submissive, O Kṛṣṇa, You have manifest Yourself in these innumerable confidential manifestations out of Your infinite mercy. Let me express my love to You by calling out Your holy names, so this love goes on increasing without any impediment."

—Śrīla Rūpa Gosvāmī, *Śrī Nāmāṣṭakam,* 5

"I love You"—such profound words. These are the words we should say to Kṛṣṇa. Here they're said in romantic frame for earthly lovers, who should have at least a tinge of the sublime. I love you. It's put in so many pop tunes, it's become cheapened. He says it to her, but six months later, they're in a fight, and they break up. She blackmails him. She said he loved her but she never loved him. She said he forced her into it. The words "I love you" don't stand long, except in the spiritual world. There, Rādhā's "I love You" is eternal, and Kṛṣṇa's is eternal in return. All the Vrajavāsīs mean it when they say it to Kṛṣṇa. And it's the meaning of the *mahā-mantra* when chanted properly by the devotees of Kṛṣṇa. Hare Kṛṣṇa, I love You. "I love you" are the most profound words possible. But it has to be meant, and it has to be directed to the right Person. Kṛṣṇa says it to us, and we say it to Him. That's called *bhakti.* And it's shown not just by three words, three little words, but by actions of the body, mind and senses. Give your all to Kṛṣṇa.

Japa should be done with much feeling. The mind should not be on automatic pilot, but one should be feeling and thinking of the holy names. One should be praying to come closer to Rādhā and Kṛṣṇa through the holy sound vibration. To just chant and count numbers is to chant the outer form of the syllables and not the actual mantra. One has to dive deep into the feelings of the heart. This may mean one has to cry pitifully, asking Lord Kṛṣṇa to release him from mechanical chanting. It takes intense pleading and entreating. It is not just clockwork but heart work. One should be thinking of all the things one has learned in Kṛṣṇa consciousness up to this point. Chant with feelings of love for Kṛṣṇa, desires to love Kṛṣṇa. One should be aware of his oncoming death and pray to Kṛṣṇa for a good next life. One shouldn't chant thinking he has a million years to live. This may be the last time, this may be the last chance. One should chant with that mentality. If sleepiness is an impediment, there's not much one can do except try to get more rest and chant at a better time. But one should be alert when chanting, crying out.

Please, Lord, let my
chanting improve. I
want these hours to be
my best.

Please don't let old age
or sleepiness set in and
ruin these last-chance years.

I learned to chant as I did
when I was a young man,
passing the red beads through
my fingers.

I pray for help in
attentive *japa* and
will try to do my part.

When you get attached to performance, then it's not good. What is it I want? Worship . . . I want to chant better. I'm not ashamed to ask it again and again. You see, that's performance-worry, when I think, "I have already written here that I want to improve my chanting. If I keep on repeating it, it will be tiresome to the reader." That's nonsense. It's important for me to keep saying it: *I want to improve,* I want to improve. I want to chant better, and I think I can do it. I can improve. I just have to take the mind from where it is and bring it back to the hearing.

I rarely do that. Very rarely do I think, "This is Kṛṣṇa, this is Rādhā." Rarely do I even hear it. I don't know what I am doing.

Overall, it's not bad; you are a nice person and all that, but for real results, we'll have to consult someone else. I mean we need a real guru, not you who can't even chant. We appreciate your honesty about it, but we need to go to a higher stage of *harināma.*

I'm going to do better. Right after I finish this page, I'll do round number nine, and then seven more on the beach. Don't despair or expect the heavens to open and Lord Viṣṇu to come down, as He did in the *yajñas* when they chanted the hymns and with devotion longed to see Him. I want to do better.

When pain comes to the eye
your *japa* retreats to the mind
but the motor keeps running
and *harināmas* abound.

Kṛṣṇa will give you another
chance to chant with clear head,
and at that time I want you
to give it your heart and soul.

Be happy you're clear and
rotate the beads in your hand—
cheerful old lad
grasping his life air
the gift of Śrīla Prabhupāda.

I am hearing about You as Rādhārāṇī's lover and how the *gopīs* insult You to give You pleasure. Only they can do that. I'm getting ready to take my early rest and hope I can sleep peacefully. I want to rise early and chant Your holy names in rapid progression. Please grant me Your mercy.

To the *gopīs*, the nectar of Kṛṣṇa's lips is the greatest thing in the world, better than any *amṛta* served in the heavenly planets or any immortal *soma* drink. And so they say "*Besame mucho,*" kiss me often. Kiss me much. Kṛṣṇa obliges because He's the *rasika* master, the King of *madhurya*, and He remains unchallenged in the nectar of His lips.

Japa is our *prāṇa*,
life force. We cannot do without it.
Be happy for the privilege and
ever thankful to the *ācāryas*.

The *rasa* dance is the topmost
līlā of Kṛṣṇa and the *gopīs*.
He refuses to dance until they
sob. Then He satisfies them,
touching their faces, thighs, breasts,
putting His arms around
their necks.

Then He leaves them, and that
produces the most marvelous effects
of all. The *gopīs* go mad and
imitate Kṛṣṇa's *līlās* and ask
the deer and trees and *tulasīs*
if they have seen Kṛṣṇa.

This is the *līlā* that conquers
lust in the heart of the sincere
hearer. It is the highest pastime
of Godhead acting like Cupid.
You can't understand if you
have dirt in your heart,
and you shouldn't even try.
But for those who have the *adhikara*,
they can delight in the
supreme bliss and
never stop.

I write it down
while listening to music
and sitting in my chair.
I'll never understand
the beauty of the *rasa* dance
as long as I'm *in the mix*.

Now you're indoors, seated before Rādhā-Govinda. Your jazz poems are done. There's time for something else. Tell us about the Swami. I can't think of anything new to say. He took the holy names around the world and induced hundreds of youngsters to join him in chanting and to sit at his feet and hear *Śrīmad Bhagavad-gītā* and *Śrīmad-Bhāgavatam.* They came to surrender to him and take up vows of initiation. Over the years, many couldn't keep it up, especially after his disappearance and disruption in the movement. Still, he reigns supreme in many hearts, and his mission is established in countries throughout the world. They haven't got it quite right, but they're offering to him.

"Tell us about Kṛṣṇa." He's the hero cowherd boy. He's captivated everyone in Vṛndāvana, especially the young *gopīs.* Sometimes He appears to leave Vṛndāvana and leave everyone brokenhearted, but it's just a way of showing them more affection. He's the Supreme, as He teaches in *Bhagavad-gītā,* and peace can only be attained when we recognize Him as the supreme proprietor, the object of all sacrifices, and everyone's well-wisher.

"Tell us about Rādhā." She's the Queen of Kṛṣṇa's consorts, the most beautiful Lady in all the worlds. By Her charming qualities and talents, She captivates Kṛṣṇa, who is always eager to be in Her company. They think of each other always, and one cannot live without the other.

Mother Yaśodā sees Kṛṣṇa lying in bed in the morning and mistakes the signs of His conjugal acts for being accidents He had in the forest. She takes the fingernail scratches from the *gopīs* to be scratches from forest thorns. But how could He have them on His lips? He must have fallen headlong into a thorny bush. He's still sleeping not because He was up all night with the *gopīs* but because He's just a little boy. His necklaces are broken and in disarray from tossing and turning in bed. The *gopīs* didn't properly clean Him yesterday. That's why He's smeared with mascara and clay *tilaka.* That's what she thinks, but actually, it's the mascara and *kunkum* from the bodies of the *gopīs.*

In the evening, Kṛṣṇa enjoys a lovingly prepared meal made by His mother and the *gopīs.* "Nanda Mahārāja went out into the cow pastures, intelligent Balarāma went to sleep, and Kṛṣṇa, singing songs, wandered about the village courtyard" (Bb 2.6.136).[56] Balarāma understood that this was a good time for Kṛṣṇa to enjoy some of His more private pastimes, and Yaśodā was also inside, busy with housework. So Kṛṣṇa enjoyed playing with the *gopīs.* But hearing the distant call of His mother, out of respect for her, He came home and went straight to His bedroom and lay down comfortably on His bed. The commentary states, "*Gaurava* means 'great respect.' Although Kṛṣṇa is always eager to consort with the *gopīs,* He is also attracted by the special love of His mother. He is *akhila-rasāmṛta-mūrti,* the embodiment of all relationships, not just the *madhurya-rasa*" (Bb 2.6.137, commentary).[57]

It is nice to hear that Kṛṣṇa reciprocates with the devotees in all the *rasas* and satisfies them. Sarūpa is not privy to Kṛṣṇa's conjugal pastimes with the *gopīs* in the evening, but he receives plenty of intimate affection as a cowherd boy, such as when Kṛṣṇa personally hands him the *manoharā lāḍus* made by Rādhārāṇī.

I may be too tired to go over and see Jayādvaita Mahārāja today as I had planned. If not, I'll go see him tomorrow. It's always pleasant to sit and talk with him.

---

56 Sanātana Gosvāmī, *Śrī Bṛhad-Bhāgavatāmṛta of Śrīla Sanātana Gosvāmī.* Trans. Gopīparāṇadhana dāsa. Vol. 3, (Los Angeles: Bhaktivedanta Book Trust, 2002), 365-366.

57 *Ibid.*, 367.

He is writing a commentary on the Old Testament book Ecclesiastes. Maybe I can recover and go after all.

Japa essay

Japa is its own world, contained as if within a glass ball. Concentrate on your business and don't go wandering off into a nowhere-land, like Antarctica. You have Rādhā and Kṛṣṇa. Do your chanting. Keep pressing down on it. You know how to chant. Perseverance and concentration. While I'm chanting, I should be wrapped up in the world of chanting. There should be nothing else going on. I shouldn't be swept away by witches and ghosts into another land where chanting is not the main thing. Don't be mesmerized by nothingness. Hearty, fixed.

Think of Rādhā and Kṛṣṇa in a simple way. Have faith that They are hearing you and are reciprocating with you. They want you in Their pastimes, and this can be achieved by chanting. Never underestimate the miraculous potency of *harināma.* So I sped along attentively, and I pronounced the sacred syllables, trusting that they would do me much good. I was a little drowsy this morning and could not keep exact timing of the rounds, but they were not very slow. If Bala doesn't come up by the time I do eight rounds, I go on chanting. Or if my head feels weak, I lie back in the chair and wait and rest. I like to have eight or more done before we leave for the beach. The best thing about the session was decent speed. The weakest thing was a touch of drowsiness.

My *japa* ebbs and flows. Sometimes it is good, and sometimes it is not as good. I am not utterly truthful about my performance, and sometimes bluff it. By "bluffing" I mean that I say that I'm doing very well when I'm not really doing very well. I speak this way this morning because I'm a little disappointed in the session. At least I did eight rounds.

How can we let the name do the chanting and not be so forcefully in control ourselves? It's a matter of surrender. You have to be in awe of the presence of the holy name and aware that the name is a person. You have to call out to Rādhā and Kṛṣṇa and ask Them to come down.

Treating Them like subjects of our chanting is not good. The names are the dominant things, not the chanter. I must call on Kṛṣṇa and Rādhā, recognizing Their supremacy over me. I am a tiny person calling out for mercy. Kṛṣṇa is willing to be present in all His majesty if I call to Him helplessly. But if I act like a big controller of the names, then I've got it backwards. The names should be controlling me. I can't contain the holy name within a seven-minute segment as if it is my performance, with me the controller. The name is controlling me, and I am trying to hold on with my cries. That is how it should be. But I chant like a bully and push the holy names around. I control them, I make them fit into a space of a certain amount of seconds. My pronunciation should be a plea, my utterance a cry. When will the day come when I will chant the holy name, addressing Rādhā and Kṛṣṇa as persons and myself as a tiny entity, asking for Their mercy? I seem to have it backwards as I beat Them into shape, finish Them according to my speed and my control. I am not the controller of the Hare Kṛṣṇa mantra, but it controls me. I run behind the mantra, chanting, "Kṛṣṇa! Rādhā! Please let me serve You." I am a servant of the name, not a cowherd rounding up cattle. This is what it means to chant the holy name in a humble state of mind, thinking oneself lower than the straw in the street.

O holy names,
please lead me.
Let me reach to You.
You are the Masters,
I am the caller;

You are the great objects,
I am the tiny subject.
I have been chanting
as if You are mere beads,
You are the Supreme Controllers,
and I have the need.

Let me worship You
as divine persons leading
and myself Your humble follower.

Begging for the Nectar of the Holy Name

It would be good if you could flow more in a particular direction with force. Or if your writing could help more in your present purpose of improving chanting. In *Begging for the Nectar of the Holy Name,* you give a glimpse into the life of a struggling chanter; you give us many relevant verses from *śāstra* and "snapshots" of Srîla Prabhupāda. But the writing doesn't result in a dramatic change of heart in chanting. You may write along and keep a record of a not-so-successful journey. In that case, the writing's sincerity is its virtue. It is a kind of victory just in attempting the *yajña* (*japa-yajña*) and in writing through your days.[58]

Death a failure? Death is also a victory for the devotee. The continued struggle of a Westerner coming to Kṛṣṇa consciousness, despite the persistence of *anarthas,* is a victory. *Begging for the Nectar of the Holy Name* will help the many devotees who are in the preliminary stages. It offers them companionship on the road rather than perfect

58 Antarctic explorer Captain Scott's diary of his last expedition is victorious in that the human will doesn't get defeated or act dishonorably, but he's a failure in that he dies. SDG. see Robert Falcon Scott, *Scott's Last Expedition* Ed. Leon Huxley, (New York: Dodd Mead and Company, 1913).

advice by one who has already arrived at the goal and is sending back messages to the poor strugglers.

> At least my arm was comfortable in the sling.
> The chanting kept apace.
> I was content with the speed and sound.
>
> I was alert and not drowsed off,
> So we say it's not so bad,
> a day of chalked-up *japa*
> in the medium range.

Robinson Crusoe

The fictional character Robinson Crusoe lived alone on an island. Finally he found a companion he named Friday because he found him on a Friday. Some hermits choose to live entirely alone in caves or huts.[59] I could never do that. You have to be very self-sufficient and take time to gather food and protect yourself from the elements, and even sometimes from wild animals. I need comforts and companions. Vaiṣṇavas are not advised to live alone unless they are in a very advanced stage. Prabhupāda says unless they are advanced, solitaries will spend their time sleeping too much, and they will not be able to concentrate on Kṛṣṇa. We are advised to associate with devotees. I like to associate with just a few devotees who live mostly alone in a hermit-like existence. We share our meals and talk together, but give each other ample time for solitude. Prabhupāda preferred that devotees live in communities and organize outward preaching, but living with a small group is an alternative. He encouraged Yamunā dāsī and

---

59 Daniel DeFoe, *Robinson Crusoe* (New York: Oxford University Press, Inc., 1999).

Dina-tarana dāsī to live alone and practice strict *sādhana*. I live mostly alone, partly because of my health limits. But I do outward preaching by writing. Prabhupāda called writing and publishing the Bṛhad mrdaṅga, after an expression used by his spiritual master. Bhaktisiddhānta Sarasvatī Ṭhākura even had a picture of a printing press as part of the logo for the Gauḍīya Math. He said the *saṅkīrtana* party, with singers and *mrdaṅga*, could be heard from only a block away, but books could be circulated all over the world.[60] I keep mostly to myself, but by the Internet, I broadcast *The Yellow Submarine* to readers all over the world. I'm not like Robinson Crusoe, isolated from all civilization, having no communication with other living beings.

Coming to the isolated beach for solitary *japa* with Nārāyaṇa-kavaca is refreshing and favorable for *japa* meditation, but I supplement it with the Bṛhad mrdaṅga.

Devotees are chanting in *japa* retreats. They report outstanding results, especially on the day when they observe *mauna-vrata* (vow of silence) and chant sixty-four rounds. A spiritual revolution. "Never before have I felt such ecstasy in chanting, after thirty-six years." "I recommend it to everyone." I attended one *japa* retreat and didn't experience a long-term resolution, but I am more serious about my quota, and trying for some extra. The retreats are a good symptom of the times.

Prabhupāda writes that we should "constantly, incessantly chant the *mahā-mantra*."[61] He prescribed that his disciples chant at least sixteen rounds on *japa mālā* of a hundred and eight beads daily. That number (1,728 mantras) takes a little over two hours a day, so it is not exactly "constant or incessant," but it is regular, and one

---

60 Satsvarūpa dāsa Goswami, *Srila Prabhupada-lilamrta*, Chapter Four, "How Can I Serve You?" in Satsvarūpa dāsa Goswami, *Śrīla Prabhupāda-līlāmṛta: a biography of His Divine Grace A. C. Bhaktivedanta Swami Prabhupāda*, Vol. 1, Second Edition (Los Angeles: Bhaktivedanta Book Trust, 2003), 704.

61 *Bg*. 8.5, purport.

is free and encouraged to chant more than the minimum number of rounds in a day. I am embarrassed to admit that I do not chant much more than sixteen rounds a day, but I think that if I chant them intensely with devotion, it will be sufficient to qualify for practicing to chant at the time of death. It would be better if I chanted more, and I could certainly improve the quality of my chanting. Prabhupāda once remarked that we could chant sixteen rounds on beads and innumerable mantras off the beads. One should be accustomed to chanting Hare Kṛṣṇa throughout the day, as much as possible.

But the time of death is particularly crucial, and so I pray for Your help in remembering You at that time. In the fifth verse of the eighth chapter of *Bhagavad-gītā,* You state that if we think of You alone (concentratedly, with no other thought or distraction) at the time of death, then without doubt we will attain Your nature. Attaining Your nature doesn't mean merging into Your existence. It means our soul will transfer to Your abode, Kṛṣṇaloka, in the spiritual world, for eternity, knowledge and bliss as Your intimate servitor. *Whatever* state of being one remembers when he quits his body, he attains that state without fail.[62] It we're thinking of something other than Kṛṣṇa, than we will get a body accordingly. Mahārāja Bharata, although a great personality, was thinking of a deer at the time of his death, and he attained the body of a deer in his next life.[63]

We are living our whole lives in preparation for the time of death. Śrīla Prabhupāda writes, "Of course, one's thoughts during the course of one's life accumulate to influence one's thoughts at the moment of death, so this life creates one's next life" (Bg. 8.6, purport). This present life is just a spot in our eternal journey of transmigration through the species of life, and we must not take it as the

62 *Ibid.*

63 *Bhag.* 5.8.

all-in-all. I must use it as preparation for my next life. That will be determined by my mental complexion at the time of death. Another point is that the time of death is usually a very difficult time, and it is not conducive for meditation. This is another reason why one should practice chanting while one is in a good state of mind during one's normal course of life.

The chanting of the Hare Kṛṣṇa mantra is the best process for changing one's state of being at the end of life. I pray to be chanting Your names at that time, and I ask Your help in my present practice of chanting so that I will be ready at the end. I must discipline my mind: "Dear brother, please chant the Hare Kṛṣṇa mantra nicely and with attentive devotion every day and you will attain the highest destination."

Guṇagrahi Mahārāja and I were reading the *Bhāgavatam* yesterday. The verses and purports kept emphasizing that a *nārāyaṇa-parāyaṇa* (Kṛṣṇa conscious) person never experiences fear. If he's in a miserable condition, he never thinks, "I am a great devotee. Why is this happening to me?" Rather, he thinks, "This is Kṛṣṇa's mercy." [64]Guṇagrahi Mahārāja kept pressing me for what it meant to be fearless. I said the greatest fear is about what will happen at death. The *Bhāgavatam* purport said that a devotee doesn't mind if he goes to heaven or hell because he goes on serving Kṛṣṇa in any condition. Guṇagrahi Mahārāja wanted a more specific explanation of fearlessness, and he mentioned a Godbrother whom he would like to discuss it with.

We are afraid of so many things in this world, and sometimes new fears are added to our present ones. Fearlessness is an advanced platform in spiritual life. At

64 *Bhag.* 1.18.2, purport.

our present stage, we can at least take shelter of Kṛṣṇa when we are afraid and try to philosophically accept our position.

Turning to Kṛṣṇa

Japa should be a time for prayer, turning to Kṛṣṇa in His holy names. It should not be just numbers and hurrying to get them done. I'm myself a little guilty of that. Nevertheless, it's a great accomplishment to get your rounds done and should not be overlooked. Early mornings are meant for this. Getting up and diving into your rounds, watching the count rise, enunciating the syllables even without thinking so much about them. The names are Kṛṣṇa and Rādhā. It's absolute, even when you're not fixed on Their pastimes. Kṛṣṇa is kind to give us this sound vibration meditation. It works, even when all you accomplish is the faithful recitation of the transcendental sound vibration. But there are three stages in chanting: offensive, clearing, and perfect. You want to improve, to think of Kṛṣṇa while you chant. Mechanical chanting is not complete. It contains a trace of the offense of inattentiveness. Complete attention means thinking of the qualities, pastimes, and form of the Lord. All you can do is keep trying. Staying awake and alert is a big advantage. It counts in your favor. Drowsy chanting is very poor, or chanting while allowing the mind to drift off to other topics. So you should not bash yourself for completing the rounds as quickly as possible and paying attention to the syllables of the Hare Kṛṣṇa mantra.

Chanting *japa* is a delight,
even in the lower stages.
You're with the Lord
in sound vibration,
and that is always good.

You aspire for more
and are disappointed
but you do not allow yourself
to fall into depression.

Kṛṣṇa has packed so much
potency in the syllables
of the names that all
His energies are there.

It's true that Lord Caitanya
says, "I am so unfortunate
that I have no taste because
I chant with offenses."
And we have to live
with that truth.

But I am still cheerful
that I accomplished
my quota and I've
got eight and more
to go to improve.

Japa is the first thing I do in the morning, and it sets the tone for the day. It is best when you're up early, and you're not rushed. There should be time to chant the mantras in a meditative mood. Rādhā and Kṛṣṇa are the focus of the *yajña*. Their names, forms and pastimes should be the focus of the exercise. It is for Their pleasure, and I am the servant of the names. Nāma Prabhu is *real* Kṛṣṇa, as good as His form in the spiritual world. Lord Caitanya has emphasized that everything in spiritual life can be accomplished by good chanting. We should be serious about His proposals in *Śikṣāṣṭakam* and chant with heart and soul. All our faculties should pull to make a good sacrifice in chanting. Just to chant your vow of numerical strength is a great accomplishment, but you should strive to do much better. Overcome reluctance and make it the best part of your day. It is the most important thing. Dear Lord, please give me the inspiration to chant nicely with an unagitated mind. This simple practice in the morning is most precious and should never be neglected. The day evolves around successful chanting of the holy names of the Lord.

In a lecture that Prabhupāda gave in June 1969 on *Śrīmad-Bhāgavatam* 1.5.11 at New Vṛndāvana, he said that literature which is composed very nicely but has no description of the Absolute Truth or the Supreme Personality of Godhead is enjoyed by a class of men who are like crows. We shouldn't divert our attention to *gramya-kathā,* any literature, tragedy, or comedy, etc. What do you gain by it? Simply agitation. It is like throwing fuel on the fire. You get no *śānti.* The aim of our life is peace. Mundane literature will simply agitate the mind. *Paramahamsas* are interested in Kṛṣṇa conscious composition, even if it is made without grammatical nicety. Students in the Kṛṣṇa consciousness movement don't play with musical exactness or with dancing training but just out of their own ecstasy. Simply because it is glorification of the Lord, it will act.

This understanding of Kṛṣṇa's pastimes or chanting has as its subject matter the glorification of Kṛṣṇa, and so it is *uttama-śloka. Śrīmad-Bhāgavatam* is full of meaning in every line. He has no material qualities, but He has transcendental qualities. They can be chanted by those on the transcendental platform. Those finished with material pleasures can take pleasure in *saṅkīrtana.* Those who still want material pleasures won't enjoy chanting.

Why should one be aloof from this chanting and hearing? The only person who avoids it is the animal killer.

He won't like it. We can analyze the animal killer in two ways. One is the man who eats meat, and one is the person who does not take care of his self-realization.

Eager Hope Against Hope

kṛṣṇa-bhakti-rasa-bhāvitā matiḥ
krīyatāṁ yadi kuto 'pi labhyate
tatra laulyam api mūlyam ekalaṁ
janma-koṭi-sukṛtair na labhyate

"Pure devotional service in Kṛṣṇa consciousness cannot be achieved even by pious activity in hundreds and thousands of lives. It can be attained only by paying one price—that is, intense greed to obtain it. If it is available somewhere, one must purchase it without delay."

—Śrīla Rūpa Gosvāmī, *Padyāvalī,* 14

My doctor told me not to be so hard on myself. He says I have served Prabhupāda well, especially through my writings. I should not feel obliged to travel and lecture. He thinks this self-deprecation might be the cause of my headaches. I listened attentively. While self-deprecation may not be the cause of my headaches, it doesn't serve me much good.

But now someone has just placed "*Dainya*—Humility, Seven Songs" from Bhaktivinoda Ṭhākura's *Śaraṇāgati* on my desk.[65] It's filled with the Ṭhākura's bitter lamentation of wasting his life in worldliness and failing to worship the Supreme Lord.

"Diseases trouble me, constant anxiety has made me feverish, and my heart burns with every want. I see no way

65 Śrīla Bhaktivinoda Ṭhākura, "Dainya," In *Saranagati*, available in digital form from www.vedabase.com

out of this predicament, for all its darkness. Now I am very much afraid.

"The current of this worldly river is strong and relentless; a frightening, gloomy death approaches. 'Finishing my worldly duties, I will worship You, Oh Lord'—that hope is now fruitless as well."

He finally states that a pure devotee came to him and told him the news of the descent of Śrī Caitanya Mahāprabhu.

"Śrī Caitanya Gosai, who is Kṛṣṇa Himself, the son of Nanda, has saved the world by freely distributing the gift of His own holy name. Go to Him also and receive your deliverance.

"Hearing those worlds, oh Lord, Bhaktivinoda has come weeping and weeping to the soles of Your lotus feet and tells the story of his life."

So his life is a self-proclaimed failure, but he takes shelter at Mahāprabhu's feet and asks not to be judged but to be given the mercy of the holy names.

A friend was telling me about his progress on a personal project. He said his work has made him realize what he wants in life. He then asked me, almost challengingly, "Do you know what you want?" I quietly answered, "Yes," and the conversation ended there. What was on my mind as my desire in life is to obtain love for You and Śrīmatī Rādhārāṇī. I pray for this goal, which I know is rarely attained by a person in this world. You award *kṛṣṇa-prema* only to a soul liberated from material desires and filled with intense *laulyam* (spiritual greed) to have that love. Śrīla Rūpa Gosvāmī has written a poem that states, "If Kṛṣṇa consciousness is available to you, then you should try to purchase it at once." But the then asks, "What is the price to attain this love of God?" He answers, "It is *laulyam,* your intense desire to possess it." And if a person thinks, "All right, then I'll purchase it," Śrīla Rūpa Gosvāmī replies that this *laulyam* is not attainable by millions of years of pious activities.

But when I was asked if I knew what I wanted, I quietly answered, "Yes," and thought of *kṛṣṇa-prema.* Am I like a blind man trying to see the moon? Nevertheless, this is my desire.

What am I doing to try to attain it? I am practicing regular Kṛṣṇa consciousness and harboring my desire for the advanced state. I am following the recommended process of chanting the Hare Kṛṣṇa mantra every day, and I am rendering service in Caitanya Mahāprabhu's mission. I am regularly hearing the pastimes of Rādhā and Kṛṣṇa in Vṛndāvana. I may not succeed in my desire in this lifetime. Śrīla Rūpa Gosvāmī says pious activities are not enough, but the practices that I am following are more than mere pious activities performed for elevation to higher planets or other auspicious material results. My practices are pure *bhakti-yoga,* as taught by Caitanya Mahāprabhu and given to me by my spiritual master, a pure devotee, Śrīla Prabhupāda.

I pray that You nurture this desire in me so that it becomes intense greed. I pray in the mood of Lord Caitanya's *Śikṣāṣṭakam,* "I do not want wealth, beautiful women, or followers. All I want in my life is Your causeless devotional service, birth after birth." My standing in devotional service may be laughably immature for me to ask for *kṛṣṇa-prema,* but that is my stubborn desire. I don't want something else. I want the best thing. I may not be serving strongly enough to deserve it, but I openly beg for Your mercy. Why should a person desire less than this? Pure love of God is the ultimate goal of life, the most desirable object.

I can only continue with my present practices and try to intensify them. In *Bhagavad-gītā,* You say, "As they approach Me, I reward them accordingly."[66] So You will

66 Bg. 4.11.

judge my devotional service and place me in a position according to my actual performance and my actual desires. Maybe You will decide that I have not proven that I truly desire to be with You and Śrīmatī Rādhārāṇī in the spiritual world. I will have to settle for less. So be it, if that is so. But I proclaim that I have fixed my heart on the ultimate goal. May the day come when my *bhakti-latā* breaks through the universal coverings and reaches Your lotus feet in Goloka Vṛndāvana and flourishes there, producing fruits and flowers to offer You in love of God.

Japa is one of the most important things in my life. It is an authorized activity. *Kīrtana* may be superior, but *japa* is the required injunction for every devotee—to chant his sixteen rounds is the most essential instruction from the spiritual master. As we do it each day, we gain incalculable riches. No one should ever lapse in their sixteen rounds, but if they do, they should quickly recover and come back up to the standard. I have had times in my life when I went below the par, but I'm now at a steady place. I don't think I will ever drop below again. We should always be grateful to Lord Caitanya for the easy method He has given us. It is so pleasurable, and there are no hard and fast rules. Unfortunately, we don't have a taste for chanting because we commit offenses, but even that can be overcome by constant chanting. The *Śikṣāṣṭakam* is the key to opening all the secrets of chanting Hare Kṛṣṇa, with all the inner and outer meanings revealed to the cogent chanter. It is a *yugala-kiśora* mantra, a mantra about the loving pastimes of Rādhā and Kṛṣṇa. When we can climb above the mechanical stage and start to relish the *ruci,* or taste, of actual chanting, then we become the most fortunate persons in the world. There's nothing more valuable than being able to taste the chanting of Hare Kṛṣṇa. No material riches, fame, power, beauty or anything in the material world equals it. In Queen Kuntī's prayers, she says that material benefits are actually obstacles to spiritual life. One should be humble and bereft of material ambitions and chant in a humble state of mind. We should not think we are great chanters. We should pray to improve from a fallen position. Feeling one's disqualifications is true humility. Without humility, we cannot advance or gain the favor of Kṛṣṇa.

Prayer means to speak to the Lord, to implore Him, to praise Him, to thank Him. He comes in different flavors. But they should come with some knowledge of who God is, who you're talking to. You *must* come with sincerity. The best prayer is the prayer of the heart. The prayer with desperation in it. The prayer with calmness in it. The prayer with the sound as sweet as the flute. The prayer stolen from Kṛṣṇa. The prayer Kṛṣṇa makes to Rādhārāṇī, and you repeat it in His mood. The prayer the spiritual master gave you and that you repeat with obedience and loyalty. The prayers you enact, which he gave you to carry out. The best prayer can be long, like the fourteenth chapter of the Tenth Canto, or it can be just one verse. Some prayers are so wonderful that most devotees are not qualified to say them. There's that prayer by Rādhārāṇī which only Mādhavendra Purī and Lord Caitanya can say. Others are not qualified to say it. We should pray as we can, not as we can't. I like the prayers by the *gopīs,* where they're thinking of Kṛṣṇa in Mathurā, with the sophisticated ladies there. They ask whether Kṛṣṇa will ever come back to them. Does He think of them? Will He ever touch them with his *aguru*-scented hand? And I like the prayer by Mahārāja Pariksit, where he says to the gathered sages, "Let the snake bird or whatever magical thing come to bite me, but you just go on praising the glories of Lord Govinda." And in the next verse, he says, "And if I have to be born again in this material world, let me be born in the association of devotees and let me be kind to all living entities, and let me love Kṛṣṇa more than anything else." Something like that. From time to time, you have different favorites. The more, the better. And of any choice of favorite prayers, you'd have to pick the prayers written by Lord Caitanya, the *Śikṣāṣṭakam.* And a little prayer that rose out of your own heart, full of pathos and sincerity. *Vandanaṁ* is one of the nine ways to perfection in the process of devotional service.

atha āśā-bandhaḥ
āśā-bandho bhagavataḥ prāpti-sambhāvanā dṛḍhā

Here comes great hope. This unshaken possibility of the realization of the Supreme Personality of Godhead is called *āśā-bandha* or the great hope against hope.

—Śrīla Rūpa Gosvāmī, *Bhakti-rasāmṛta-sindhu,* Eastern Wave 3.34

Dear Lord, I have faith in the scriptural statements about chanting the holy names. Even by imperfect chanting one gets rid of all his sinful reactions. The proof is in the history of Ajamila. But removal of sins is not the ultimate goal. It's Kṛṣṇa-*prema*, pure love to You, that only comes by chanting without offenses.[67] It seems easy enough to avoid the ten offenses, but it is hard to control the mind and be attentive and prayerful. It takes great practice. I like to chant, especially early in the morning. I feel occupied, warm and intimate. I feel like I'm in the presence of my

67 Śrīla Bhaktivinoda Ṭhākura lists ten offenses in the Chapter Twenty-four of the *Jaiva Dharma* titled "Eludication of Nāmāparādha, Offences against Śrī-harināma." In Śrīla Bhaktivinoda Ṭhākura, *Jaiva Dharma*. Trans. Sarvabhāvana Dāsa (Vrindavana: Brhad Mrdanga Press, 2004), 498.

parents, my true beloved parents. But do I cry out like a child calling for its mother? That is the recommended attitude. Śrīla Prabhupāda says that Mother Hara hears the chanting of the sincere devotee and rewards him with Kṛṣṇa consciousness. I go on chanting in the hopeful mood.

The taste is a desire to be with You and Rādhā. I think once we have the mechanics in place—careful enunciation, attentive hearing—then we are ready for crying out to You. And when we cry, we taste. Sometimes the taste is in remorse that we have neglected good chanting. We grieve that we have committed offenses.[68] Sometimes the taste is a happiness that we are coming closer to the existential truths of chanting—that You the person are the same as Your name "Kṛṣṇa." Because You are All-Blissful, this contact with You in sound vibration makes *us* happy. As Lord Caitanya, You also express this in the *Śikṣāṣṭakam:* "When will tears flow constantly from my eyes, and when will the hairs of my body stand on end, and when will my voice choke up just by the utterance of Your name?" This is taste.

Painful chanting creates a bar, but
a sincere desire persists, and I
manufacture mantras from deep within
my will. They are not offensive, and
they count as true *japa.* My eye is
inflamed, but my soul is clear.

I call out to Rādhā and Kṛṣṇa to please
accept my cry, which is like a child

---

68 *nāmāparādha-yuktānāṁ/ nāmāny eva haranty agham/ aviśrānti-prayuktāni/ tāny evārtha-karāṇi ca.* "If one becomes determined, and continues his chanting of the holy name, and does not give up the process of chanting, the holy name will remove all his sins, and grant to him, the most valuable spiritual benefit." Śrīla Baladeva Vidyābhūṣaṇa, *Nāmārtha Sudha Bhaṣya*, 192.

for the mother, helpless but needy,
distracted but loving.

HOW MANY DAYS DO YOU HAVE LEFT TO LIVE? Mahārāja Pariksit had seven. Mahārāja Khaṭvāṅga had only a moment. If you had forty days to live, what would you do? Would you go to Vṛndāvana and spend it there? Hope to surround yourself with devotees chanting the holy names? What would you do with your last forty days? Forty days is a lot. But looked at another way, it's a little. It's enough time to become Kṛṣṇa conscious, under the direction of the spiritual master. Lord Caitanya taught Śrīla Sanātana Gosvāmī for a month, and He taught Śrīla Rūpa Gosvāmī for ten days at Daśāśvamedha Ghāṭa. You have to spend your time well.

I kept waking up during the night almost every half hour, coming out of dreams. I got up at 3:00 A.M. and started chanting. After about the fourth round, I got a headache but subdued it. My chanting was on track, clickety-clack. But I wasn't crying out, "Oh Rādhā, oh Kṛṣṇa, please engage me in Your service. I am fallen. Please accept me." Instead it was a rigid kind of chanting, paying attention, moving speedily at six and a half minutes per round. I was chanting, but not chanting deeply. It has to go to the heart and not just the lips and chest. You have to take it out of the mechanical realm and put it into the devotional realm. Nevertheless, I'm pleased with the accumulation of the rounds and the attentiveness to the sounds.

Chanting Hare Kṛṣṇa is a simple thing,
but it's difficult to chant with *bhāva.*
You need to surpass the mechanical stage
where your mind is absent of devotion.
Be eager for Kṛṣṇa as you call His
name, be eager for Rādhā. *Laulyam*
is the price for pure bhakti *japa.*
The mechanical will disappear,
and you'll be merged in bliss.

In a lecture Śrīla Prabhupāda gave on *Śrīmad-Bhāgavatam* 1.2.12 on August 5, 1972, in Los Angeles, he said: "People ask, 'Can you show me God?' Yes, but you must have the qualifications. How can I see God if I don't have qualifications?" A mechanic can see what's wrong with a machine, but an ordinary man cannot see it. They want to see God without qualifications. God says, "I am not exposed." One must be faithful, eager. It is not a frivolous thing. One must think, "I must see." There's an interesting story that illustrates this. One professional reciter told how Kṛṣṇa was living in Vṛndāvana and was highly decorated with valuable jewels. A thief in the audience heard this and decided that he would go to Vṛndāvana and steal Kṛṣṇa's jewels. His qualification was that he was thinking, "I must see Kṛṣṇa." When he went to Vṛndāvana, Kṛṣṇa appeared before him. The thief flattered the boy and said, "You are so nice. May I take Your ornaments?" Kṛṣṇa said, "No, My mother would be angry." Then, by Kṛṣṇa's association, the thief became a pure devotee.

The *gopīs* came to Kṛṣṇa because He was such a beautiful boy. They loved Him heart and soul. They didn't care for their husbands or children. They went to dance with Him when He played His flute. We must be very eager. Some of the *gopīs* who were prevented from getting out of the house gave up their lives.

Kṛṣṇa will respond if you are attracted to Him. Śrīla Rūpa Gosvāmī has written a verse in which one *gopī* addresses another: "There is a boy, Govinda, standing near Keśi ghāṭa playing a flute. Please don't go there, because if you have a tendency to enjoy with your family, it will all be ruined." Dhruva Mahārāja saw Kṛṣṇa and said, "Seeing You, I now have no more mundane desires." Śrīla Rūpa Gosvāmī wrote another verse that stated that if Kṛṣṇa consciousness is possible, you should purchase it immediately. But what is the price? Your eagerness is the price. This eagerness, however, cannot be achieved by pious acts in millions of years. But it can be achieved by association of devotees. This life is meant for seeing Kṛṣṇa. By eagerness, you achieve knowledge and detachment from matter.

na premā śravaṇādi-bhaktir api vā yogo 'tha-vā vaiṣṇavo
jñānaṁ vā śubha-karma vā kiyad aho saj-jātir apy asti vā
hīnārthādhika-sādhake tvayi tathāpy acchedya-mūlā satī
he gopī-jana-vallabha vyathayate hā hā mad-āśaiva mām

O Gopījanavallabha, the beloved Lord of the Gopīs! I have no pure love (*premā*) for You, nor have I any wealth of spiritual practices, such as ability to hear and chant Your name. Nor can I meditate or concentrate on Your name. I have nothing, nor do I possess any knowledge about You in truth; I can not serve the devotees and I am bereft of auspiciousness, and I do not even possess a high birth or a caste, so I am unqualified to worship You. Even then, because You do meet the needs of those who are humble and insignificant, I maintain my unshaken hope for attaining You, but this hope gives me the greatest pain.

Alas! What shall I do now?[69] Śrīla Viśvanātha Cakravartī Ṭhākura makes a short comment to this *śloka*. He says that the qualification for the *āśā-bandha* that is described in this *śloka* is the hope without any admixture of yoga, *jñāna* and karma and aimed only at the service of Kṛṣṇa in selfless love. He said that there can be no second explanation to this.

MY DEAR LORD, I chant early in the morning with a clear head, and I pray that my *japa* not be impaired with headaches or sleepiness. Try hard to focus on deeper chanting. I don't have to think of amorous details and love sports of the Divine Couple—I'm not qualified for that—but things I am qualified to think of, I want to think of. I can think of You two touching each others' hands or Rādhārāṇī teaching You to play the flute (Rādhā's brother Śrīdāmā claims Rādhā taught You this art, but You became so expert at it that Your flute playing seems to transform the hearers more than Rādhārāṇī's). I pray to be able to one day hear Your flute playing, which is described as the most mind-blowing, transforming experience possible, even to Lord Brahmā and Lord Śiva and the cows, and especially to the *gopīs*. It cleanses the heart and helps us to taste the nectar for which we are always anxious, just as *harināma* does.

My dear Lord, I pray to one day associate with You in Goloka Vṛndāvana. It may be as a bird in the treetops looking down upon You as You play Your flute and exchange words with the *gopīs*. In that case, I would be in ecstatic meditation with my eyes closed, but somehow be able to take in the whole scene. I would talk with the other birds about what was going on. One bird would say that You had said, "Don't talk." A group of birds didn't stay any longer but flew off to tell Candrāvalī the good news. But

69 Śrīla Rūpa Gosvāmī, *Bhakti-rasāmṛta-sindhu*, Eastern Side, 3.35.

it was not good news for Candrāvalī. You had said, "Don't talk with Candrāvalī, but I want to talk with Rādhārāṇī." The *gopīs* in Rādhā's party were very happy, as were the birds in Her party.

This is a fantasy prayer. My notebook page is streaked with pen marks, and I have difficulty reading it because it is coming out of a semi-conscious state. I have heard from authoritative sources that the birds in Goloka sit in the upper branches like meditating sages and behold the pastimes of Rādhā and Kṛṣṇa. It sounds like an enviable position. But I would like to be more actively engaged, like a *gopī mañjarī.* I would like to be in Rādhā's party competing against the intrigues of Padma and Śaibyā, the clever cohorts of Candrāvalī. I would prefer to be working under Lalitā and Viśākhā and Rūpa Mañjarī. These are fantasies because they are so far above my realizations. Still, a blind man can hope to see the moon in the sky, and it can be granted to him if Rādhā and You desire. Even Jesus Christ gave sight to a blind man in the temple at Jerusalem, and it caused a great controversy, because some of Christ's enemies claimed the miracle was bogus.

I pray in my fantasy mood to reach the topmost position. Why not? I don't deserve it, but I dare to pray for it. Is that blasphemy? Or is it *āśā-bandha,* great hope—hope against hope. Śrīla Rūpa Gosvāmī's prayer: "I have no love for Kṛṣṇa nor for the causes of developing love for Kṛṣṇa—namely, hearing and chanting. And the process of *bhakti-yoga*, by which one is always thinking of Kṛṣṇa and fixing His lotus feet in the heart is also lacking in me. As far as philosophical knowledge or pious works are concerned, I don't see any opportunity for me to execute such activities. But above all, I'm not even born in a nice family. Therefore, I must simply pray to You, Gopi-Janavallabha Kṛṣṇa, maintainer and beloved of the *gopīs.* I simply wish and hope that someone way or other, I may be able to approach Your lotus feet, and this hope is giving me pain, because I think myself quite incompetent to approach that transcendental goal of life." The purport is that under this heading of *āśā-bandha,* one should continue to hope against hope that someway or other he will be able to approach Your lotus feet.[70]

So apparently it is not blasphemous to maintain a wild hope for high achievement, even though you don't deserve it. But that hope will give you great pain? Why? Guess. Because you know you can't attain it? Because you want it, and the yearning for the impossible disturbs you? Because you have dared to achieve the topmost (*gopī mañjarī*), and you are well aware of your disqualifications?

In this fantasy prayer, I imagine myself a meditating bird on the treetops, liberated and living in Vraja and observing the *sṛngāra rasa.* I'm pushing the envelope where I may even doubt such a position exists—and this is greatly disturbing. Why don't I make a prayer that is simple and with ardor? "Now I lay me down to sleep, I pray the Lord my soul to keep, and if I die before I wake, I pray the Lord my soul to take." Just pray to be saved and take birth in any capacity, not as a love bird in the treetops or a *gopī mañjarī.*

I HAVE SPECIFICALLY PRAYED FOR SOMETHING that is beyond my reach, to be a meditating bird in a treetop overlooking the *gopīs,* to be a *gopī mañjarī.* It came by allowing my uncensored thoughts to have free rein beyond the level of mere intellectual reasoning. I would like to pray like this again, but you can't just turn it on mechanically. It has to come with actual freedom of thought, like in a dream. One might say it's a fantasy, but

70 Śrīla A.C. Bhaktivedanta Swami Prabhupāda, *Nectar of Devotion,—The Complete Science of Bhakti Yoga* (New York: Bhaktivedanta Book Trust, 1970), 137.

I actually control it. Or it could be a genuine free fall. I free fall for a while, and then I pull the parachute ring. It comes out Kṛṣṇa conscious and lands safely on the ground, but it is an exciting ride. "I will manage to come to Kṛṣṇa because I'm trying my best to follow the principles of devotional service, and I'm sure that I will go back to Godhead, back to home"[71] I fantasize that you will be a follower of Rūpa Mañjarī and I imagine what that will be like. By following the routine principles, your sure that you'll attain your *svarūpa siddhi.* This is *āśā-bandha,* and it is one of the symptoms of steady *bhāva.* You tell others what it is like to practice Kṛṣṇa consciousness. You're a preacher in Kṛṣṇa consciousness, and you tolerate getting insulted when you try to present it. Lord Nityānanda and Haridāsa Ṭhākura used to go out every day and tell people to chant the Hare Kṛṣṇa mantra. Sometimes people swore at them, and Jagāi and Mādhāi chased them, and then Mādhāi struck Lord Nityānanda on the head with a clay pot and drew blood. Śrīla Prabhupāda went out begging to collect money to print his first volumes of *Śrīmad-Bhāgavatam.* Not everyone gave, and he spent long hours begging to distribute his magazines and books. Once he faltered in the New Delhi heat and almost became unconscious, but a passing doctor intervened. Countless ISKCON devotees have risked getting rebuffed on book distribution. Kṛṣṇa is very pleased with them for their efforts. "Anyone, however, who tries to present *Bhagavad-gītā As It Is* will advance in devotional activities and reach the pure devotional state of life. As a result of such pure devotion, he's sure to go back to home, back to Godhead" (Bg. 18.68, purport).

Fantasize going back to Godhead as a result of preaching. It's a sure bet. There will never be a servant more dear than he who teaches this message to the devotees. In December 1977, I continued preaching in the spirit of mourning Śrīla

---

71 *Ibid.*, 137.

Prabhupāda, talking of the details of his disappearance and our loss. Most went out to "double it" in a Christmas marathon to show their loyalty by distributing more of his books than ever before. Both services were worthy. "He lives forever by his divine instructions, and the follower lives with him."

kintu bhāgyaṁ vinā nāsau bhāva-cchāyāpy udañcati
yad abhyudayataḥ kṣemaṁ tatra syād uttarottaram

"But by the appearance of which there is some gradual unfolding of fortune or bliss, even that reflection of pure devotion does not appear in the heart without a great fortune of the chanter."

—Śrīla Rūpa Gosvāmī, *Bhakti-rasāmṛta-sindhu*, Eastern Wave 3.51

Yesterday I had four headaches, two in the morning and two in the afternoon. When I went to bed, I woke up at 10:00 P.M. with another headache. I've been enjoying peaceful nights of complete rest for over a week, so this was a change and a disruption. I got up at 2:00 A.M. and began chanting. I felt tired. I've chanted thirteen rounds, so I've kept up a pretty good pace. My attention has not been the best. I may be a little under the weather with congestion of the sinuses. I've been paying attention to the syllables of the name, but not in a deep way. My overall impression is one of fatigue and inability to chant with vigor. This produces a general distraction and lack of focus on the target. I'm accumulating my quota and will get the prescribed rounds done before too long.

I could not get beyond the counting to begging Rādhā and Kṛṣṇa for Their service. It is all I can do. I lack deeper feeling. In the back of my mind, I lament. I do the rounds perfunctorily. I don't think of other things while I chant. I distinctly hear each mantra in my mind. Each one passes through my attention. Like a schoolboy reciting his verses or multiplication tables. I don't cry. I dry cry that I don't cry. I ask myself when I will reach the further stages. What will it take? I am very peaceful and content to be alone and chanting in my room. I know it is the best thing. But I don't cry for intimacy and mercy. I am not a topmost chanter, but I am grateful that I can at least chant mechanically with alertness.

He chants and counts
them up. He's cheerful
and attentive. He keeps
a lively pace. So glad
to be up early in *japa.*

But he knows something
vital is missing, his cries
to *Nāma Prabhu.* He's
unfeeling in the place
of the heart. But there's
nothing he can do.

He goes on cheerfully counting
while something like lead
weighs him down.
Kṛṣṇa, let me write for You.

So many poets are writing
of music and love in the
material world. The Vaiṣṇava
poets are read mostly only
by devotees. It would be
nice if they were widely read and
people knew the most beautiful
person and object of supreme poetry.

If I could do it, I would write for
the people of the world. But
as soon as you say "Kṛṣṇa," they
shy away. They are *mūḍhas.* But
someday Kṛṣṇa poets will
find a way to spread His
glory to wider applause.

Tell how he's everywhere, in everything,
but also the prince charming of the *gopīs*
and the teacher of *Bhagavad-gītā.*
May I play a little part
in that spreading of Kṛṣṇa
to the people of the world
in accessible lines
that catch the eye
and heart of readers of poems.

From Vrindavana Journal

I woke up in the middle of the night and couldn't get back to sleep. Finally, I did. I got up from bed at about 2:35 A.M. I had no head pain, but chanted slowly and not so attentively. I'm still in a slough. But I persisted and gradually accumulated my rounds. I've only done eight rounds. I'm on my ninth round. Rādhā and Kṛṣṇa are not close to me.

Be careful not to bash yourself. I still have a lot of rounds to do and can improve. I should take heart and get back to the chanting of the beads. I should speed up more. Put your consciousness in the utterance of the names. Call out to Rādhā and Kṛṣṇa to be engaged in Their service by the exercise of chanting Their names. I'm going along. It's not so bad, but it could be much better. I will now stop and go bathe and hope that will improve my chanting quality. It's a shame to have a mediocre report. I wish I could be chanting first-rate, but I have to tell the truth. At least I'm chanting regularly and paying attention to the syllables, chanting in my mind.

"Oh Rādhā, oh Kṛṣṇa, please engage me in Your service." What service? The service of chanting itself, among others. The translation of the *mahā-mantra.* I found a Catholic television station. A priest was lecturing on the power of saying the rosary. They had people chanting the whole rosary, the Hail Marys and the Our Fathers. They were holding up their beads. It was appealing, like our *japa.* The show was put together well. They have a vast, worldwide congregation. ISKCON should have a TV station. They were advertising books, videos, pictures. In India, it might be possible, and in countries with large Indian immigrant populations, like Mauritius and Guyana.

Nārāyaṇa-kavaca made a list of points to prove that it is beneficial for me to chant my *japa* in Vṛndāvana *dhāma,* even if I am experiencing difficulties in doing so. The list is as follows:

Time spent in the dhāma has benefits that are so great that is it not possible to enumerate them. Thus the chanter becomes more pleasing to his personal nāma prabhu, having improved himself via the special benefits of the dhāma.

Associations, impressions, benefits and boons, liberations, purifications, realizations, austerities all prepare one to be a more pleasing chanter and to be able to bring the dhāma within our minds wherever we must go.

Meeting Kṛṣṇa in the most intimate place where He is Himself removes the chanter from the inherent formalities of Kṛṣṇa in other settings and allows the chanter to take away this intimacy when he returns in his other place of service.

The benefits of devotional service (of which the principle one is the chanting of mahā-mantra) performed in the dhāma are astronomically increased. So even if we feel a disruption or difficulty in the routine of our chanting, the benefit that we receive, the degree that Kṛṣṇa is pleased with our chanting, is greater regardless of what difficulty we may feel. This increase in the benefits of devotional service in the dhāma is frequently and variously promised in many authorized scriptures.

Another point is that the chanting of Hare Kṛṣṇa is given to us by Lord Caitanya Mahāprabhu and should be done in the mood of separation. By coming to Vṛndāvana, worshiping our nāma prabhu in His original and natural setting, we will naturally feel separation when we are not here. Also, we may feel separation from our prabhu-datta deśa of regular chanting when we come here in the dhāma.

WHEN LORD ŚIVA FINISHED HIS PRAYER, he said to the Pracetās, "A devotee of Lord Kṛṣṇa whose mind is always absorbed in Him, who with great attention and reverence chants this *stotra* [prayer], will achieve the greatest perfection of life without delay" (*Bhag.* 4.24.74). Śrīla Prabhupāda writes, "Any devotee of Lord Kṛṣṇa can attain all perfection, material gains and liberation simply by offering prayers to Him." Śrīla Prabhupāda says further, "As far as devotional service is concerned, even hearing and chanting is as good as acting with our body, mind and senses. Actually, hearing and chanting are also activities of the senses" (*Bhag.* 4.24.78, purport). Lord Śiva concludes, "My dear sons of the king, the prayers I have recited to you are meant for pleasing the Supreme Personality of Godhead, the Supersoul. I advise you to recite these prayers, which are as effective as great austerities. In this way, when you are mature, your life will be successful, and you will certainly achieve all your desired objectives without fail" (*Bhag.* 4.24.79).

The Supreme Lord spoke to the Pracetās. "Always engaging in the activities of devotional service, devotees feel ever-increasingly fresh and new in all their activities. The all-knower, the Supersoul within the heart of the devotee, makes everything increasingly fresh. This is known as the Brahman position by the advocates of the Absolute Truth. In such a liberated stage (*brahma-bhūta*), one is never bewildered. Nor does one lament or become unnecessarily jubilant. This is due to the *brahma-bhūta* situation" (*Bhag.* 4.30.20).

In his purport, Śrīla Prabhupāda writes, "A devotee is inspired by the Supersoul within the heart to advance in devotional service in a variety of ways. The devotee does not feel hackneyed or stereotyped, nor does he feel that he is in a stagnant position. In the material world, if one engages in chanting a material name, he will feel tired after chanting a few times. However, one can chant the Hare Kṛṣṇa *mahā-mantra* all day and night and never feel tired. As chanting is increased, it will come out new and fresh. Śrīla Rūpa Gosvāmī said that if he could somehow get millions of ears and tongues, then he could relish spiritual bliss by chanting the Hare Kṛṣṇa *mahā-mantra.* There is really nothing uninspiring for a highly advanced devotee" (*Bhag.* 4.30.20, purport).

The Supersoul exists in everyone's heart, but in the heart of the devotee, He reveals Himself as ever increasingly new. By the grace of the Lord, the devotee gets inspiration.

At the risk of becoming repetitious, I want to write some more about my discussion with Nārāyaṇa-kavaca about chanting *japa* in Delaware and in Vṛndāvana. It's a fact that my chanting has not been as good in Vṛndāvana. I am not as attentive, I do not time my rounds accurately, I do not chant with speed, I am drowsy. This has made me depressed and desire to return to my *bhajana kuṭīr* in Delaware, but Nārāyaṇa-kavaca has pointed out some profound reasons to appreciate my chanting in the holy *dhāma* and not regard this as something lesser or something to be eager to leave. He has referred to the *śāstras,* which repeatedly tell us that Hare Kṛṣṇa in Vṛndāvana is superior and brings you close to Kṛṣṇa. Even a little time spent chanting in Vraja brings you immeasurable benefits that cannot be found outside. We have to take these statements on the authority of the scriptures, sadhus and gurus. And the personal feelings that I am having are also auspicious.

I am feeling separation from my own *bhajana-kuṭīr,* and that is a good thing. When I return there, I will also be able to feel separation from Vṛndāvana, even though I am not feeling the pleasure of it now. The impressions, purifications, and austerities that I am undergoing will all be there for me as rewards when I return to the USA. So I should not regard it as a waste of time or a negative thing to chant Hare Kṛṣṇa, even though it is difficult, and even though the performance is less in Vṛndāvana. Be happier here and be benefited by immense advantages, *japa* in Kṛṣṇa's abode. It is not something you have to immediately perceive, but it is a fact. And I am gaining every day that I chant here. I will surely notice it when I return to the yellow submarine. I have a fear that I will not be able to return to the perceivable standards I was keeping in Delaware, but I should not be afraid. After some initial adjustment, I will surely be able to chant better there, and the memories of Vṛndāvana will increase my standard rather than confuse me or reduce it. Therefore, each day that I struggle here is a gain, and it is being noticed by Kṛṣṇa. I am begging Him to grant me increased devotion for *japa* here and after I return to Delaware. And I desire to return to Vṛndāvana again and chant better than I am doing this time.

1

Rādhā, my dear,
You are the dearmost
to My heart. Your movements
make Me dance.
Your eyes put Me in a trance.
You are My most beloved
gopī, and always will be.

You are ever fresh and the
Queen of Vṛndāvana. I submit

to You, My flute is just
to please You. Please be
kind to Me and quell
Your anger over My offenses.
I cannot live if You do
not smile upon Me with
Your lovely face. Please
play with Me in the groves
of Vraja, which exist
just for Our pleasure.

2

Rādhā, my sweet,
it is so nice roaming
the paths with You.
You make the world shine
with Your effulgence,
golden like the sun.
Please never leave
Me but stay by
My side. When
I embrace You,
I am complete.

You are the gopī par excellence,
the rāsa dance is pale without You.
Don't think I'm unfaithful, I only
think of You.
Other gopīs exist just
to enliven My desire for You,
they are Your servants.
Let us share this swing
together.

When I have pain, I face an alternative: to chant through the pain or to stop and wait until later in the day, after the pain has cleared up. I prefer to chant through the pain, because I never know how long the pain may last. I don't want to go late into the day with my quota not reached. I can chant with pain by chanting silently and going to a small place in my heart where the pain doesn't affect me. I call out to Kṛṣṇa from there, and I'm not affected. I sit back in a comfortable position and try to relax and say the rounds at a moderate pace. I pray to Kṛṣṇa to allow me to do it nicely and to forgive me for the inevitable lack of perfection. Kṛṣṇa stays with me, and we chant together. I used to get migraines that would last twenty-four hours. So there's no question but that I have to persist in chanting during those times. I can't hold up the white flag of surrender to no chanting, but I chant as best I can and count on Kṛṣṇa's leniency and compassion. I can still pay attention to the syllables and chant silently in my mind.

Chanting under duress
is a bit of a mess.
You can't concentrate clearly
because the pain blocks you nearly.
Rather than stop, you push on,
and you're happy to get them done.
Wounded *japa* is better than none,
and you feel you have actually won.

At least you hope you continue chanting the Hare Kṛṣṇa mantra. That's your *laulyam* for *japa.* How horrible to go years without chanting or knowing Kṛṣṇa. You can't force a little baby. You never hear of infants being born chanting. They are not developed. It takes years before they can chant sixteen rounds. There must be some exceptions. Those who go straight to Kṛṣṇa have no such problem. Gopa-kumāra always chanted his Madana-gopāla mantra even before he reached Goloka Vṛndāvana. In Goloka, you don't stop chanting, but you have so much more! Be humble and don't presume to know where you'll go. Just persist now as best you can to be a sincere devotee. Kṛṣṇa places you where He desires.

I would like to print books. I would like to chant with devotion. Lord Caitanya (in *Śikṣāṣṭakam*) and Bhaktivinoda Ṭhākura prayed to manifest symptoms of ecstasy while chanting, such as flowing tears, choked voice, and hairs standing on end. Śrīla Bhaktivinoda Ṭhākura writes, "Becoming overwhelmed with *bhāva,* when will my color fade, and when at last will I lose all consciousness? Regaining my consciousness once again, I will maintain this life simply by taking shelter of Your holy name. Crying incessantly, this Bhaktivinoda, who is devoid of all intelligence, says, 'Will there ever be such a day for this unfortunate soul'?"[72]

A life of *bhajana* is not boring but is filled with waves of emotion. Simply by hearing about Rādhā and Kṛṣṇa and chanting Their names, the advanced devotee swims in the ocean of transcendental bliss. The *vaidhī-bhakta* performs his devotional activities because he is supposed to, but he doesn't relish ecstasies. He seeks happiness elsewhere, in external things. He likes to dress and eat nicely and maybe watch a movie. But when he arranges for a public festival or collects funds for the propagation of his spiritual master's mission, he is not engaging in external affairs.

72 Commentary to *Śrī Śikṣāṣṭakam*, In Śrī Caitanya Mahāprabhu, *Śrī Śikṣāṣṭakam* (Mathura: Gaudiya Vedanta Publications, 1995). 94.

These efforts are as good as solitary *bhajana,* and they may produce the same results, if Kṛṣṇa is pleased.

Sometimes when you begin your *japa*, you feel reluctant. It just doesn't have a taste. The only solution for that is to keep going resolutely. The taste eventually comes, always. The lack of taste may be due to many things, often physical. You may be tired from lack of sleep or some physical malady. Mental lack of taste is due to your poor Kṛṣṇa consciousness. It may be prominent on a particular day just because of the whims of the *cañcala* mind. It is a sad reflection to reveal to you that you're just not a good chanter. There is no excuse for it, you just must keep chanting and overcome the bad state of the mind. It's sad that we are not instantly excellent chanters in the morning, and that some mornings find us with the blues. During the chanting we can pray to Kṛṣṇa to help us out of this slump and bring us to our rightful position. Chanting is a kind mechanism. With a little effort, we'll find ourselves back on track. Those are the days to push with extra effort to find our rightful place. Determination is required and the strength not to become overwhelmed with depression at our poor state. Don't take it as such a terrible thing, just work through it and come to the right position.

This morning I found this tastelessness when I began, but it did not last long. Within a couple of rounds, I was feeling better and cheerful, and I was chanting at a good speed. I didn't give in to the poor start, which could have lasted longer. Maya is always waiting to catch us and tell us that the chanting is not working and that we are worthless and might as well give up. But actually we are just having a little bump in the road that we can overcome with persistence. It is just a temporary mood that can easily be overcome by chanting several rounds of *japa* without quitting. Kṛṣṇa does not want to withhold the sweetness of the holy names, and He is just testing us. He is showing us our low state. He will allow us to overcome it in short order.

Keeping the company of good, likeminded devotees is a sharp antidote to wrong action. Spending a good amount of time chanting Hare Kṛṣṇa *japa* keeps you on the safe side, and engaging in congregational *saṅkīrtana* is an excellent emergency measure to engage in regularly. You have recommended all these acts, and I shall follow them to save myself. Staying out of maya is of prime importance because we need to practice thinking of You at the time of death—which is fast approaching.

O my Lord, a beautiful woman is the quintessential symbol of maya. When Pūtanā, the horrible-looking witch, wanted to gain entry into Your presence as a baby, she assumed the form of a shapely woman with beautiful features and was permitted to enter Your room, although she was a stranger. Although all the Vrajavāsīs were tricked by Pūtanā's apparent beauty, You saw through her disguise and killed her by sucking out her life. Another demon infiltrated Your presence in the disguise of a cowherd boy, and another came in the form of a charming calf, but You saw through these facades and killed these dangerous demons. I pray that You will give me the savvy to see the approach of Māyādevi in my life so that I will be able to act as You and Balarāma acted and not be befooled by outer appearances.

A poor beginning will
not last for the gutsy
chanter of the Names.

Soon the soothing balm of
Nāma Prabhu covers the
rough patch with its nectar.

Like a bad dream, the
faulty start evaporates
and a cheerful sunrise
appears through the beads.

All that was required was
that I show Kṛṣṇa I'm
sincere and not a fair-
weather chanter—I
can endure a bad first inning.

2:03 P.M. I think one of the best things in my recent *Vṛndāvana Journal* which I just read are the statements by Nārāyaṇa-kavaca as to the benefits of chanting *japa* in Vṛndāvana. I was complaining that my chanting was not as good in Vṛndāvana as it is in Delaware. He gave very learned and realized statements about the glories of chanting in Vṛndāvana. One of the best ones was about the feeling of separation. He said Lord Caitanya taught us to chant in separation from Kṛṣṇa. So after chanting in Vṛndāvana, when I am back in my *prabhu-datta-deśa* in the West, I will feel separation for chanting in Vṛndāvana. And furthermore, when I'm in Vṛndāvana, the feelings I have of separation for my *prabhu-datta-deśa* in the West are also an enhancement.

N.K.'s point of view was that even if I didn't perceive my chanting in Vṛndāvana as proficient and enjoyable, it nevertheless possessed an almost unexplainable superior quality over chanting anywhere else. And that quality could be appreciated even after one left Vṛndāvana.

Māyāvādīs say that worship of Rādhā and Kṛṣṇa is imaginary and that the Absolute Truth has no form. They don't know that the Absolute Truth has *vigraha,* form. Some Māyāvādīs worship Viṣṇu and want to become one with Him. The sunshine is many millions of small particles of sunshine, but the particles are different. We are different and have different identities. In the *Bhagavad-gītā,* Kṛṣṇa says that all of us existed in the past, present, and future—as individuals. We are parts and parcels of Kṛṣṇa eternally. The devotees want to remain in their constitutional position. If you have strong *bhakti-yoga,* you are not in a material body. You are in a spiritual body. The Māyāvādīs are not *bhaktas.* They want to become Nārāyaṇa and enjoy Lakṣmī. Even Brahmā and Śiva are not equal to Nārāyaṇa. The Māyāvādīs are saying that Lord Nārāyaṇa is equal with *daridra* (the poor man).

It is very rare to attain Goloka Vṛndāvana. Sometimes I write that I want to go to Goloka Vṛndāvana, and I express things like, "hope against hope," or going there on Śrīla Prabhupāda's interceding for me and allowing me to attain it with his "key to the back door." When I read the statements of how rare it is to attain, I think maybe I should hold my tongue. But a blind man can talk of seeing one day.

Goloka Vṛndāvana is so charming that it is pleasing merely to talk about it. We are encouraged to hear about it and read authorized books in disciplic succession about the glories of Goloka. Śrīla Prabhupāda had the BBT print his spiritual master's translation of the *Brahma-samhita,* which is all about the glories of Goloka. *Cintāmaṇi-prakara-sadmasu kalpa-vṛksa laksavṛtesu.*

Gopa-kumāra made it
to Goloka on the strength
of his determined
chanting of the
Madana-gopāla mantra.

Wherever he went, he
remained unsatisfied
and went on chanting to
Madana-gopāla.

The Hare Kṛṣṇa mantra is just
as good, and if I were
determined and never gave up
chanting, could I
not reach Goloka?

But he must have been
very determined.
The Hare Kṛṣṇa mantra
can deliver a soul
to Goloka Vṛndāvana.
But he has to chant
without offenses
and with pure love.

I am not such
a chanter, and I don't know if I
ever will be,

but the opportunity
is open: Chanting
Hare Kṛṣṇa without
the ten offenses
and in pure love.

Sarūpa taught his
friend how to do it,
and by submission
and discipline, his
friend, the Mathurā *brāhmaṇa,*
made it too.

By the power of
association with a pure
devotee, a raw neophyte
can become a *paramahaṁsa*
and follow his mentor
to the spiritual world.

Early Morning

It is difficult to give up the opportunity to chant, even if I have a pain. Chanting in the morning is so rare. I don't want to give it up. Even if the chanting is a little inferior, I want to get it done, I want to stay on quota. It's an easy practice and so can be kept up even with an impediment. Chanting can actually soothe the mind and sometimes reduce a headache. It is good not to quit if I can help it. Chanting more relaxedly helps.

But if an eruption of pain comes, I have to be sensible and stop my *japa* for a while. I should rest assured I'll get it done later. If I can continue with minor disruption, that is best. We are so eager to chant *harināma*, we don't want to be stopped.

You don't want the hours
to pass without the names.
Smooth, uninterrupted flow
is your desired pace,
but you fight to
keep a lesser standard going.
Depending on Kṛṣṇa to respond
to your call, you endure
and get them done.

Early-morning chanting is the gem of the day. I especially like to get eight rounds done by 4:45 A.M. We are trying to get something done in Vṛndāvana. Nārāyaṇa-kavaca said it looked like Rādhārāṇī would let us do it. I was surprised and pleased to hear him say that, and I remembered the conventional wisdom that nothing is accomplished in Vṛndāvana without the permission of Śrīmatī Rādhārāṇī. Even ordinary things are thought of as not possible without Her mercy. So I thought I should chant here in Lewes, Delaware, for the accomplishment of things in Vṛndāvana. Try to please Rādhārāṇī by chanting Her names clearly and with devotion. Kṛṣṇa is never alone. He's always with Rādhārāṇī, and this is true also in the Hare Kṛṣṇa mantra.

Think of Śrīmatī Rādhārāṇī standing beside Kṛṣṇa, as in the *mūrti* forms. Initially, I forgot to wake up Rādhārāṇī and Kṛṣṇa and set Them on the altar, but then I remembered, and with bodily weariness, I did it. Kṛṣṇa's crown is a little crooked, and I will try to straighten it. They are very nice to chant to. They accompany me through my difficulty. It is nice to have your own Rādhā-Kṛṣṇa Deities to chant to.

Chanting to Rādhā and Kṛṣṇa,
you relax and speak Their names.
They reciprocate with Their delicate beauty,
and you stay awake in Their sight.

Rādhā and Kṛṣṇa are Hare Kṛṣṇa
and Hare Rāma,
and you try to
recall Their presence in your life.
You pray for Rādhā's permission
that things will turn out all right.

Two things

We should be doing two things when we chant the Hare Kṛṣṇa mantra on beads. We should be hearing the syllables of the mantra, and we should be meditating on Rādhā and Kṛṣṇa. We've heard it is enough to be fixed simply on the syllables of the name. But are you doing that, or is the mind thinking over yesterday's events and today's events-to-be? If we cannot fix our mind rigidly on the syllables of the name, we should be meditating on Kṛṣṇa. How? Think of Rādhā and Kṛṣṇa as our protectors. Adore Them. Think of Their pastimes, if possible. Keep the chanting of the syllables fixed in mind. But who are you chanting about? Stay in Kṛṣṇa's protection. That is why I like to chant in front of my Rādhā-Govinda Deities. I see Kṛṣṇa's three-fold bending form and Him holding the flute, and I see Rādhārāṇī beside Him. I think of Them as I chant. It is not absolutely necessary, but some meditation on Kṛṣṇa is advisable. Chanting should be deep. The mind should not be wandering while we chant the syllables. If it is not wandering, then where should it be? Fixed on Rādhā and Kṛṣṇa. Plead to Them to reciprocate with our chanting. Have faith They are reciprocating. Enter the mysterious realm of exchange through the mantra. Make it a complete meditation.

Sometimes when I am chanting, I am only thinking of the numbers and the accumulation. This is not enough, and I can do better. It is not a numbers game. It is meditation on the lotus feet of Kṛṣṇa. Śrīla Rūpa Gosvāmī has said, "How much nectar is in these syllables Kṛṣ-ṇa." We should try to enter the nectar of the sounds. Think of the Lord. Chanting, after all, is a meditation through sound vibration on the names, forms, qualities and pastimes of Kṛṣṇa. At first, we should be locked on the names themselves, the sound of Hare, Kṛṣṇa, and Rāma. As we gradually become absorbed in those syllables, we think of Rādhā and Kṛṣṇa and Their mastery of our lives. The Hare Kṛṣṇa mantra is complete meditation.

Who are we chanting to
in the Hare Kṛṣṇa mantra?
Is it a sound to the void,
a mere number calculation?
It is "Hare" and "Kṛṣṇa,"
the Divine Couple, and
we are calling to Them for
Their mercy.

Please enter my life,
please fill my mind
with Your names and
forms and qualities.

I'm not passing the time
in a numbers game, but
praying to Persons who
protect and rule my life.

I should think of Them
and worship as I chant.

The *gopīs* came to Kṛṣṇa, being captivated by His beautiful features. They came to Him out of lust. They loved Kṛṣṇa heart and soul. They heard His flute, and when their husbands, brothers and fathers tried to stop them, they didn't care. They ran out of the house to join Kṛṣṇa. Some *gopīs* were stopped, and they gave up their lives. You have to have eagerness, either out of lust or wanting to steal His ornaments, or whatever. Śrīla Rūpa Gosvāmī has composed a poem of one *gopī* talking to another. She says, "My dear friend, there is one boy, Govinda, standing by the Keśi ghāṭa playing His flute in the moonlight. Don't go there, because if you have a desire to enjoy with your family, if you once see Kṛṣṇa, you'll forget all material enjoyment."

If you are eager, you will see Him. Śrīla Rūpa Gosvāmī also said that if it is possible to purchase Kṛṣṇa, then do it at once. But what is the price? You must have eagerness, *laulyam*. It is not so easy. It cannot be achieved by practicing pious activities for millions of years. But it is possible by the association of devotees. You have to think, "I must see Kṛṣṇa in this life." This life is not for being like hogs and dogs. You'll achieve knowledge and detachment. This is the only institution giving this knowledge. It is the knowledge to stop death. As soon as one gets this knowledge, you become detached from all nonsense.

When you develop your love of God, then you will feel nice. If you practice religion and develop love of God, then it is actual religion. If you don't develop love of God, it's not religion.

The method is very simple. You chant the Hare Kṛṣṇa mantra. Prabhupāda said that his students were Christians and Jews, but he has given them the Hare Kṛṣṇa transcendental mantra. "*Mantra*" means to deliver the mind. The chanting of Hare Kṛṣṇa is so nice. Experiment for one week: Hare Kṛṣṇa Hare Kṛṣṇa Kṛṣṇa Kṛṣṇa Hare Hare, Hare Rāma Hare Rāma Rāma Rāma Hare Hare.

You can't demand that Kṛṣṇa be your love. It's a strong request, however. Please, Kṛṣṇa, be my love. Kṛṣṇa enjoys the entreaty and the dance. Yes, I'll be your love, He says. You love Me, and I'll love You. That will be our reciprocation. There are millions of devotees who sing this song to Kṛṣṇa. Not many are qualified to do so, but still there are so many who are qualified. Kṛṣṇa accepts their sincere request, and He becomes their love. "Be my love, Kṛṣṇa." Kṛṣṇa agrees, and everything is perfect. He agrees, it's unanimous. Kṛṣṇa is your love, just because you ask for it. He's that malleable. All you have to do is ask Him, "Be my love," and He will be. But you have to give Him your love fully. That's the catch. You love Kṛṣṇa, and He'll love you. Just like Śrīla Prabhupāda said to me. It's a two-way street, a lovely two-way street decorated with flowers and arches and trees. The scent of mangos. It's the road of love, where Kṛṣṇa exchanges with those who love Him. The imperative is not wrong. It must be true. He must respond, because that's His inclination.

Hare Kṛṣṇa, Hare Kṛṣṇa, Kṛṣṇa Kṛṣṇa, Hare Hare. A man wrote to me and told me he chants a different mantra instead of Hare Kṛṣṇa, a chant composed of the names of Lord Caitanya. I told him we should chant the Hare Kṛṣṇa mantra because it's recommended by the *ācāryas* in the Gauḍīya *sampradāya.* It's the *yugala-mantra*, made of the names of Rādhā and Kṛṣṇa, and it is the supreme mantra.

We should chant the Hare Kṛṣṇa mantra and not another. I like chanting Hare Kṛṣṇa, and I've been doing it for forty years. I wouldn't dream of chanting another mantra. So lay your head back and try your best, even on this bad day, to chant your favorite mantra and plead with Lord Caitanya to appear in His names.

Hare Kṛṣṇa mantra
is the supreme sound vibration.
The *ācāryas* say it's so.
My spiritual master gave it to me,
and I've put it in my heart.

Even on a low day, I embrace
it and rush through, chanting
Hare, Kṛṣṇa, and Rāma
as the thing to do.

Deeper Desire

Is there any deep desire to improve the *japa-yajña?* Yes, some. Then please acknowledge that. There are many advantages in chanting *japa* in the yellow submarine.

We read how Mādhavendra Purī, in a contrite mood, left the Remuṇā temple and went to chant his *japa* in the marketplace. Śrīla Prabhupāda writes, "This chanting can be executed anywhere, either inside or outside the temple." (*Caitanya-caritamrta*, Madhya 4.125, purport.) The Gosvāmīs chanted under the trees. Besides, the yellow submarine is a temple.

Don't forget the importance of chanting and the fact that yours needs work—there are some people out there who are looking to you. Now do something about it. Let me put down the pen and pick up the beads—and put the mind on the names.

Feeling sorry for yourself
that your *japa* isn't better.
But you must keep up your
courage that you will return.

Remember the former days when
you were chanting in the groove,
hearing Hare, Kṛṣṇa and Rāma?
Assure yourself you can come back
to that. Relaxed effort, not so
tense, yet overcome the drowse.

I know it's not so easy to put
the elements together, but you
have to run the risk and with
attentive mind, *pray* again
to Rādhā-Kṛṣṇa in supplication.

4:40 A.M. When you're behind in your quota, you tend to rush, and this is not good. You should be sure that you get your rounds done in the course of the day at the regular pace. Try to go deeply into thoughts of the Divine Couple. Hear each syllable. Don't let your mind get distracted to other thoughts. I was able to slow down and control my anxiety and chant nicely. I was wide awake and enjoyed the chanting of the holy names. Just don't worry about your quota; it will be done. Chanting Hare Kṛṣṇa is at once comfortable and yet intense. You say the mantras with ease and polish and try to have the larger awareness of what you're doing. You're going beyond the comfortable hours spent on the beads to depths of meditation. You're seeking to stay with Rādhā and Kṛṣṇa in Their most merciful forms.

Japa is a workout. It's like working on a punching bag, exercising your faculties and getting good exercise in the holy names. You move through them quickly and try to remember to pray, but you don't always do it. Praying means calling on Rādhā and Kṛṣṇa to reveal Themselves in the holy name and to reciprocate with you. You have to cry out to Them and not just go through the "calisthenics." Chant the syllables on time, emotional and spiritual content is needed.

To attain a high level, you have to do more than easy-going *japa*. You have to be willing to work.

In Separation

vilikhya sakhi dattani
sa jīvita-suhṛttamaḥ
virahartas tavemani
japan namani śamyati

"She wrote down these names in red sindura ink and gave the writing to Your life-friend Kṛṣṇa. When He is anguished in separation by not being able to see You, He chants these names and becomes pacified."

—Śrīla Rūpa Gosvāmī, *Vṛndāvaneśvarī-nāmāṣṭottara-śata-nāma-stotra*, 4

My dear Lord Kṛṣṇa, I feel lonely, and I am not willing to do something to alleviate it. I know association with likeminded friends is the remedy, and serving the nondevotees by offering them Kṛṣṇa consciousness. But I am disinclined to mix with others. I think to myself, "If I had a live, loving relationship with Rādhā and Kṛṣṇa, my problem would be solved." But it seems I cannot reach Them on my own without going through the devotees, my seniors, my peers, and my juniors. I was going to go out and mix with devotees in Philadelphia today, but I had all those headaches in the morning, and I was afraid that if I traveled two hours and reached out, it would bring me too much strain and more headaches.

Can I write to You and alleviate my loneliness in that way? Surely my loneliness will be ultimately solved by my association with You. I could try reading *The Nectar of*

Devotion. I could also ask Bala to work with me and try on the new outfits for Rādhā-Govinda. I just asked him, and he said he would work with me in an hour. We will work from 4:00 P.M. to 5:00 P.M., and then I'll start my lonely one-and-a-half hours of *japa.*

In the *japa,* I can be with You because You are not different from Your names. All Your qualities and forms and pastimes are present in Your names. I will not be able to realize that, but I'll be trying to do something that is certainly worthy and not being alone. So I have only this present hour alone, in which I can write to You. Why did I fail to contact You in Vṛndāvana? Why do I become so isolated, leading to anxiety? If I were Kṛṣṇa consciousness I could just look at a picture of Rādhā-Kṛṣṇa or gaze upon my Rādhā-Govinda *mūrtis* and I would feel Your presence. If I were a pure devotee, like a true follower of the Six Gosvāmīs, I could be satisfied seeing Kṛṣṇa standing in His threefold bending form holding His flute and wearing a peacock feather in His crown. I would be delighted to see Rādhārāṇī standing beside Him bending slightly and extending Her right hand to Him. Śrīla Prabhupāda writes in *Bhagavad-gītā* that a yogi never feels afraid or lonely, even if he's living by himself in the jungle. He realizes Kṛṣṇa is in his heart, and he is protected and happy with his Lord.

I feel Your absence. I wish I could say it was an ecstasy of feeling separation from You. This is the goal of the Gauḍīya Vaiṣṇavas—they relish "painful" feelings of separation from Rādhā and Kṛṣṇa. This is valid loneliness: "I am feeling the world to be all void in Your absence." [73]Please grant me love and attraction to You so that I feel a bit of Rādhā's separation from Kṛṣṇa.

You two are my most longed-for company. You are what I am missing. With thoughts of You, I am consoled.

---

73 Śrī Caitanya Mahāprabhu, *Śikṣāṣṭakam*, 7. Trans. Śrīla A. C. Bhaktivedanta Swami Prabhupāda, in Introduction to *Śrīmad Bhāgavatam*, Vol. 1 (New York: Bhaktivedanta Book Trust, 1987), 41.

I pray that You will always give me the opportunity and intelligence to serve You. The first-class service to You is to be among Your eternal associates in Your spiritual abode, Goloka Vṛndāvana. There, one serves You in Your form as the original person, the cowherd boy, Śyāmasundara. Equally good, although different, is to be among Your eternal *parisads* (associates) in Navadvīpa, where You manifest as Lord Caitanya and engage in the *saṅkīrtana* (congregational chanting) of Your holy names. If one is not qualified to serve You in the spiritual world, he can serve You in separation in the material world. Service in separation, when done in full surrender and fervor, is just as potent as service in union with You. Service in direct union with You is called *sambhoga,* and service in separation is *vipralambha-sevā.* Even in the spiritual world, Your devotees sometimes serve You in separation. The *gopīs,* or cowherd damsels of Vṛndāvana, had many pastimes with You in direct union. The most famous is the *rāsa* dance, where the *gopīs* danced with You in the evening in the Vṛndāvana woods. But when You were sixteen years old, You left Vṛndāvana for Mathurā and did not return for many years. The *gopīs* apparently suffered painfully in separation from You. But in actuality, when You were not present, the *gopīs* meditated on their pastimes with You and felt Your presence more intensely than when You were actually present. Paradoxically, Your absence produced a higher ecstasy for the *gopīs* than Your presence. Lord Caitanya appeared in this world for the confidential reason of experiencing *vipralambha-sevā,* Rādhārāṇī's mood of ecstasy in separation from You. His followers, the Six Gosvāmīs of Vṛndāvana, also cultivated *vipralambha-sevā* and always remained unrequited in their search for You. They would cry out, "Where is Kṛṣṇa? Where is Rādhā? Are They on Govardhana Hill? Are They at Rādhā-kuṇḍa?"[74] They would remain in the mood of searching for You without

74 *he rādhe vraja-devike ca lalite he nanda-sūno kuta/ śrī-govardhana-kalpa-pādapa-tale kālindī-vane kutaḥ*. In Śrīnivāsācārya, *Śrī Śrī Ṣaḍ-gosvāmy-aṣṭaka*, 8.

finding You. The spiritual masters in the Gauḍīya Vaiṣṇava *sampradāya* teach their disciples to cultivate *vipralambha-sevā* and consider it the highest spiritual ecstasy.

But whether one cultivates service in separation or service in union with You, it is the *quality* of the service that counts. We are taught to serve You for Your pleasure, not our own sense gratification. A sincere devotee wants to please You. The *gopīs* felt pain when You were away because they thought You would be unhappy without them. When they are together in the *rāsa* dance, the *gopīs* try to please Your senses. The disciples try to serve the spiritual master so that he will please *his* spiritual master, which they know is their *guru mahārāja's* topmost desire.

I don't have much to say right now. Kṛṣṇa wrote love letters to Rādhā in red rose ink: I write in black ink with no such love. But I like to hear of His letters and the letter which Rādhā wrote to Him, even before They met!

I began chanting at 2:35 A.M. A dull headache set in my forehead, but I continued chanting. There is always a bit of initial resistance to the effort. But it melts away quickly as my strength for chanting kicks in. By the end of the first round, I am ready for an improved, quicker second round. And even during the first round, my mind pays attention to the mantras. I am very pleased when my mind doesn't wander. In the afternoon chanting, my mind wanders more and I feel more resistance. Today some of my rounds were under six minutes, but the eight rounds averaged approximately seven minutes per round. I was mainly occupied with the headache and hearing the syllables and noting the accumulation. But I also thought of the importance of chanting. Therefore I wanted to do it nicely, with concentration. If I chant well, I will feel Kṛṣṇa's presence, and that will be my perfection. As I progressed, I watched cautiously for signs of drowsiness and hoped it wouldn't come. Fortunately I stayed alert. All the instructions I have heard about the holy names and all the years I have been practicing are producing an effect. I also hoped my headache wouldn't build, so I chanted gently, though quickly. I don't know how many years it will take me to chant on a pure platform. I'm not there yet. Kṛṣṇa doesn't easily give the full nectar of ecstatic chanting. You have to cry out for it. "When will tears flow from my eyes from chanting Your holy names, and when will my voice choke up at the utterance of Your names?" When will the whole world seem like a void in Your absence? These are the statements of Śrīmatī Rādhārāṇī, expressed through the mouth of Śrī Caitanya Mahāprabhu in His *Śikṣāṣṭakam,* and they are all about the chanting of the holy names. Just yesterday in Lord Śiva's song, I heard that everything can be attained by chanting. So I should give my daily *japa* my very best effort. Today I felt the lack of joy and bliss in my utterances. I struggled with the headache. But the best thing was the dutiful completion of the rounds.

Don't you remember the hopes of going to Kṛṣṇaloka? Now you're interested in another "ism." You're going to school now. You've got a new job. You're embroiled in family life. Or you've just . . . changed. You're not interested anymore in what I'm interested in. Our rapport is gone. You even look different. You dress differently. You talk differently. We can't make it together anymore. We've gone our separate ways. But maybe in the future, things will change again. I'm hoping for that. You've changed once, you could change again. Rādhārāṇī hoped that about

Kṛṣṇa, that He wouldn't stay in Kurukṣetra, that He'd come back to Vṛndāvana and change again so She wouldn't have to remain sad and mournful. It wasn't that He'd changed so much, it was that the place changed. If He could just go back to Vraja, then He'd change again. When someone changes like that, the bottom drops out, and it's just very sad.

Kṛṣṇa comes "out of the blue", that is. His bodily hue is like a gray-bluish rain cloud. Sometimes the *mūrtis* are painted black, and the Sanskrit word *kṛṣṇa* means "blackish". But He is far more beautiful than persons with blackish or whitish complexions in the material world. In different *yugas*, He appears in different hues. At Kṛṣṇa's name-giving ceremony, Gargamuni said, "This boy appears white in Satya Yuga, red in Dvāpara Yuga, and black in Tretā Yuga. Golden is His hue in Kali Yuga as Gauraṅga, Lord Caitanya Mahāprabhu." Kṛṣṇa's cowherd boyfriends in Goloka Vṛndāvana are described as appearing in many colors—green, orange, etc. The *gopīs* are mostly white or golden. All these varieties are pleasing to Kṛṣṇa. The demons who come to kill Kṛṣṇa in Vraja often take unusual shapes, like a beautiful woman, a duck, or a horse, but their uncovered forms are often ghastly and monstrous—black bodies with copper-red hair, sharp teeth, and long nails. They have *siddhis,* or magical yoga powers, which enable them to change shapes and assume heavy bodies like Tṛṇāvarta.

By Kṛṣṇa's agent Vṛndādevī, or *yogamāyā,* He changes the spiritual world to appear different and more attractive, such as by a change of seasons or sudden occasional celebrations. When Kṛṣṇa left Vṛndāvana for many years, the *dhāma* appeared to lose its glamour and dry up, due to the grief-stricken feelings of separation of its residents.

Free writing can imagine the sound of the flute. Without actually hearing the flute, it can daydream that it hears it.

> The flute is heard in the inner
> ear, and I think of Kṛṣṇa in Vraja.
> He is standing in *tribhaṅga* on
> Govardhana Hill, and He fingers the
> holes in the bamboo.
>
> I swoon to hear it
> and run in the direction,
> stumbling with joy and confusion.

The prayers of the gopīs *are very sad. They are remembering Akrura's coming to Vṛndāvana to take Kṛṣṇa away to Mathura. They refer to His līlās with them. If one actually enters the mood of the prayers, he will feel transcendental emotions. They are not just rhetoric spoken by sentimental girls. They are direct expressions they shared with Kṛṣṇa, the killer of the Aghāsura demon. They are accurate reports of mental states of Kṛṣṇa's lovers.*

Kṛṣṇa tells Uddhava that if He did not always meditate on the *gopīs* in love, he would not be Kṛṣṇa. Thus He proves that He has not become hardhearted by leaving the *gopīs,* but He thinks of them always and feels extreme pangs of separation, just as the *gopīs* feel for Him. Kṛṣṇa is not ungrateful toward the *gopīs,* but He praises them as the topmost devotees, greater than the yogis in *samādhi.* The impersonalists attain a stage where they forget their bodies and identities and become one with Brahman, but they do not think of Kṛṣṇa. There is ultimately an empty center to any realization that is not Kṛṣṇa conscious.

I'm lonely for You, wanting You. You are the ultimate goal of Kṛṣṇa conscious association, and I am not so close to You. I don't have a ready, affectionate relationship with You, and that leaves me lonely. "I am feeling the world all void in Your absence." It could be a sign of my growing more advanced in spiritual life that I'm feeling lonely without You.

Where are You? Are You on Govardhana Hill? Are You at Rādhā Kunda? Why aren't You present on my tongue when I chant Your holy name? I cannot see You because my eyes are not anointed with the salve of love of God.

Please live closer to me and let me feel Your association, even if I do not have much other association. You are all I need.

ohe naba-ghana-śyāma kebala rasera dhāma
kaiche raṁha kori mana jhure
caitanya celaya jāya hena anurāga pāya
tabe bandhu milaya adūre

"O Kṛṣṇa, dark like a new monsoon cloud, O abode of nectar, I stay here and weep. I'm loosing My consciousness. O My friend, from far away please return to Me."

—*Śrī Hari-nāma-cintāmaṇi*, 15. *Suhai-rāga*[75]

This is Rādhārāṇī's song. She is yearning for Kṛṣṇa to return. He is Her Prince. She has hope against hope, *āśā-bandha*. He said He would return in a day, but now years have gone by, and He has not come back. He has married

75 Śrīla Bhaktivinoda Ṭhākura notes on this verse in his *Śrī Hari-nāma-cintāmaṇi*: "A devotee who thinks his only wealth is Lord Kṛṣṇa and who is expert at tasting nectar will always taste the nectar of the holy names Hare Kṛṣṇa with ecstatic love. The holy names are described in the words given below, words that are a song in the 183rd part of the *Pada-kalpataru*, a part entitled *Ardha-bāhya-daśā-pralāpam* (Words spoken while halfway in external consciousness.)"

16,108 queens. There is no reason to think He will come back, but some day. . . . She maintains a hope because He said He would return. The *sakhīs* maintain Her life by giving Her assurances. Sometimes they send notes to Kṛṣṇa admonishing Him for His cruelty. Kṛṣṇa has His own reasons. He had to stay in Mathurā and Dvārakā to do political business and to assuage Devakī and Vasudeva. And He was increasing the love of the *gopīs* by being away from them. Rādhārāṇī knows this in Her heart. She knows He will return, and so She sings, "Someday My Prince Will Come." She's actually happy because She knows it's true. One day Kṛṣṇa will appear, wearing His glittering yellow garments, and He will take Her in His arms. It will happen, for sure.

Śrīmatī Rādhārāṇī's condition of anxiety in separation from Śrī Kṛṣṇa also described in *Kṛṣṇa-karṇāmṛta* by Bilvamaṅgala Ṭhākura: "What shall I do now? To whom shall I speak? What is the purpose of holding on to the futile hope of receiving His *darśana*? Please speak about something better. Aho! But how can I possibly stop talking about He who is contained within My heart? His gentle, sweet smile is a festival for the mind and eyes. My longing to see this form of Śrī Kṛṣṇa increases moment by moment."[76] Śrī Rādhā asks Her *sakhīs* to abandon talk about ungrateful Kṛṣṇa. But as She says this, Kṛṣṇa manifests to Her internal vision. Distressed, She cries, "Oh what suffering! Kṛṣṇa is lying in My heart and looking at Me with His sidelong glance, which is imbued with a sweet, gentle smile. This glance, full of laughter, is a great festival for the eyes and minds of all *gopīs*."

The devotees of Śrīmatī Rādhārāṇī feel pain in hearing of Her distress. But paradoxically, they know that She is experiencing the greatest happiness of love of Kṛṣṇa in separation. I do not understand these mysteries, and perhaps I should not even inquire into them. But Sukadeva

---

76 Śrī Bilvamaṅgala Ṭhākura, *Śrī Kṛṣṇa-karṇāmṛta*, 42. see *The Kṛṣṇa-karṇāmṛta*, Ed. S. K. De (Dacca, 1938).

Gosvāmī says at the end of the *rāsa* dance that the affairs of Kṛṣṇa and the *gopīs* are capable of banishing all lust from the heart. So I repeat them, along with my own prayers, and pray for clean motives. May the prayers of Lord Śiva, my own words, and the pastimes of Rādhā-Kṛṣṇa shine in my heart and release me from bondage.

When your lover has gone, you're bereft. You're alone and sad, but they play it with soul and upbeat. That's the meaning of the blues. You take the hard times and you weave it into something sweet and lively. Even the departed lover becomes a pretty tune. Not exactly pretty but hard and swinging. When your lover has gone, you burn in the fire of separation. You wait for him to come back. You wonder if he'll ever come back. You remember the times you had together, and they make you cry. You experience *sphūrti*, visions of being with him again. So in a sense, he's never gone. That's the way it is in Goloka. The lover never goes, but He stays in His *bhāva* incarnation. They say it's even better than when He's with you. When your lover has gone, it's bittersweet because he's still with you, and yet, in the other sense, you don't see him, you don't touch him. It's the great mystery of bhakti, and it's created by Kṛṣṇa. It stimulates love.

When Kṛṣṇa blesses you with a good *japa* session, you should be very grateful. It may become a rare opportunity. When young, you think you'll always be fit for vigorous *japa.* Later it becomes almost a rarity. When it comes, be grateful and take full advantage. It's like bathing in a smooth, warm river—the Yamunā. The water courses past you, and you utter the sacred syllables. The birds are chirping, and everything is sublime. It's like the descriptions of Goloka from the *Bṛhad-bhāgavatāmṛta.* You can be with Kṛṣṇa and Rādhā. I'm looking at Them on

Their altar. The Hare Kṛṣṇa mantra is so easy and efficient. It brings you into the company of Kṛṣṇa without your even noticing it, without your even making much of an effort. Your chanting is still preliminary. Try to go deeper. Go under the Yamunā. Immerse your head. Kṛṣṇa will protect you. Go on chanting and accumulating and enjoying His blessings.

Toward the end of my eight rounds, I felt the beginning of a headache. But I'm doing my duty, up early and performing the *yajña.* It's the best I can do now, and I don't hate myself for it. I trust that Kṛṣṇa and Rādhā are hearing me and appreciating my struggle. I know the importance of the chanting, and that's why I get up so early and attempt it. I cannot neglect it, at least not in my schedule, so I continue to attempt as best I can each morning. At least I'm not behind on my rounds, and I will have time to chant a few more before I have to take my 5:30 A.M. bath. Instead of going on the walk, I may try to get some extra rest to curb the cold.

Janmāṣṭami Appearance Day of Lord Kṛṣṇa — 3:56 A.M.

I woke at 12:30 A.M. wide awake and couldn't sleep anymore. I lay in bed until 1:45 A.M. and then got up and began chanting. I've now done fourteen rounds, which is good for Janmāṣṭami. I can chant some extra rounds today. I'll probably have to crash later because I woke up so early, but so far, I'm alert. I'm chanting all right. I've been chanting my rounds at under seven minutes per round, focusing on the syllables of the mantra. There'll be extra *kīrtana* and *japa* today, and reading of Kṛṣṇa's pastimes. A spiritual celebration. As the rounds accumulate, I hope to go deeper. I pray to Rādhā-Kṛṣṇa to please engage me in Their service. Extra chanting usually means extra focus, extra benefit. So I look forward to that today.

Today is the day that Kṛṣṇa appeared on the earth. Let it be the day that He appears in my heart. Like a New Year's resolution, like a reform, He can take birth in me today. A renewed presence.

At the beginning we try to understand Kṛṣṇa by chanting His names. Then, when purified, we understand His form, His qualities, and His activities. But none of it can be understood by our material senses. How can it be understood? When we take to transcendental, loving service, the Lord reveals Himself. Therefore, the first business is to engage the tongue in the service of the Lord. How? By chanting and glorifying His name and qualities. Then the other senses can perceive Him.[77]

This human body is a great opportunity. By engaging the tongue, we can make advancement. It cannot be done in any other species of life. To have a human body is a great boon for getting out of the clutches of maya by always chanting the Hare Kṛṣṇa mantra. This sound is not different from Kṛṣṇa. People consider Kṛṣṇa an ordinary human being. He is not different from His name or anything connected to Him. As soon as my tongue touches the holy name of Kṛṣṇa, I am with Kṛṣṇa. If you constantly keep yourself in contact with Kṛṣṇa, just imagine how you can purify yourself. Another way to engage the tongue is to eat food offered to Kṛṣṇa.

Sanātana Gosvāmī states, "Material existence is full of various miseries, but devotional service at the Lord's lotus feet (*padayoḥ*) eradicates them all (*vyasanardanaḥ*). Of if we take *padayoḥ* to modify *vyasanardanaḥ*, the meaning of the two words together is 'that which destroys the pain felt by the feet.'" This interested me because I always feel pain

---

77 *Padma Purāṇa* verse, *ataḥ śrī-kṛṣṇa-nāmādi/ na bhaved grāhyam indriyaiḥ*, is quoted in Cc. *Madhya*, 17.136. and *Bhakti-rasamrta-sindhu*, 1.2.234. see Rūpa Gosvāmī, *The Bhakti-rasāmṛta-sindhu of Śrīla Rūpa Gosvāmī* Vol.1. Trans. Bhanu Svami (Chennai: Sri Vaikuntha Enterprises, 2005), 267-268.

in my left foot. Sanātana Gosvāmī goes on to say, "Kṛṣṇa's *rāsa-līlā* is mostly a festival of dancing, and dancing means moving the feet. By entering the *rāsa* dance, one will be relieved of the distress they feel from doing other things."[78] Of course, to enter the *rāsa* dance, you'd get a body free of arthritic feet (and impure heart).

Kṛṣṇa plays in the spiritual world
where there is never a hint of distress.
His separation from Vṛndāvana
is a great mystery because
it appears to throw the Vrajavāsīs
into deep misery of separation.

Their feelings are actually the
highest ecstasy, as He increases
their love for Him.
I miss Kṛṣṇa in a simple
way that is not as great as *viraha*.
I want to be with Him
but can't swim the ocean of separation.
Kṛṣṇa breaks hearts out of a
desire to increase the *bhāva*.

He's not actually cavalier
or cruel. What He does
cannot be understood by a fool.
I'm on the outside looking in.
I support Kṛṣṇa's acts
and defend Him against the critics,
but I am not crying

---

78 Sanātana Gosvāmī, *Śrī Bṛhad-Bhāgavatāmṛta of Śrīla Sanātana Gosvāmī*. Trans. Gopīparāṇadhana dāsa. Vol. 3, (Los Angeles: Bhaktivedanta Book Trust, 2002), 564.

that He's not coming.
"That's just His way,"
I say, and carry on
with a tepid *bhakti-yoga.*

Kṛṣṇa never leaves a
step out of Vraja. He
remains there in His *bhāva*
expansion. But the
Gauḍīya Vaiṣṇava teachers
are meant to create the
mood of separation in
their followers. If you cry tears for
Kṛṣṇa, you're a great success. Don't ask,
"But I thought He never left?"
Deepen your feelings of distress
that you're not with Him now
feel happy that He's with you
and don't ask foolish questions.

Buddhists sometimes speak of emptiness. We speak of separation. We know Your names and faces and forms and Your place of residence. We theoretically know what we will do with You when we join with You in some future birth. We long to be with You in Your *yugala-kiśora* as Rādhā and Kṛṣṇa. We have heard of Your appearance as Śrī Caitanya Mahāprabhu, and we've heard that this is Your most merciful (*audarya*) form. In this form, You fully distribute love of God. There is no emptiness in Your abode or in the process to reach You. The means and the goal is the chanting of Hare Kṛṣṇa.

As I consider these facts, I begin to understand that there is no reason for me to feel bereft or neglected. You are with me if I want You. Please create the urge in me to desire Your company always. Then even if You do not appear before me, I may cry tears as symptoms of my love for You. Only a fool neglects the attempt to break his loneliness by reaching for You, Śrī Śrī Rādhā-Kṛṣṇa, Śrī Śrī Gaura-Nitāi, and Śrīla Prabhupāda and all the *ācāryas* in disciplic succession.

Where are You, Kṛṣṇa? Are you hiding in my heart? Are you hiding in the kuñjas? Why are You not before me? Are you trying to increase my love for You? But it's awfully hard not to be with You now, not to see You, not to touch You. Where are You? I know You are everywhere—in the sun, in the moon, in the water, in the beach. So the answer is given by You: You're everywhere. But I want to know where You are in Your cowherd form. Are You running somewhere with the boys? Are You off with the gopīs? Where are You, Kṛṣṇa? Please give me a hint so I can go there and be with You. Give me the privilege. Surely You will let me see You and be with You. It's just a matter of time. This song is only four minutes and eleven seconds long. Is that enough time for me to meet You? Is that enough time for me to find You? Is that enough time for the answer to the question, "Where are You?" I know You're not playing games, at least not malicious games. You're teasing. You want me to increase my love before You appear to me. You want me to cry out with tears and yearning. Where are You? But I know You are present everywhere, so I'm not really bereft. I know You're here. I'm just asking this question so You'll be my hero when You appear in Your yellow dress, carrying a lotus. Then I'll say, "Oh, there You are. Where were You all this time? Where were You? Thank You for appearing."

YOU CAN'T JUST CRY FOREVER. You have to let it calm down eventually, return to some normalcy. But the *gopīs* couldn't stop crying. Neither could Mother Yaśodā. She cried until she became blind. When Kṛṣṇa left them, they were in such sorrow out of separation that they couldn't "dry."

What about ourselves? We rarely have tears. Sometimes we cry tears of self-pity or tears that we're just sorry we're not better devotees. That's rare, and that's good. Those tears dry eventually also. Tears are good. It's good to cry for Kṛṣṇa. Better that we "soak our couch with tears," as Bhaktisiddhānta Sarasvatī Ṭhākura said. You can't actually do it, but that should be the mood. Gour Govinda Mahārāja used to say that Kṛṣṇa consciousness was a "school for crying." Our hearts should be crying for the Lord. Crying out, as in crying out in *kīrtana,* is another way to cry. Cry like the child cries for its mother. That's the recommended method for chanting Hare Kṛṣṇa. So Kṛṣṇa consciousness is not a staid thing. It's a yoga of emotion. We want to reach Kṛṣṇa and Rādhā, and for now, we can't. Nothing to do about it but let the tears dry and hope they'll come back again. Don't resign yourself to just forgetting the whole thing and saying that you're not capable of crying to Kṛṣṇa, and there's no use entering that emotion. Some people fake crying just to get a reputation. We're not talking about that. We're not talking about crocodile tears. Tears of joy, tears of sorrow, tears to Rādhā and Kṛṣṇa.

In *The Nectar of Devotion,* while discussing "further features of ecstatic love for Kṛṣṇa," Śrīla Rūpa Gosvāmī quotes from the *Haṁsadūta:* "One day, when Śrīmatī

Rādhārāṇī was feeling much affliction because of Her separation from Kṛṣṇa, She went to the bank of the Yamunā with some of Her friends. There, Rādhārāṇī saw a cottage wherein She and Kṛṣṇa had experienced many loving pleasures, and by remembering those incidents, She immediately became overcome with dizziness. This dizziness was very prominently visible."[79] Śrīla Prabhupāda remarks, "This is an instance of confusion caused by separation."[80]

A crying song. It reminds you of Śrīmatī Rādhārāṇī crying out for the absent Kṛṣṇa. Ornette cries on his horn. The lonely woman has no one in the world to turn to. She cries tears down her face. She's restless and doesn't know what to do with herself. At least Śrīmatī Rādhārāṇī had lots of *sakhīs* to console Her. But they couldn't reach Her, not Her loneliness, and She cried out, "Where has Kṛṣṇa gone? When will He come back? He promised He will return. Will He ever return? Will I ever feel the touch of His *aguru*-scented hand again?"[81]

Loneliness is a sad state. All you've got is memories, burnt-out memories. There's a popular song, "The way you wear your hat, the way you sip your tea, oh no, they can't take that way from me."[82] There are some memories that they can't take away even if you are lonely and without the person.

---

79 Śrīla Rūpa Gosvāmī, *Śrī Haṁsadūta*, 1.3. cited in *Nectar of Devotion—The Complete Science of Bhakti Yoga. (A Summary Study of Śrīla Rūpa Gosvāmī's Bhakti-rasāmṛta-sindhu)* (New York: Bhaktivedanta Book Trust, 1970).

80 *Ibid.*

81 *Bhag* 10.47.21 also cited in *Caitanya-caritamrta*, Adi, 6.68.

82 George and Ira Gershwin, "They Can't Take That Away From Me," 1937.

The residents of Vraja were lonely. Only they *knew* the *viraha*, the separation from Kṛṣṇa. Only they knew the core of loneliness because they loved Kṛṣṇa so much. It's a great mystery in Kṛṣṇa consciousness how this loneliness is actually a great treasure to them, because when they weren't with Kṛṣṇa, they were *actually* with Him in a more intense way. As Lord Caitanya, He told His mother that He used to go and visit her every day and take lunch from her, and so she should be confident of it and not cry. But she was lonely without her Nimāi. Kṛṣṇa asked Sudāmā to wait for Him and that He would come back to Vraja. Sudāmā stood there and waited and waited for many years, but Kṛṣṇa never returned. His heart broke with loneliness. But it's that *viraha*, a gem of joy within the lonely heart because he recalls, and in that way he's actually present more intensely with his Beloved. Yet only the lonely feel such pain. They have no more times with their beloved. He's gone. Life is not worth living. That's how they feel. It's hard to understand. You have to be a lover.

What about Prabhupāda? He was present as the giver of the holy name. He handed me the *mālā* of big, red *japa* beads after chanting on them. When he gave me my beads, I bowed at his feet and swooned, chanting the mantra: *nama oṁ viṣṇu-pādāya kṛṣṇa-preṣṭhāya bhūtale/ śrīmate bhaktivedānta svāmin iti nāmine.*

APPRECIATION IN LOVE

śrī-dayita-dāsa, kīrtanete āśa,
kara uccaiḥ-svare 'hari-nāma-rava'
kīrtana-prabhāve, smaraṇa svabhāve,
se kāle bhajana-nirjana sambhāva

"This Dayita dāsa[83] simply desires to be absorbed in the nectar of chanting the glories of Kṛṣṇa's holy names. My dear mind, now let's loudly chant the holy names of Kṛṣṇa so we can continuously remain in the ocean of transcendental nectar. The congregational chanting of the holy names of Kṛṣṇa awakens the transcendental quality of natural spontaneous loving remembrance of Śrī Kṛṣṇa. At this moment the confidential realization and the pure practice of "solitary" loving devotional service to Their Lordships Śrī Śrī Rādhā-Kṛṣṇa becomes possible."

—Bhaktisiddhānta Sarasvatī Ṭhākura, *Vaiṣṇava Ke*

ONCE, IN A BIG CLASS OF DEVOTEES, someone asked Śrīla Prabhupāda, "Prabhupāda, what will really please you the most?" Some devotees were anticipating that Prabhupāda would say, "That you distribute my books." But Prabhupāda answered, "That you love Kṛṣṇa."

Japa is the quiet prayer. You say it loud enough so you can hear it, but it's mostly for yourself. Rādhā and Kṛṣṇa can hear you. They're close by, so you don't have to shout.

83 "*Śrī-dayita-dāsa*"—name of Śrīla Bhaktisiddhānta Sarasvatī Ṭhākura—the humble servitor of the all-merciful Śrīmatī Rādhārāṇī.

But They're listening carefully, so you pronounce with great care. Put your heart into it. "Hear me, Lord: Hare Kṛṣṇa, Hare Kṛṣṇa, Kṛṣṇa Kṛṣṇa, Hare Hare/ Hare Rāma, Hare Rāma, Rāma Rāma, Hare Hare. Over and over the thirty-two syllables are repeated. You bear down on them like a baseball pitcher who's come in to save the game. The pressure is on you to strike them out. You keep your composure, fast but not too fast. Pace yourself. It's also mental. It's not just throwing out the names. It's saying them so you can hear them and Kṛṣṇa can hear them.

Śrīla Prabhupāda taught us how to chant. Don't touch the beads with the index finger, use your thumb and third finger and rub the beads between them. The index finger pokes through the hole at the side of the bead bag. You rub and rub. Sometimes you rub a blister. Come to the end of the circle of the beads and then stop at the head bead and start back. Keep careful to count so you know how many you've said. Don't be slack in that. Don't chant on the head bead,[84] but stop just before it and then head back. Head back quickly. At first, you've only done a few, but then you're one third through, then one half through, then two thirds through, then you're almost through again. Another round. You're at the head bead again, and you turn back and go the other direction. Don't think of it just as a mechanical thing. You're going and coming are just your routine. The main thing is to get deeper into the meditation on the holy names. Deeper and deeper, hearing the sound. Gradually you begin to awaken to the fact that the name is Kṛṣṇa, and all you have to do is say it clearly. It's easier than you thought. You increase your concentration, and you pick up speed. Other thoughts leave you. Drowsiness leaves you. Your head is clear. You're chanting successfully, by Kṛṣṇa's grace. More and more, you accumulate the rounds, and

---

84 One *mantra* is said for every bead. When arriving at the head bead, the largest bead, usually with the tassel, one turns the *japa-mala* beads around and then goes back in the same direction.

more and more you hear them in your mind. This is how to chant successfully.

My dear Lord Kṛṣṇa, I finished my sixteen rounds. But I will not be able to chant the extra hour and a half. I want to spend some time writing to You. I know You through the scriptures. For the devotees, You are the swift deliverer from death. In Your original form, You are humanlike—a beautiful adolescent in Your topmost form. Everyone loves You in Vṛndāvana, and Śrīmatī Rādhārāṇī loves You the most. Even the cows and trees love You, and Your parents and younger and older *gopas* and *gopīs.* This is your confidential form in Goloka Vṛndāvana. It is rare for a spirit soul to enter this spotless *nara-līlā* with You, but it is possible for all living beings. One has to contact a pure devotee spiritual master and take shelter of him. He can recommend you to Kṛṣṇa. But we have to be a hundred percent detached from material pleasures and a hundred percent inclined to satisfy You. If we hold onto the lotus feet of the spiritual master, You may accept us even if we are not perfect. That is why it is so important to follow Śrīla Prabhupāda, exactly as he trained us, so that he will recognize us and recommend us to his Lord.

Rādhā and Kṛṣṇa are the epitome of service and worship. Their pastimes are the purest and most sublime and may be appreciated only by the rarest connoisseurs of spiritual culture. You, Rādhā, and You, Kṛṣṇa, are my Lords. Your relationship is the sweetest thing in all the worlds. I beg to be cleansed of material dirt so that I can approach You in Goloka Vṛndāvana.

Words cannot describe the beauty
of Kṛṣṇa's face. Words cannot describe

the thrill the *gopīs* feel in His embrace.
Words cannot describe the pain
that Rādhārāṇī feels in Kṛṣṇa's
separation.

Words cannot describe Her hot tears,
the uselessness of words
of consolation.

Words cannot describe Her joy
on seeing Him return in the evening
with the cows and Their exchange of
sidelong glances.

Words cannot describe Rādhā's joy
at Kṛṣṇa's touch. Words cannot describe
because the feeling is too much.
Words cannot describe the lover's bliss
in their tryst. Words cannot describe
but I'll attempt it if you insist.

It's like the happiness
a million times better than when Śiva
and Pārvatī get together.
It's like the ocean of bliss
increasing, it's like
the highest taste unceasing, increasing
until there's no end in sight,
it's like an unending night of love
that words cannot describe.

gītvā ca mama nāmāni vicaren mama sannidhau
iti vravīmi te satyaṁ krīto 'haṁ tasya cārjuna

"They who chant My name and thus live with Me – I promise to you, that I give Myself to them, O Arjuna!"

—Ādi Purāṇa[85]

I united Rādhā-Kṛṣṇa to Hare Kṛṣṇa by the simple method of seeing the Deities and having faith that the name is Rādhā and Kṛṣṇa. I had some desire to chant well and invested my feelings in the chanting. I paid attention to the syllables of the mantra and didn't wander to other things. But it was hard not to be distracted by my shoulder. On Thursday I will find out what's wrong with it and what further work has to be done. Until then, my mind will be occupied with it. So the best thing was that I did chant at a decent pace. The weakest thing was my lack of concentration.

I'm waiting for the miracle,
the big change to take place. My chanting
will transform to *śuddha-nāma,* and
I'll see Kṛṣṇa's face.

I"m waiting for the miracle, my change
into a preacher bold who speaks to many
people and converts them to devotees.
I'm waiting for the miracle, where ISKCON
becomes a loving home of friendly,
noncompetitive people.

---

85 As quoted in *Bhakti-rasamrta-sindhu*, 1.2.231.

I'm waiting for the miracle where
millions will start chanting
Hare Kṛṣṇa and stop eating meat.
But better not expect the miracles
to take place. Be realistic and work
humbly at an average pace.

It's up to Kṛṣṇa to make miracles,
and all that we can do is stay at our duty
and be true to our guru.

Lord Kṛṣṇa manifested His all-pervasive form so all the cowherd boys could simultaneously massage His legs when He was fatigued. They sang sweet songs in soft voices about His pastimes, putting Him to sleep. The boys were free from sins, and their only desire was to please Kṛṣṇa. They are called *mahātmās,* and the word also applies to Kṛṣṇa. Mother Yaśodā was the most fortunate of all of Kṛṣṇa's mothers, including Devakī, because she got to enjoy Kṛṣṇa's babyhood and boyhood pastimes, and more than any other mother, she gave Kṛṣṇa her breast milk to be sucked by Him.

Sanātana Gosvāmī gives half a dozen meanings for a word in his *Bṛhad-bhāgavatāmṛta* commentary. In one verse, he addresses Mahārāja Pariksit as "*mahā-rāja.*" In addition to expected meanings regarding "*mahā-rāja,*" another meaning is as follows: "Or else the term may indicate that the fondness cherished by the cowherd boys for Kṛṣṇa is supremely splendid; it is the *mahā-rāja* of loving sentiments. Although this *sneha,* or love, is always present within the boys, in this setting of intimate service, it now rises to the peak of its potency. It radiates with infinite brilliance, leaving all contamination far behind."[86]

86 *Bb* 2.7.125, commentary in Sanātana Gosvāmī, *Śrī Bṛhad-Bhāgavatāmṛta of Śrīla Sanātana Gosvāmī.* Trans. Gopīparāṇadhana dāsa. Vol. 3, (Los Angeles: Bhaktivedanta Book Trust, 2002), 736-737.

5:14 A.M. I had trouble getting to sleep last night because of troubling thoughts. I woke up at a little past 3:00 A.M. and hurried to the bathroom. Nārāyaṇa-kavaca came up, and we had a conciliatory talk, which was nice. Because I began my *japa* late, I concentrated on speed and accumulation. I glanced frequently to my Rādhā-Govinda Deities. We changed Their outfits yesterday. They are wearing simple Vṛndāvana village-like outfits made by Mother Surabhi.

They are a turquoise color with orange trim, but not so much in the Lakṣmī-Nārāyaṇa style as in the Vraja style. They caught my attention during the whole *japa* period, which was nice. I chanted quickly, six and a half minutes per round. I was alert the whole time and paid attention to the mantras. I can't say more than that. Deeper absorption into Nāma Prabhu will have to come in the future. But I was bright-eyed and bushy-tailed during the whole period. I did not lag.

The chanter looks at
the *arcā-vigraha.* They
encourage him, "You
are chanting to Us." The
names merge into Their forms,
and it's a pleasing combination.

He vibrates and looks upon
the peeping lotus feet of Kṛṣṇa,
he utters and sees Rādhā's delicate hand.
You could do much better,
but to have your own
Rādhā-Govinda cheering

you on is a fine benediction,
and you're grateful for it.

Someday you'll get better
in fixing the mind on
the deeper meanings of
this combination, and
you'll be really chanting Hare Kṛṣṇa.

Reality

It's not just a dream, it's reality to be here writing. It is spiritual reality to see Prabhupāda's picture on the desk. I'm still tied to this world via my body and my identification with its dreams. When my chest feels cold and I can't sleep, that becomes my reality. The *gopīs* of Vṛndāvana forget everything except Kṛṣṇa. They think of Him—His pastimes, form, name and qualities. They have no need for "soul searching" or writing methods or performance of *bhakti-yoga* as done by Śrīla Vyasadeva. The *gopīs* were in *sahajya samādhi,* natural trance. If they spoke to someone, they were in Kṛṣṇa conscious *samādhi.* Neither do they perform *sādhana.* They always think of Kṛṣṇa and their desire for His happiness. They want to make Him happy. Remembering Kṛṣṇa is their "meditation" or *dhyāna.*

It's not false to rise and want to write, but I must purify any impure motives. Remember the best pastimes of Kṛṣṇa; service those *līlās* by faithfully hearing and chanting.

In a sense, writing is a warmup to chanting. I beg that my mantra chanting may be filled with thoughts of Kṛṣṇa in Vṛndāvana.

Our delight is to sing *kīrtana,* to utter
names, to write poems about Kṛṣṇa.
To walk with a friend in predawn chanting.
we have down time in this body with
pains, but delight is the greater factor.

Our delight is to see Rādhā-Govinda in
the half-light. They emanate Their
peaceful, conjugal communion in the
arcā vigraha. We experience delight in
hearing music from the holy sphere,
driving and swinging wordless *kīrtanas*
from our heroes.

A devotee has a life of delights, even as
he grows old. He takes on burdens for
Kṛṣṇa, but feels satisfied to take
the responsibility.

Delight is not always outward, it's
inward in a silent, private way. It's
between you and Kṛṣṇa.
If you know you please your spiritual
master, that's a delight for sure:
his pleasure.

Our delight is not in sense gratification,
it's not taking a drink or a woman or
making a lot of money.

Our delight is in devotional service to
Kṛṣṇa, getting an inkling that He's
present in our life, in our daily acts

performed for Him.

Our delight is ecstatic, touching the
supreme enjoyer in a service mood.
It's delight to spend time on the beads
pronouncing His names and counting
up the quota. If we lack delight,
it's because we're in the neophyte
stage and do our service as mere duty.

To taste delight, you need the greed to
service the Almighty in His
friendly form.

Delight is in Goloka, where walking
is a dance, the flute is the constant
companion, and speech is song.

Please find delight by giving up
the attempt to find it in the body
and the selfish mind.
Serve others and take delight from
delightful Govinda.

THERE IS STARDUST IN THE SPIRITUAL WORLD. It floats in the sky and illuminates the pastimes of Rādhā and Kṛṣṇa. It is a spiritual illumination, unlike the stars in the material world. When there is too much stardust, Rādhārāṇī wears Her white clothing so she will not be seen as She travels incognito to the rendezvous.

Kṛṣṇa is Rādhā's lover-man. Without Him, She dries up like an unwatered lotus flower, and Her *sakhīs* have to save Her life by extreme measures. She needs Her lover-man.

Flowers are blooming in Goloka. The does and bucks and fawns are wandering on Govardhana Hill. The cowherd boys are herding their unlimited numbers of calves, and Kṛṣṇa is leading them all.

There are no worries in Goloka, only rumors of demons. The boys play with Kṛṣṇa, take lunch and bathe in the river. When they eat, they sit in a circle, and each boy is thinking that Kṛṣṇa is looking only at him. Summer is in the air, and everything is slow. It's hot, but not overbearing, because it's the spiritual world. They can always go for a dip in the Yamunā. The calves walk delicately and wander in search of better grasses. Sometimes the boys neglect to follow them, and Kṛṣṇa has to go alone and gather them. These are summer pastimes, enjoyable to Kṛṣṇa and His devotees everywhere in the world. There's a nice melody that accentuates it.

Chanting Hare Kṛṣṇa, coming through the fog.
Don't be afraid
to push the accelerator, it won't do you harm.
Turn your head to Rādhā-Govinda
and think of Their love.

Immerse yourself in
pastimes and qualities
along with the form and shape of the syllables,
the speed and the accumulation.
Don't go forgetful,
don't go off the road and
do all these things
and you'll improve
and lose your anxious
fall-behind mode.

Chanting *japa* calmly with a physical impediment is peaceful. I'm careful not to push too hard. I hear each syllable carefully. It's a little slower than usual. I take shelter of Kṛṣṇa and sail along through calm waters. Chanting should not be frantic. It should be a fixed process, keeping an even pace. If you have Deities to look upon, that's an added benefit. They shine upon you, giving grace and reminding you Whose names you're chanting. Rādhā-Govinda are lovely and give me peace. I keep awake and alert, even though in the comfort zone. That is very important. Don't doze off in the name of peaceful chanting. I keep my mind optimistic and try to look at the good side of things. I don't think of myself as a bad chanter. Strive well. You can urge yourself, "I'm chanting nicely," and actually do it. The time goes by, and I accumulate the rounds, and that's good news. It was good to get up early. I got a jump on things. I'll now chant my *gāyatrī* and then continue chanting at a moderate pace.

You are the most merciful in Your forms of Gaura-Nitāi. You deliver the Hare Kṛṣṇa mantra, the easiest form of deliverance. I did not chant it well today. But I will have another chance this afternoon. All you have to do is utter the names and pay attention. It can bring you back to Godhead.

Back to Godhead is where Kṛṣṇa plays in His humanlike form. Sometimes the *gopas* and *gopīs* predominate Him. His mother scolds Him. He loves this treatment the most. Love in awe and reverence cripples the affection because there is too much formality. Kṛṣṇa prefers the familiarity of His dear ones. "What kind of a big man are You?," say His pals, and they climb onto His back. "Don't let Kṛṣṇa come into the *kuñja,*" says Rādhārāṇī, and She forbids Her dearmost from entering. "Kṛṣṇa! Tie Him with ropes," says His mother, but the ropes come up two finger lengths short.

Kṛṣṇa, You are my Lord. You are the one I trust. I read about Your splendor and how You control the material and spiritual worlds. I am isolated without You; I am lonely without You. I am guilty from not associating more with Your devotees. But You allow me to come to You also. You see my attempt to reach You as sincere.

I approach You, and You do not kick me away. You extend Your hand to me. You accept my voice. You believe my words. You take me to You. I believe all this because You are the most honest and trusting person, and You want me to live with You. Therefore You are the most wonderful person, and I offer myself to You. I pray that in the future, I will be awakened to take up personal service to You and run by Your side forever.

In free writing, you daydream that you reach Kṛṣṇaloka on a swan-carrier plane. You are taken there by hearing the nectar of Rādhā-Kṛṣṇa from a guru like Sarūpa. He transforms you from a raw recruit to a lover of Madana-gopāla. You give up all material attachment and anxieties and go to the highest spiritual planet. It happens in less than a second. You are in the forests of Vraja, and you hear the flute and fall down unconscious in transcendental bliss. Then the Lord approaches you and picks up your body and caresses you. You swoon, but He brings you to consciousness again and speaks to you. He says He has been waiting a long time for you to come. He says, "You can stay with Sarūpa and live in Goloka," and the other boys are cheered to hear this. You have never been so happy, but you don't know what to do, so you place your head on His feet. He lifts you and looks you in the face. You are given the service of assisting with the cows.

The calves have long eyelashes and big eyes. They are not troubled by mosquitos. They suck the milk from their mothers' udders. When they hear the sound of Kṛṣṇa's flute, they stop sucking the milk and stand there, transfixed by the sound vibrations. The birds fly overhead and cry out with blissful melodies. The does and bucks walk forward together to glance at Kṛṣṇa's form. Even the lions and tigers watch peacefully with no enmity toward the other creatures. The peacocks open their wings into a fan and dance with their consorts. The boys play games with balls and wrestle with Kṛṣṇa and tease the demigods. From their houses, the *gopīs* cast sidelong glances at Kṛṣṇa, and He glances back at them. These glances with the *gopīs* are the most intense exchanges.

Premāññjana-churita-bhakti-vilocanena.
With eyes of love, you can see
Kṛṣṇa in Vṛndāvana.
The eyes have to be smeared
with the ointment of *kṛṣṇa-prema.*

It's a cosmetic not available in
a beauty shop for lovely girls.
It's an eyewash that comes
from the mystical heart of
the *prema-bhakti* yogi
who drops every kind of
beauty aid and perceives only the cowherd boy
and Rādhārāṇī on the path
to the Yamunā. He cries out, "Oh when
will They pass again
across the pathway

to my eyes?" Otherwise,
he sees the world as void.

With me, I see all
shiny things and men
and women with
candy and cigarettes. I'm not straining to block
out the maya and only see the best.
Where is Kṛṣṇa?
Who has seen Him last?

Is He at Govardhana or
in the temple Deity
or in a pure heart best?
Who is seeking Him out,
and Rādhā, too? He's not at the zoo
or the baseball park
or the TV show,
don't look for Him there.
Learn not to see Him
with your material eyes,
and seek Him in your heart
in the sound of *harināma*
in the yearning mind. Surely you will find
Him where the pure devotees
dwell. Go to the well
of His pastimes,
go to your lonely heart.

All the young *gopīs* of Vraja fall in love with Kṛṣṇa. He satisfies them with the *rāsa* dance, the topmost of His pastimes. They dance in a circle, and Kṛṣṇa expands Himself and stands between each *gopī* holding her hand. By the power of *yogamāyā*, each *gopī* thinks that Kṛṣṇa is dancing alone with her. Dissatisfied that Kṛṣṇa is not with Her alone, Rādhā leaves the *rasa* dance. Kṛṣṇa becomes dissatisfied with the dance and leaves in search of Rādhā. He finds Her, and they walk together. He makes a flower garland for Her, but suddenly deserts Her, leaving Her in great distress. The other *gopīs* find Her, and in sympathy, they all go searching for Kṛṣṇa in the forest. After experiencing madness in separation, they finally settle on the bank of the Yamunā, singing songs of Kṛṣṇa. Then Kṛṣṇa, moved by their grief, returns to them, and they sit together talking. They again take up pastimes, and the *rāsa* dance goes on for the duration of a day of Brahmā. The dawn finally comes, and each *gopī* returns to her home.[87]

The *rāsa* dance is told in the Tenth Canto of the *Śrīmad-Bhāgavatam,* and many of the *ācāryas* have put it in their poems. In the *Śrīmad-Bhāgavatam,* at the end of the *rāsa* dance, Sukadeva Gosvāmī says that anyone who hears it will be free from lust in the heart.

In just a few minutes, I get into my space capsule and shoot off into the spiritual world of *japa-yajña.* This will be the first hour for today. All paraphernalia is ready—the altar, the *japa-mālā,* the stopwatch, my willingness. I know I'll hit the brick wall and will disperse in many directions. I can't prevent that. But I can keep going and keep trying for a break in the weather conditions. I mean *looking* for a break. It may not occur. He may handle me roughly in His embrace. (What a statement! If He does embrace me, why complain, "It was rough. He's not gentle." Be glad you are embraced.) Or He may neglect me and not come before me as I chant His name. Even in pure sound He may not be willing to come.

87 *Bhag.* 10.33.

Then I chant the covered sound or *nāmā-ābhāsa,* or *nāma-aparādha.* Face the facts of my limits. Go on. See the virtue in *utsāhān niścayād dhairyāt.* Enthusiasm and patience.[88]

This is a warm-up. I hope to be a little more aware than usual. I hope to not so fully allow myself to think over memories and plans while chanting. Then why not get the benefit of being here? I'm here, now make an effort, some gain, at least whatever is possible by my endeavor. It may be very small, but try for it.

Japa should not be chanted on automatic pilot. It should not be done unconsciously. It is a conscious deliberation. Unless you're conscious, you can't go deep. Going deep means thinking of the mantras and their meaning, listening carefully to the enunciation of the syllables. I think this is a very important distinction I just covered: unconscious and conscious chanting. Nārāyaṇa asked me if I was worried about anything. I told him I was disturbed by my late chanting. He said that won't do any good, and of course, he's right. I should be assured that I'll get my rounds done when I come back from the beach. Just don't ruin the chanting by rushing and chanting without thought. There's no point in rushing the rounds. I have enough time in the day for good chanting, for deep chanting. Go all the way down to thinking that you're chanting to Rādhā and Kṛṣṇa, and be eager for Their reciprocation through the sound vibration. Don't push the mantras through your mouth so quickly so that it's like eating quickly, which is a bad habit, and unhealthy. Chanting quickly is fine as long as you keep your concentration and your meditation. If you find yourself just chanting to get them done, then you know you're going too fast or too thoughtlessly. The idea that I have to have eight or ten done before I leave

---

88 Śrīla Rūpa Gosvāmī, Verse 3 in Śrīla A.C. Bhaktivedanta Swami Prabhupāda, *Nectar of Instruction* (London: The Bhaktivedanta Book Trust, 1975).

the house is an artificial construction. Just be patient. Everything will get done.

I wanted to chant with care in my moral or spiritual feelings towards Nāma Prabhu. Seeing Rādhā-Govinda helped because They are tenderness personified. I wanted to chant like a lover. I chanted in a subdued way, because I had to because of my head. But it also lent itself toward feelings of warmth and sympathy, gentle and delicate. One should handle the holy name in that way. It was a nice feeling. I'd like to always chant in that way. Nārāyaṇa-kavaca was in and out of my room, kindly arranging my things, but I continued to chant. I've chanted twelve rounds. They were good rounds, listening to the holy names and trying to appreciate as they passed through my mind. Kṛṣṇa's so kind to come in this way. The early morning is such a great opportunity.

I finished sixteen rounds by 4:50 A.M. It was a satisfying session. The most important thing was that I was alert and awake. Drowsiness is deadly. I skipped through the mantras with rapid accumulation and attention to the syllables.

The path from Mathurā to Vṛndāvana is described to Uddhava by Kṛṣṇa as He asks Uddhava to go there to give relief to the *gopīs*. The places of His favorite pastimes are pointed out. This is in *Uddhava-sandesa*[89]. The opposte route, from Vṛndāvana to Dvārakā, is pointed out by Lalitā *sakhī* to the swan in *Haṁsadūta*[90]. The swan can see the *rasa stalis* from the sky. Suddenly I thought I was taking part in Kṛṣṇa's pastimes. The words of the poet brought me

89 Śrīla Rūpa Gosvāmī, *Uddhava-sandeśa*, 3-35.

90 Śrīla Rūpa Gosvāmī, *Śrī Haṁsadūta*, 6-97.

into Kṛṣṇa's presence. He was crying tears of pity and love from His eyes. He didn't want to cause pain to the cowherd people by letting them know the pain that He was in.

I just took a nap, and now the morning is getting late. Rādhā-Govinda are wearing lovely yellow and blue outfits that were sent from Vṛndāvana. Yesterday, Nārāyaṇa, with my help, bathed the Deities, polishing Them with *gopī candana,* and changed Them into Their new outfits. I am grateful They are here and lift up my spirits. They bring a Vṛndāvana atmosphere to the yellow submarine. My inability to put something into the free write speaks of the emptiness of my life. But it is just a superficial silence. There is a covering over a bubbling, interesting consciousness. It is a writing block. I have an interest in life, but it is covered by a pot-covering. It is foolish to think I have nothing to say. If I allowed myself, I would gush force with expressions from many worlds.

As you chant, you come to life again. I'm glad it's this way. Chanting has become such an important part of my life. I must begin to chant on waking. I panic when I wake late, and this isn't necessary, because I always catch up. The anxiety is there because I so much prefer the early beginning. The mantras are offered to Rādhā and Kṛṣṇa, and I'm aware of this. Nothing could be more important. I don't have to figure out why it is so. It has just developed that way in my life. Prayers to the Lord come first. Not just one prayer, they have to accumulate, up towards the quota. And I strive to do them with quality, paying attention and staying awake. I was able to do this this morning, so I have some relief in my mind. But I have a long way to go. Let me pray not to become drowsy but to keep up the pace I've begun so far and not lapse into a dreadful slow pace, as

I did in that last round. I'm happy to be chanting and to be alive in the holy names. There is nothing so refreshing and life-giving as chanting the *mahā-mantra*. This is my religion, and my religion is the most crucial element in my life, beyond eating and sleeping. And so I've come out of a *zombie state*, and I'm a human being again, sailing in the *japa* waters.

Japa is the life breath,
the form of meditation
of the Gauḍīya Vaiṣṇavas.
I'm a chanter among them,
breathing for life, living for chanting.

Kṛṣṇa'll be pleased with me
for chanting His names—
Rādhā and Kṛṣṇa
Rādhā and Kṛṣṇa.
The Divine Couple who reciprocate with me
when I utter Their holy names.

6:45 A.M. The concept that becoming a *gopī mañjarī* is the highest goal for all Gauḍīya Vaiṣṇavas was intriguing, but when I went on to read *Ujjvala-nilamani.* I found the amorous details to be too intimate, and they disturbed me, so I stopped reading the book. A devotee quoted to me a saying by Sridhara Swami: "Don't think that if you don't read *Ujjvala-nilamani,* you can't become a pure devotee." I'm still interested in the *madhurya* rasa, but I'm not reading any of the pure *rasika* books right now. It seems these interests come in phases at different times in your life, when you feel you need them or you don't.

Tonight Guṇagrahi Mahārāja is coming to visit me, and we will do some reading. We haven't chose yet what to read, but I would like to save *Bṛhad-bhāgavatāmṛta* for the mealtime readings. Reading books is the perfect activity for those few hours after I finish the journal and before I start my evening *japa.*

Not a Dream

Śrī Rūpa Mañjarī's
verses like "I do not
know how much nectar
these two syllables contain"
and ". . . my mind hankers
for the forest by the
banks of the Yamunā,
where the fifth note of His flute
reverberated softly within my heart."

The great devotees
gathered at Haridāsa Ṭhākura's house
and savored these verses
and praised the humble *kavi.*
Swamiji was in his room,
and we read some poems
to him. Mine had a line
that when I'm chanting Hare Kṛṣṇa,
my pleasure is so great
I'm afraid I'll be swept
across the sky and
taken to Indra's planet.
It was NYC beat style
free verse. He smiled
and nodded, "very nice."

Then I *was* ready to
fly across the sky!
He said it could go in our
Back to Godhead.
Oh Swamiji! You
approved that kind
of poem![91]
You were so liberal
and literary
and kind.

Early morning is the most crucial time of the day for chanting Hare Kṛṣṇa. I try to keep alert. Soon we will be going down to the beach, and that will be a testing time, as I tend to get drowsy then. Still, it's a good time. I take great pleasure in the accumulation of the rounds but get a little anxious about pushing to get them up. I should not be so obsessed in upping the count but should concentrate more on the beauty and meaning of the names. Hare Kṛṣṇa is an all-around practice, including saying the names clearly with your mouth and tongue and absorbing your mind in thoughts of Rādhā and Kṛṣṇa. All the *ācāryas* in the line of Lord Caitanya have given great emphasis on the importance of their chanting, and I'm following in their footsteps. They achieved the platform where they were completely in love with chanting and said things in their prayers that indicated the chanting was everything to them and that they loved it deliriously. They knew that chanting was Kṛṣṇa Himself. They were involuntarily attached to the repetitions of the names. They couldn't let go. They were captured. I have a little of that quality,

91 *Back to Godhead* Magazine, 6 (January 20, 1967).

too, where I can't let go of the chanting and go on and on with it for my quota. It's a wonderful thing to be attached to the chanting, where you can't let go. You don't want to be interrupted by anyone else's talking. You want to concentrate and not be distracted by other events. You just want to chant. This is a good sign of the advancing stage. Oh chanting of Hare Kṛṣṇa, don't let me go, don't let me stop, keep coming through my mouth. Let me think of you more deeply. When this attachment grows, you feel good about it. You press on to increase it and stick like glue to the *mahā-mantras* ("Please don't bother me, I'm chanting Hare Kṛṣṇa").

From the Japa Log

I woke up at 11:30 P.M. last night and couldn't get any sound sleep thereafter. I got up from bed at 1:45 A.M. Fortunately, I was alert and awake during *japa*. But I didn't have a feeling of tenderness in chanting the holy name that I had yesterday. It was more like a shovel tractor digging up macadam on a city street. But I was consistent, working constantly name after name. I chanted all sixteen rounds in a row. I was not distracted. My mind was too scrambled to keep count of the individual rounds, but it was speedy, although not rushed. I think it was a conscientious morning workout, although not done with finesse or deep meditation. I leaned heavily on the names themselves and trusted in their potency. I'll do this every day for the rest of my life.

> Chanting vigorously through
> sixteen rounds in two hours. A
> no-nonsense session of a blue-collar
> worker. He didn't stop to gaze

upon Rādhā-Govinda but trusted that
Nāma Prabhu is as good as His form.
No delicate savoring today, but
pushing like a farmer with his
ox and plow. There are many varieties
to *japa* on your different days.
On this one, I worked muscularly
and lacked a finer sense.

When Gargamuni first saw baby Kṛṣṇa, his body manifested ecstatic symptoms. His hair stood erect, and he experienced mental bewilderment. He thought he had come there to do the name-giving ceremony, but if his joyous state continued, it would be impossible for him to do it. He thought if he held onto Kṛṣṇa's feet, people would think, "Gargamuni has gone crazy." If he embraced Him to his chest, they would say he was acting frivolously. If he held back and did nothing, he would be filled with anxiety and lose his patience. "But never mind," he thought. Today his life had become really fortunate. His eyes had attained perfection, his learning and exalted birth had become blessed.[92]

There are no hard and fast rules in chanting the holy names of Kṛṣṇa. You can even sit in a chair if you have a bad back. Śrīla Prabhupāda didn't like to see devotees rapidly jouncing their leg. He would even point it out and say, "Sit properly," or "Don't move your leg." He also didn't like it if he saw a whole room full of young men slouching. But I think any posture in which one is not indulging in "sleepy time" positions is acceptable. Devotees can even walk back

92 Śrīla Kavi-karṇapūra, *Ānanda-vṛndāvana-campū*. Trans. Bhanu and Subhag Swami, Ed. Mahanidhi Swami (Mayapur, 1999), 51.

and forth if they get tired. The main point is not to assume a particular asana but to keep awake and to chant with attention. Chanting with attention means hearing the chanting with your ears and keeping your mind focused. It means not dwelling on other thoughts, aside from the syllables of the Hare Kṛṣṇa mantra. Thinking deeply of the meanings of the words and meditating fondly on Rādhā and Kṛṣṇa is even better.

Śrīla Prabhupāda once imitated slurring chanting and said, "Not like that, but with *prīti*, with love."[93] We should take the care to make the proper enunciation. "Kṛṣ-ṇa" should not be cut off to "Krish." "Rā-ma" should not be cut off to "Ra." And we should not become so inattentive that the actual order of the words is mixed up. When you roll quickly in a smooth rhythm, these problems are ironed out. It doesn't happen automatically or mechanically but with mental supervision of what you are saying. One cannot keep it on automatic pilot. Always steer your "plane" through the full mantra. "Am I chanting fast enough?," "Am I hearing all the names?," "Am I thinking of Rādhā and Kṛṣṇa?"—these should always be on our mind.

Hearing sweet sounds
and enjoying them,
working with attention,
in a serious mood—
these are the components
of a successful *japa* session,
and always remembering Rādhā and Kṛṣṇa
the objects of the meditation.

It's an easy exercise,
but must be kept up at length,
a marathon of speaking,

93 Śrīla A.C. Bhaktivedanta Swami Prabhupāda, Lecture on *Bhag. 1.10.2* (Mayapur, India, June 6, 1973), available in digital form from www.vedabase.com

a fixation on the hearing,
it's a pleasant way to pass the time
and the profoundest way to reach the Lord.

I should not be so anxious about being so far behind in my rounds due to rising late. Otherwise, I will spoil the rounds by trying to rush them. Be confident I have enough time in the day to do all my duties. It is probably even good to sleep later.

For so many years, I used to rise at midnight after four hours' sleep and catch an hour nap later in the day. I'm not able or inclined to try that routine again. It is too much stress, and my doctor wants me to get seven hours of uninterrupted sleep. He feels it is an important factor in the chronic headaches, but I am too stubborn to give up early rising and early chanting. I feel the early-morning *japa* log is a good service to devotees, and some of them told me how it helped them in their own struggles to chant early.

The benefit of spiritual duties and the *brāhma-muhūrta* hour[94] an is emphasized in the scriptures. It is also experienced by any devotee who is able to chant at that peaceful hour of the day. So I'm going to try continuing "early to bed and early to rise," even if it creates a strain on the body.

6:47 A.M. In Vṛndāvana, Śrīla Prabhupāda took the devotees on *parikramā*. In each place, he told the pastimes of Kṛṣṇa in a very animated way, and the devotees were delighted.

94 *Brāhma-muhūrta* refers to an auspicious period of the day just before dawn, from one and a half hours to fifty minutes before sunrise. It is especially favorable for spiritual practices.

Kṛṣṇa used to take the *gopīs* out in a boat on the Yamunā. He would play tricks on them, telling them that the boat was going to sink unless they took off their jewelry and heavy clothing and threw off all the pots of yogurt that they were carrying. Then they finally discovered He was Kṛṣṇa and not just an ordinary boatman, and they became ecstatic. Kṛṣṇa was such a trickster. But they loved it. His voyage was the voyage of maidens, the cowherd maidens. But He took them many times across the Yamunā, and they loved it every time. Sometimes He said that a storm was coming, and sometimes He told them that the boat could not move because it was too heavy. He tried all kinds of tricks to get them to become more intimate with Him, and He always succeeded. One time He parted the water, like the Red Sea in the Bible, and they crossed without any effort.

Japa essay

As the hours go by and I stay within myself, I feel myself getting closer to the Lord and Śrīmatī Rādhārāṇī. I am more aware of the speed and the accumulation of the rounds than when I am with others. I'm able to concentrate without distraction from loud chanters. I chant humbly and call on my Lord in the sound vibration. My tendency is to chant at a low volume. It helps me to hear myself when I am alone. This is just one person's opinion, but if it helps me, then it's good.

Prabhupāda used to criticize
persons who went alone,
chanting for fame as a
great saintly person.

He also criticized those who
didn't help others but

tried only for their own
salvation.

But I don't think he would mind
a solitary *japa* chanter
who didn't look for fame
but practiced modestly
alone.

As long as he did other
preaching, the chanting alone
is not forbidden.
It is a peaceful way
for concentration,
hours spent alone with the Lord.
It's a way of looking always
to the Lord of the heart
and listening for His response.

I can't do those advanced techniques such as thinking the first pair of names, Hare Kṛṣṇa, means Rādhā and Kṛṣṇa are in *sambhoga* union, and the second pair of Hare Kṛṣṇas means something else, and "Kṛṣṇa Kṛṣṇa" means something else, I *just hear.* I trust the wonderful things are happening while I chant, and now I can glance at Rādhā-Govinda. I am aware that I am at a novice stage, and I'm aware that even the novice stage brings great benefits. Hare Kṛṣṇa is the most powerful kind of devotional service, even when done with some offense. In addition to counting the numbers, you are feeling your desire to chant with devotion. But I don't know what happened today. I lost count and chanted four rounds less than usual. Baldeva asked me if I had been chanting the whole time, and I said yes. He then suggested I give myself credit for the eight rounds, so I'll do so. He said, "I do it all the time." Just as we got ready to go, I developed a headache.

4:30 A.M. I woke up at 10:30 P.M. and then intermittently at 11:00 P.M., 12:00 A.M., and 1:00 A.M. I got up from bed at 1:30 A.M. and began chanting. Despite my sleeplessness, I chanted alertly. It was a typically good session, glancing at Rādhā-Govinda, keeping the *mahā-mantras* close and personal. I chanted at an audible whisper. I did not think of something else but kept focused on the syllables. Nārāyaṇa came up at 3:00 A.M., and we talked considerably. It was nice. But I got back to chanting. I've finished fifteen rounds. It's the best way to spend the early morning.

Alert chanting on your mental toes,
moving quickly through the mantras,
holding them close to your heart,
wherein Kṛṣṇa dwells, as He dwells
in the sound, and you're immersed
in His world of protective piety.

Japa is the art of saying Rādhā and Kṛṣṇa's names with devotion. What do we mean by devotion? You're saying Their names with concentration. You practice to hear them devotionally. In the higher stages, you say them with devotion for the Supreme Persons Rādhā and Kṛṣṇa, with thoughts of Their pastimes together throughout the eight divisions of the day. You are familiar with what They do together, and you meditate on them—the *rāsa* dance, the swing pastimes, the pastimes in the water, amorous pastimes, etc. But in the beginning of *japa*, devotion can mean devotion to the practice of simply hearing the sounds of Hare, Kṛṣṇa, and Rāma. You know at least that this practice is the topmost and easiest *yajña* in Kali Yuga. You have faith that you reciprocate with Rādhā and Kṛṣṇa when you say Their names, so you concentrate on the syllables themselves. It is best not to jump over to prematurely meditating on Rādhā's and Kṛṣṇa's amorous pastimes instead of concentrating on the sound vibration. The powerful sound vibration will lead to the higher realizations.

It is best to sit erect and enunciate the names and hear them stream from your lips and teeth. Have confidence that everything will follow from that. Śrīla Prabhupāda occasionally made remarks that we could think of Rādhā's and Kṛṣṇa'a pastimes while chanting. But his main emphasis was "just hear." Hear with attention and wait for the higher revelations to come. Be humble, and the stages of seeing Kṛṣṇa, meditating on His loving exchanges with Rādhā, thinking of His qualities, and hearing with ecstasy will naturally come.

Japa time is treasure time,
measured out in gold,
done with your best intentions,
keeping on the goal,
Japa time is treasure time,
so don't use it carelessly.

Put your best effort into it
even though distracted
it will count in your favor.

Japa is like a big lake, Rādhā Kuṇḍa. Sometimes you don't feel worthy of bathing in the lake, and you just put drops of water on your head. *Japa* is like a big electric generator, but sometimes you don't need it because the power is on, and you just run on electricity. Sometimes you can't fix your mind on the deeper meaning of *japa* in a mood of servitude, enunciating syllables but not going further than that. Sometimes your body is tired, and that affects the spiritual vibration. After all, it is a bodily function. You need to be fit. It's hard to judge a particular *japa* performance. You get your rounds done so you think it's all right, but in your heart, you know you weren't really praying. But you don't want to bash yourself. After all, you did your quota. The best *japa* players are fast and expert, like good hockey players. You sit back and let *japa* conquer the mind. It has to be an attentive act. The range of *japa* goes from poor to excellent. Excellent *japa* is *samādhi, kṛṣṇa-prema.* Poor *japa* is offensive. Still, it grants you connection with the Lord's holy names. Don't be too hard on yourself or get depressed. You can always bounce back. But there's a place for remorse.

Japa rounds go round
the *mālā*. The mind stays
fixed on the utterance.
You want to chant from your chest
and be filled with vigor, but
sometimes you're not making par.

At times like this, hold
on to the mother monkey,
hold on for dear life
and don't fail in your grip.
Pray for counting
your quota and accumulate your rounds.
Quality is foremost.
It's all the mercy of *gurudeva*,
so cling to his instruction
and call for his grace.

8:43 A.M. You've got no headache, so you've got no excuse. You've got to worship Rādhā's *sakhīs* if you wish to reach Śyāma. No other way is possible. They sarcastically joke with Govinda. You can take their words to mean different things—either, "Govinda, we love You dearly, don't crush the creeper of our devotion to You, please give us service," or "We don't care for You, You are a debauchee who are after other men's wives, we are chaste women, keep away, we're going home." But in their hearts, they're ready to give up everything for Him. They've received the *darśana* of His hair, which is partly exposed under His turban, and when He takes off His turban to rest, they see His hair flowing over his face, and they've seen the other beautiful features of His body, such as His chest, His mouth, His arms, and His feet. These have captured them like birds in nets.

They pick the flowers of Vṛndāvana, and Kṛṣṇa calls them "thieves" of His garden, but they protest that the Vṛndāvana garden belongs to Rādhā. A quarrel ensues between the *gopas* and *gopīs* in which they quote scriptures as to who is actually the ruler of Vṛndāvana. Rādhā comes out triumphant but says She does not want to sit alone on a throne. She wants to share it with Kṛṣṇa and rule Vṛndāvana with Him.

Japa is an all-around function. It involves counting the rounds, being careful to enunciate the syllables, and beyond that, meditating and crying out. You must remember Rādhā and Kṛṣṇa. You are not just an accountant or a statistician. You are a prayer-maker. The counting is necessary to keep order in *vaidhī-bhakti* to assure yourself that you're doing the required quota. But chanting is more than that. Each mantra is a precious jewel, and you examine the facets of the diamond as you utter the mantra. Each mantra is a personal call to Rādhā and Kṛṣṇa, and you beg to reciprocate with Them through the sound vibration. You have trust in the words of the *ācāryas* and the scriptures that the sound vibration is as good as the personal form of the Lord, so you are on very holy ground when you are chanting. You should be alert and reverent in the presence of the vibration. You're making the vibration from your own body, but it is allowed and granted by Kṛṣṇa and Rādhā. They are allowing you to associate with Them through this means. You are not tracking a racehorse with a stopwatch. You are going deep into the mine of love of God, following in the footsteps of great chanters like the Six Gosvāmīs of Vṛndāvana and Haridāsa Ṭhākura. They knew what the chanting was about, and you are their humble follower. You say, "meditate" and "cry out," and you try to follow the words with the appropriate emotions. This is real chanting, the *yajña* of celebrating Kṛṣṇa's presence in the transcendental sound vibration.

"Meditate" means go deeply,
think of what you're doing,
going to Rādhā and Kṛṣṇa.
Don't leave Them out.

"Crying out" means the call.
Like Coltrane, you wail,
you genuinely emote,
seeking to join yourself
to the Divine Couple.
As Swamiji first invited
you with the sign in his
window at 26 2nd Ave.,
it's the "transcendental sound vibration,"
and you're still learning
what it means.

Will Kṛṣṇa let me be
with Him? The answer
is "yes." You have only
to cry clearly and find
your heart.

I get distracted when I'm chanting near a loud chanter. I need to concentrate on my own sound vibration in my own ear drum. It's such a private thing. You're talking to your God and want it to be private, like the penitent in the confessional booth. That's how it's different from *kīrtana,* where everyone wants to join their voices and hear each others' harmonies. I used to like to chant in the car with Bala, who chanted softly. And I can do that with Nārāyaṇa-kavaca also, if he would chant softly. But gung-ho, loud chanters distract me.

You want to savor the sound and meaning of each word. "Hare" is an address to Rādhā, and you want to be able to concentrate on that. And you want to think of Kṛṣṇa distinctly when you say His name and not be intruded upon by someone else's "Kṛṣṇa." And "Rāma," meaning Kṛṣṇa the enjoyer, you want in your own space also. You want to roll out the mantras one after another in your private world. At least that's how I feel about it. I can chant with other quiet chanters, not with loud ones. They seem intrusive and overbearing. Maybe I'll ask him to chant a little more quietly, without being rude about it. Thus we can have consideration for one another.

Chanting mantras in your own world,
you invite Kṛṣṇa to live with you.
Private *bhajana* between you, Rādhā and Kṛṣṇa,
and your reciprocation is intimate.
Kīrtana is public
and *japa* is private.

Both have their place
in the *bhajana* of the holy name.
Some folks like to chant *japa* loudly together.
I'm not one of them
but prefer to snuggle close to my Lord
in my own *bhajana-kuṭīr*
where I talk for His hearing alone.

Kṛṣṇa likes to stroll. He walks along the paths in Vraja with His friends. They pick flowers and minerals, with which they decorate their bodies. They stroll with their cows. It's fun walking along with Kṛṣṇa. Sometimes we stroll in this material world with a friend. That's also fun. But to walk with Kṛṣṇa is something unimaginably sublime. He dotes on His friends and shows them so much affection. They swim in bliss. Strolling with Kṛṣṇa in the pastures of Vraja is the wished-for goal of every living entity, except we don't know it. We look for something else. Kṛṣṇa cries out sometimes when He walks, and the boys laugh. Sometimes while strolling they walk right into a demon, but there's nothing to fear. Kṛṣṇa finishes him off playfully, like breaking a toy doll, and they resume their strolling. They stop only for lunch. Otherwise, you'll find them strolling through the pastures, up the hill, by the riverside, moving the cows before them at a leisurely pace

The boy or girl claims that the other one took advantage of them. "You attracted me to you, and then took advantage of me. You used me for your own purposes." Is this serious? Rādhārāṇī doesn't mean it seriously. She likes it when Kṛṣṇa takes advantage of Her. She wants only to please Him. In the material world, it's different. A man really takes advantage of a woman, uses her for his selfish purposes, for his sense gratification, and then he leaves her. Or the woman does it to the man. But in Kṛṣṇaloka, it's all play. Kṛṣṇa took advantage of the *gopīs* when He took them out on the boat. He told them the boat was too heavy and they had to throw out all their butterpots, and even their heavy jewelry. They were in the middle of the river with Him, and so He took advantage of them in their precarious situation. But when they found out that the boatman was actually Kṛṣṇa, they were delighted and glad to be taken advantage of. Many times, Kṛṣṇa took advantage of the *gopīs*, using His superior power, and they appeared peeved and angry. He even arranged rendezvous with Rādhārāṇī and then didn't show up. She got angry with Him and called him a *lampaṭa,* a debauch. But in Her heart, She never changed Her steady love for Him.

Japa is meant to be concentration on the syllables of the Hare Kṛṣṇa mantra, hearing the words "Hare," "Kṛṣṇa," and "Rāma" and thinking of Rādhā and Kṛṣṇa. An errant chanter allows his mind to drift off into worldly topics and to wander all over the universe. This is offensive chanting. When you chant the mantras side by side with worldly thoughts, you still get the benefit of the chanting, as Ajāmila got the benefit of chanting the name of his son, Nārāyaṇa. You can be cleansed from your sinful reactions even with offensive chanting. But you cannot gain love of Kṛṣṇa by that kind of chanting. Love of Kṛṣṇa comes in the offenseless stage when your mind is fixed on Rādhā and Kṛṣṇa and is free of worldly dross. The more you read news magazines or watch television, the more likely you'll be to think of those things when it's time to chant. A good *japa* chanter keeps his mind chaste without indulging in worldly activities and worldly topics. But do we need to keep informed of the world we live in? Isn't it important to know of the emergencies and catastrophes and political topics? The answer is no. Prabhupāda was once browsing through a *Time* magazine when his servant came into the room. Śrīla Prabhupāda pushed the magazine aside and said, "They make the illusion seem so real."[95] All the pictures and expertly written articles make you think that this is the reality, whereas actually, it is not. Reality is that we are Kṛṣṇa's servants, but that by misuse of free will, we have been put into this world, which is like a prison. All the prisoners are interacting on a false platform. Nationalistic propaganda and wars are fought in the realm of maya. They have a reality, but they are temporary and therefore false. The plane of true reality is the eternal soul's attempt to get free of temporary history, which takes place in the cycle of repeated birth and death. Freedom from the temporary "reality" is gained by turning to Kṛṣṇa, our eternal master, and engaging in spiritual servitorship. In the age of Kali, the only way to do this is by chanting the Hare Kṛṣṇa mantra: Hare Kṛṣṇa, Hare Kṛṣṇa, Kṛṣṇa Kṛṣṇa, Hare Hare/ Hare Rāma, Hare Rāma, Rāma Rāma, Hare Hare. Chanting Hare Kṛṣṇa while engaging in material activities is like pouring water while trying to light a fire. Pure devotees teach the world that political affairs are maya and that we should engage our energy strictly in the service of the Lord. Those who have been informed of the reality and are convinced of it from *Bhagavad-gītā* and other Vedic texts should preach Kṛṣṇa consciousness and keep aloof of material news while concentrating on their chanting.

---

95 Śrīla A. C. Bhaktivedanta Swami Prabhupāda, *Room Conversation* (New York, June 1976), available in digital form from www.vedabase.com

What is real?
The daily news, as reported on TV,
or the news of the spiritual world?
Devotees avoid the temporary news
and pay attention to the eternal.

The daily news is a shifting phantasmagoria,
a world of names and Maya's puppets.
They read the news as *Śrīmad-Bhāgavatam*
where the truth personified
frees us from the shadows
Of the temporary show.

They chant God's names
and release themselves from material bondage
by the transcendental sound of Truth. The few
who know this
should stay true to the process
and tell everyone they meet the difference
between the shadow and the light.

If you have purchased a ticket for an intermediate station, you cannot go all the way to California. If you want to go to Goloka Vṛndāvana, you have to worship Him. What is the difference in that planet? The supreme planet is that from which one never returns. In the material world, even if you go up to the higher planets, you have to come down. Just as we are changing different dresses or bodies, similarly, we transfer to different planets. We should try to go to that planet from which you never come back. Those who worship the Supreme Lord go to Him. They will never come to this place of miseries. At the time of death, whatever my mental condition is will determine my next body. Practice thinking of Kṛṣṇa for the time of death. If we want to transform, then like an apprentice, we have to practice. A good student is already guaranteed to pass and go back to Godhead.

How to perform Kṛṣṇa consciousness? Make friends with Kṛṣṇa. If you want to make connection with someone great, you have to prepare a relationship. We have to prepare love of God. We can't claim anything without love. There are six principles of loving exchange. You give something; you take something; you give something to eat; and you take something to eat; you disclose your mind; and you receive your friend's confidential mind. We worship God in that way. We offer to God, *patraṁ puspaṁ phalaṁ toyam.* We offer God a leaf, a flower, fruit, and water. These things are available universally, even to the poorest person. But they must be offered with devotion.

Seeing Kṛṣṇa in person
with the eyes is the perfection
of spiritual life, say the
agents of Vaikuṇṭha.

It's the goal of the nine processes
of devotional service: hearing, chanting, etc.
You can do it in this body
by His *karuṇya-śakti*, mercy-
bliss and by devotional service.

It's better than meditation in
the mind, it's been attained
by Prahlāda, Brahmā, and others.
I will agree. I will long for
the glimpse of His lotus feet,

His hips, His chest and arms,
His smiling face with pearl-
like teeth, His lotus-like
eyes.

Seeing Kṛṣṇa is the goal,
and you can do it
in this lifetime, bringing
unforgettable bliss.

I've written many books, so if they ask me, I could write a book. I'd like to write a book about Rādhā and Kṛṣṇa, but I'm not qualified. There is a book, though—*Śrīmad-Bhāgavatam*. And there are books by the Six Gosvāmīs that tell about the way Rādhā and Kṛṣṇa walk and whisper and look. It tells how They met in a way that the world will never forget. The simple secret of the plot is just to tell the people that They love each other a lot. Then the world discovers, as the book ends, how to make two lovers of friends. If they ask me, I could write a book about my days in Kṛṣṇa consciousness; my struggles. It wouldn't be so wonderful, but it would be true. And I'm writing that book. It's telling how I chant and how I hear and how I try to serve my spiritual master. As the book ends, I'm not sure how I wind up. I try to approach the two lovers in the spiritual world. The end of my book will have to be discovered at the end of my life.

BENGALI AND SANSKRIT SOURCES:

Ānanda-vṛndāvana-campū, *Kavi-karṇapūra.*

Bhagavad-gītā (Bg),
trans, A. C. Bhaktivedanta Swami Prabhupāda.

Bhakti-rasāmṛta-sindhu, Rūpa Gosvāmī.

Bhakti-sāra-pradarśinī-ṭīkā, Viśvanātha Cakravartī Ṭhākura.

Bṛhad-Bhāgavatāmṛta, (Bb) Sanātana Gosvāmī.

Gitavali, Bhaktivinoda Ṭhākura.

Govinda-līlāmṛta, Kṛṣṇadāsa Kavirāja.

Haṁsadūta, Rūpa Gosvāmī.

Harināma-cintāmaṇi, Bhaktivinoda Ṭhākura.

Kṛṣṇa-karṇāmṛta, Bilvamaṅgala Ṭhākura.

Nāmāṣṭakam, Rūpa Gosvāmī.

Prārthanā, Bhaktivinoda Ṭhākura.

Śaraṇāgati, Bhaktivinoda Ṭhākura.

Śikṣāṣṭakam, Śrī Caitanya Mahāprabhu, trans, A. C. Bhaktivedanta Swami Prabhupāda.

Śrīmad-Bhāgavatam/ Bhagavata Purāṇa (Bhag), trans, A. C. Bhaktivedanta Swami Prabhupāda.

Vaiṣṇava Ke, Bhaktisiddhānta Sarasvatī.

Vidagdha-mādhava, Rūpa Gosvāmī.

BIBLIOGRAPHY:

A. C. Bhaktivedanta Swami Prabhupāda, *Bhagavad-gītā As It Is*. New York: Macmillan Publishers, 1972.

——, *Śrīmad-Bhāgavatam*, Vols. 1-30. New York: Bhaktivedanta Book Trust, 1987.

——,*Śrī Nāmāmṛta: The Nectar of the Holy Name*. Los Angeles, CA: The Bhaktivedanta Book Trust, 1982.

——,*Nectar of Devotion—The Complete Science of Bhakti Yoga (A Summary Study of Srila Rupa Gosvāmī's Bhakti-rasamrta-sndhu,)* New York: Bhaktivedanta Book Trust, 1970.

——, *Nectar of Instruction*. London: The Bhaktivedanta Book Trust, 1975.

Bhaktivinoda Ṭhākura, *Prārthanā*. Kolkata: Touchstone Media, 1999.

——,*Śrī Harināma-cintāmaṇi*. Trans. Sarvabhāvana Dāsa. Vrindavana: Rasbihari Lal & Sons, 2001.

——,*Jaiva Dharma*. Trans. Sarvabhāvana Dāsa. Vrindavana: Brhad Mrdanga Press, 2004.

Bhaktisiddhānta Sarasvatī, *Prākṛta Rasa Śata Dūṣiṇī*. Mayapur: Sajjana Toṣanī, 1916.

By Anonymous. *The Way of a Pilgrim*. Pasadena, CA: Hope Publishing, 1993.

Kavi-karṇapūra, *Ānanda-vṛndāvana-campū*. Trans. Bhanu and Subhag Swami, Ed. Mahanidhi Swami. Mayapur, WB, 1999.

Kṛṣṇadāsa Kavirāja, *Śrī Caitanya-caritāmṛta of Kṛṣṇadāsa Kavirāja Gosvami*. Trans. Śrīla A.C. Bhaktivedanta Swami Prabhupāda. Madhya Lila, Vol. 8. Los Angeles: Bhaktivedanta Book Trust, 1996.

Nityananda Dasa, *Prema Vilasa - Pastimes Of Love*. Kolkata: Touchstone Media, 2006.

Rūpa Gosvāmī, *The Bhakti-rasāmṛta-sindhu of Śrīla Rūpa Gosvāmī with with Durgama-saṅgamanī-ṭīkā, a commentary called "Resolving the Difficult" by Jīva Gosvāmī, and the Bhakti-sāra-pradarśinī-ṭīkā, a commentary called "Revealing the*

Essence of Bhakti" by Śrīla Viśvanātha Cakravartī Ṭhākura. Trans. Bhanu Svami. Chennai: Sri Vaikuntha Enterprises, 2005.

Satsvarupa Dasa Goswami, *Begging for the Nectar of the Holy Name,* Port Royal: GN Press, 1992.

——, *Japa Reform Notebook,* Port Royal: GN Press, 1982.

VERSES INDEX:

ACKNOWLEDGEMENTS:

I would like to thank the following disciples and friends who took part, helped produce and print this book on japa: Yadunandana Swami, Nārāyaṇa-kavaca, Baladeva Vidyābhūṣaṇa, specifically Kṛṣṇa-kṛpā and Gurudāsa for proofreading the text, Sureśvara and Krishna Ksetra Prabhus for writings for the front matter and Caitanya Candrodaya for editing and design.

I am grateful to Gopinatha Dāsa for his kind donation to print this book and Śyāma Gopāla Dāsa and Śiromaṇi Devi for the support.

5487079R0

Made in the USA
Charleston, SC
22 June 2010